PHILL,
AKA MICHAEL MYERS
JASON NEVER DIES!
SLASHER FAMILY x

JASON 1

TO PHIL
STEVE DASH
THE REAL JASON
11

On Location in Blairstown:

The Making of Friday the 13th

by

David Grove

Foreword by Tom Savini

www.AuthorMikeDarkInk.com

Published by *AuthorMike Ink*, 9/13/2013

www.AuthorMikeDarkInk.com

AuthorMike Ink, *Dark Ink* and its logo are trademarked by *AuthorMike Ink Publishing*

CONTENTS

FOREWORD

by Tom Savini

A long time ago, in a Connecticut city far away, I met with Sean Cunningham to discuss how I was going to kill all these good-looking teenagers wandering around Camp Crystal Lake.

But first I suggested doing something about the ending.

The script had a perfunctory ending where the bad guy, in this case the bad woman, was done away with. I had just seen the film *Carrie* and I thought it would be a good idea to have an end scare like that movie. You know, you think the movie is over, and even the music makes you think the credits are going to come up any second...then WHAM...you hit the audience with something completely unexpected, like *Carrie* did with that hand coming up out of the grave.

The consensus was the villain is dead, so how do we come up with such an ending? I suggested it would be a dream. You can get away with almost anything when what you have just seen is a dream...BUT...you get to show whatever the hell you want, and that is how we got Jason, the unseen (except for flashbacks), hideous kid to jump out of the lake and grab Adrienne King before she snaps out of it in the hospital. Audiences flew out of their seats.

The shoot itself was great fun. I had just done *Dawn of the Dead,* and I spent most of that film in the winter inside a mall. Now I was outside at Camp No-Be-Bo-Sco, in the Pennsylvania Poconos. The cast and crew stayed in a nearby hotel, but I, and my assistant, Taso Stavrakis, stayed at the camp, in some old Boy Scout hut. We had canoes and my motorcycle, which we raced down very narrow paths in the woods, and the great outdoors to play with, but I must say it did get creepy at night. Another reason we stayed there was to be close to the workshop and the kitchen where, in pizza ovens, we baked all the foam latex heads and appliances that would be part of how we killed the teenagers.

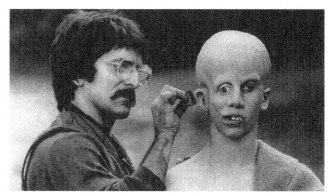

Tom Savini touches-up Ari Lehman's makeup for the filming of the climactic lake scene. (Photo courtesy of Tom Savini)

So we hit a teenager in the face with an axe, cut throats, skewered Kevin Bacon with an arrow through his neck, stabbed and punctured people left and right, but most of all, I got to create one of the all-time horror icons we still have running around today.

JASON.

However, I objected to Jason running around in the second movie when they sent me the script, as the killer in the first movie is the mother, Betsy Palmer. Jason was just her mongoloid kid, who drowned in part one. To bring him back as the villain seemed too odd to me and I turned down that movie and did *The Burning* instead.

They didn't offer me *Part 3*, but when it came to the fourth movie and the franchise was waning, they did offer me part four and I got to finally kill Jason in a movie called *The Final Chapter*.

Yeah, right. It made so much money that I am sure there is going to be a *Friday the 13th Part 13.*

Speaking of money, the special makeup effects budget on part one was around $15,000 and out of that came materials, travel, and paying my assistant. That's all I received because all I wanted at that time in my life was a big screen TV. That was my motivation for doing that movie. Finally, a big screen TV!

Then this low budget movie comes out and makes a gazillion dollars. What pissed me off was reading the reviews and almost all of them said: "The star of this movie is Tom Savini's makeup effects." So I made what was left of the $15,000 and they made gazillions, and THAT is one of the many reasons I like this book. It gives the credit where credit is due as far as my contribution to this franchise. (By the way, I made up for it on part four, *The Final Chapter*. I asked for a ridiculous amount of money....and got it.)

Some of the highlights of what I remember:

Harry Crosby playing guitar in the back seat of the car Taso and I used. He was always with us, wanting to learn stunts and fighting. When we drove, we never turned on the radio 'cause Harry was our music from the back seat.

When we killed Harry, we pinned him to a door with lots of arrows; one in his eye and the rest all over his body. I designed his death, but for some reason I wasn't there when it was executed. I remember getting a call that he had to go to the hospital because the blood got into his eye and burned it a bit. After a couple of days he was fine.

In front of an archery target, Sean asked me how I was going to make an arrow hit the target close to Laurie Bartram for a scene. I said I would just shoot it. He looked scared. I grabbed my bow and a target arrow and backed off and asked him to point on the target where he wanted it to hit. As he pointed, I pulled back the arrow on the bow and shot it one foot from his finger. Scared the hell out of him, but that's how I did it for the scene.

Robbi Morgan was the girl in the woods who gets her throat cut, and it was late in the day and Sean asked how long it would take to get her ready. The light was fading and they were deciding whether to do it or not. I said a half hour and they said, "Do it." Taso and I applied the tubing and the appliance, and painted it, and Robbi jumped on the back of my motorcycle and I rushed her to the location exactly one half hour later and Sean was impressed that we'd said a time and stuck to it.

Robbi was kind of a gymnast and Taso had a crush on her so we were together a lot and every now and then you would see the three of us doing handstands or walking on our hands down a road or to the set.

The bathroom set was just that: a set. It's where we staged and shot the scene with the girl who gets the axe in her face. Nothing functioned as it was just a set. One weekend, a Boy Scout troop came through the camp and used that bathroom. You can imagine the mess with toilets that were just non-functioning props.

One day, Taso found a rattlesnake and casually carried it into the production office, scaring the bejesus out of every woman working there. It was the snake used when the kids find a snake in their cabin.

But Jason is still running around in the movies, and here in this book, even though he doesn't exist.

He died in the first movie.

He can't still be running around, killing naked teenagers in the woods with household implements. I've had this conversation with Betsy Palmer, who did a lot of soul-searching and character-building before she played his mother, and she told me, in her mind, "Oh, they never found his body." Well then, I argued, "You mean he came out of the lake, disoriented, and here is this misshapen kid living off crayfish or something and nobody saw him, and for 35 more years he is out there still, racking up a body count?"

The simple answer is...yes.

Tom Savini
July 9, 2013

INTRODUCTION

by David Grove

I discovered the film *Friday the 13th* in 1982. It was a Friday night. A Seattle television affiliate, KSTW, that broadcasts to British Columbia, Canada, where I lived, showed the "exploding glass" sequence between every commercial break, a very effective touch. It made the commercial breaks tense and uncomfortable. The film itself terrified me from start to finish. One particularly traumatic scene was when Alice (Adrienne King) discovered Bill (Harry Crosby) mounted to the door of the generator cabin with arrows, only moments after he'd left her. What upset me was the whole lead-in to the gruesome reveal of Bill on the door.

Atmospheric shot shows an eerie bank of mist threatening to overtake Camp No-Be-Bo-Sco, which doubled for Camp Crystal Lake in the film. (Photo courtesy of Henri Guibaud)

I remember Bill as friendly and nice; he told Alice everything would be okay. He'd be right back. At nine years old, I didn't know this was a death sentence for a character in a horror film. I also didn't know that Bill was in a generator cabin. The way I remember it, Bill was in a garage, fixing a car that he and Alice were planning to drive away in. Oh well. We remember influential films we saw as children through the prism we had when we were that age.

Betsy Palmer's performance made the most lasting impression on me. Palmer's surprise appearance, indeed the unexpected reveal of a middle-aged female killer, was a real showstopper with her deranged intensity and steely eyes. Never has laughter seemed so diabolical. Never has a smile seemed less reassuring. Although it seems implausible that any woman could've had the strength to hang poor Bill on that door, with Pamela Voorhees it's believable. She was so crazy. Pamela Voorhees was, and remains to this day, one of the scariest villains in film history, and while the thought of her doesn't make me hide under the covers anymore, like I did in 1982, she still makes me cringe.

The other element that distinguished *Friday the 13th* was the effects sequences. Besides being gory, they were shocking, like a jack-in-the-box poised to attack at any moment. Not knowing anything about makeup effects back in 1982, it all seemed real. The Kevin Bacon scene. The decapitation. Never been done before. Never been seen before. How did they get away this? It was years later when I heard of makeup and special effects expert Tom Savini and learned how he created the film's memorable effects. Looking back, it was more fun when I didn't know anything.

I'm 40 now, and I've aged with *Friday the 13th*. We bond with films that made an impression when we saw them as kids. Then we watch them over the subsequent years. We grow old with them. They're a time capsule. A trip down memory lane. *Friday the 13th* is definitely that kind of film.

I watched *Friday the 13th* countless times throughout the 1980s, mostly on television and then on video. In 1990, when I was in grade eleven, I caught a midnight screening in my basement. I remember thinking then that the film's shock value hadn't "held-up" for me compared to years earlier.

My relationship with *Friday the 13th* dwindled to a crawl in the early 1990s. I went to college and established a career as a writer. I think I saw the film once during this period, as a video rental. I remember watching the film again in 2000, during the heat of the American presidential debates between George Bush and Al Gore, with an eye on doing a retrospective of some kind. By this time the film had lost most of its shock and visceral power for me and had become more like a childhood friend I'd kept in and out of touch with over the years.

In 2001, I was the first journalist to do any serious retrospective on *Friday the 13th*. I interviewed members of the cast and crew and unearthed information that had never been made public before. In May 2002, I published a major article on the film in the American horror film magazine *Fangoria*. I was the first and only journalist to interview the likes of

The silhouette of the axe that kills Marcie. (Photo courtesy of Henri Guibaud)

Peter Brouwer, Harry Crosby, Sean Cunningham, Victor Miller, Robbi Morgan, Mark Nelson, Betsy Palmer and Tom Savini in the context of "looking back" at *Friday the 13th* and its impact.

In 2005, I was the first journalist to publish a book on the film, *Making Friday the 13th: The Legend of Camp Blood*. It covered the entire *Friday the 13th* series, with several chapters devoted to the "first" film. In the subsequent years, both the book and the magazine article have been referenced in various books, DVDs, online and research projects. It seems like everyone I talk to, from fans to Hollywood filmmakers, has a copy of the book.

In 2010, I decided the original *Friday the 13th* film warranted a book of its own, entirely devoted to the execution, filming, legacy and planning that went into the creation of the 1980 film. I wanted to create a book in the vein of other wonderful books, such as David A. Szulkin's *Wes Craven's Last House on the Left: The Making of a Cult Classic* and Stephen Rebello's *Alfred Hitchcock and the Making of Psycho*.

Having completed *On Location in Blairstown: The Making of Friday the 13th*, I'm proud to say this book will be a shocking revelation to the most passionate fans of the 1980 film, but also to film historians in general. It's full of untold production stories and recollections that shatter many long held beliefs about *Friday the 13th* and answer many questions about the film and the time period in which it was conceived and born.

This book bears its title *On Location in Blairstown: The Making of Friday the 13th* not because I was present in Blairstown, New Jersey during September and October 1979, but because I wanted the title to indicate the book was written to capture the place and time when *Friday the 13th* was brought to life.

I also wanted to highlight the lives of the cast and crew who collaborated on *Friday the 13th*, not just in the context of the making of *Friday the 13th* itself, but also in terms of their careers and lives prior to and after *Friday the 13th*'s release in 1980.

Since I've interviewed virtually the entire production unit who worked on *Friday the 13th*, some of whom are now dead, this was, in many ways, the most interesting part of writing this book, especially since I've grown close to many of the cast and crew members over the years.

One thing I seek to avoid in this book is to "defend" *Friday the 13th* in any way or put the film in any kind of critical context. I set out to document and report the elements that went into the creation of *Friday the 13th*, without any of my own personal commentary.

As the scope of the book - and the title - mandates, I avoid discussing the *Friday the 13th* sequels in any meaningful detail except in the context

Betsy Palmer's appearance in *Friday the 13th* was a shock to audiences and to the actress herself. (Photo courtesy of Henri Guibaud)

of how the rest of the *Friday the 13th* franchise has affected the 1980 film. This book is focused on the 1980 film, the original *Friday the 13th*-- the only film in the series that holds my true passion.

I was stunned by the amount of new material I was able to gather. If this hadn't been the case, I wouldn't have finished. During the writing of this book, I barely looked at the previous published materials, except for accuracy and fact-checking.

I hope *On Location in Blairstown: The Making of Friday the 13th* will be accepted as "the final word" on *Friday the 13th*.

David Grove

May 15, 2013

CHAPTER 1

THE PERFECT DAY FOR TERROR

"I like pictures that have the audience talking when they leave the theater. What they're saying, I don't care."

- Philip Scuderi

"To think...this is my contribution to western civilization."

- Director/Producer Sean Cunningham

Toward the end of August 1979, a skeleton crew of filmmaking professionals, surrounded by a much larger group of complete amateurs, descended upon Blairstown. It was a quaint little township inside of Warren County, New Jersey. The invaders were there to work on a low budget horror-slasher film called *Friday the 13th*. Under the leadership of director/producer Sean Cunningham, principal filming on *Friday the 13th* began on September 4, 1979, the day after Labor Day.

No one imagined their work in Blairstown would result in a film that would escape New Jersey and travel all around the world. *Friday the 13th* revolutionized the horror film genre and the world of independent cinema. It brought exploitation into the mainstream and popularized the slasher film genre. It redefined the way Hollywood did business. It cemented the name *Friday the 13th* in pop culture.

Cunningham brought a palpable sense of desperation and weariness to *Friday the 13th*. This was a project that represented, in many ways, the end of the line for the then down-on-his-luck filmmaker. Cunningham (born in New York City on December 31, 1941) was 36 years old when he began developing *Friday the 13th* in 1978-- an age where a man takes stock of his life, and measures how much he's amounted to. "All I was trying to do was make a potboiler," Cunningham said. "To put it bluntly, I couldn't pay the rent. I asked myself, 'What's the scariest phrase in the English language?' It's got to be *Friday the 13th*."

Sean Cunningham risked all of his capital, both emotional and financial, to bring *Friday the 13th* to life.

Prior to *Friday the 13th*, Cunningham's biggest commercial success came as a producer on the exploitation-horror film *Last House on the Left* (AKA *The Last House on the Left*). The film was directed and written by Cunningham's friend and mentor, horror kingpin Wes Craven.

Filmed in 1971, and released in 1972, *Last House on the Left* was a bitter, merciless, perverse, uncompromising film that became a cult success. It also labeled Cunningham a sleaze merchant. "After producing *Last House on the Left*, I told myself that I didn't want to become identified exclusively with the genre," Cunningham says. "So I began doing other things. I always knew that I could go back to horror if I wanted to."

The success of the film *Halloween* (1978), combined with his past failures, pushed Sean Cunningham back to genre filmmaking and towards the creation of *Friday the 13th*. (Photo courtesy of Kim Gottlieb-Walker www.lenswoman.com)

While the genre experience Cunningham gained from the making of *Last House on the Left* laid the groundwork for *Friday the 13th*, the success of *Friday the 13th* was a result of execution, marketing and more than a little luck. Cunningham found the latter in the form of makeup and special effects expert Tom Savini. Savini's jolting work in *Friday the 13th* set it apart within the horror genre. Neither audiences nor the cast and crew who worked on the film were prepared for the gruesome creations that Savini unleashed in the film.

Cunningham's hiring of Savini was his smartest decision and key to the film's success. "Sean let me improvise a lot of stuff in the film," Savini recalls. "We would invent things on the spot, anything that entered my imagination, and that improvisation and inventiveness inspired us to conceptualize some amazing effects that hadn't been seen before in horror films."

Savini's work brought graphic realization to a story that was very straightforward. Developed out of collaboration between Cunningham and screenwriter Victor Miller, *Friday the 13th* tells the story of a group of would-be summer camp coun-

Halloween creators John Carpenter and Debra Hill established a formula that Sean Cunningham sought to duplicate with *Friday the 13th*. (Photo courtesy of Kim Gottlieb-Walker www.lenswoman.com)

selors stationed at a remote campsite, Camp Crystal Lake. Over a twenty-four period, they are systematically pursued and slaughtered in increasingly bizarre ways by a vengeful psychopath.

The plot was a variation of the premise established in Agatha Christie's novel *Ten Little Indians*: a group of characters, trapped in an isolated setting, are killed one by one. Simple. This is when the similarities end. Agatha Christie was certainly never a topic of conversation in Blairstown.

Although Sean Cunningham engineered this premise to closely mirror the babysitters-in-peril storyline of the virtually bloodless horror film *Halloween* (1978), *Friday the 13th* savagely diverted from this and other inspirations. It morphed into a uniquely gory and shocking creation that not even Cunningham envisioned when he planned *Friday the 13th*. "The only inspiration *Halloween* provided was its formula for success," Cunningham says. "*Halloween* is more of an artistic effort. *Friday the 13th* is more meat and potatoes and dark. In that sense, the two films are like apples and oranges."

The creative directions of *Friday the 13th* and *Halloween* matched the respective backgrounds of their filmmakers. John Carpenter, *Halloween*'s co-writer and director, had grown out of the sanitized backdrop of the University of Southern California (USC) film school prior to making *Halloween*. Cunningham toiled in the genres of exploitation and porn from the early to mid 1970s and had the scars to prove it.

The plot synopsis of *Friday the 13th* reveals a base, primitive blueprint that mirrors the coarse and ragged filmmaking experiences that Cunningham and his colleagues brought with them to Blairstown.

Friday the 13th was a date that made history.

THE STORY

One of the major differences between *Friday the 13th* and *Halloween* is how the two films established the legend or origin for each of their stories. This narrative defines the ground rules that – as seen in most of the slasher films following *Friday the 13th* and *Halloween* – serves to introduce the film's "boogeyman" or villain, along with their grudge or motive.

A confined setting – or slaughtering ground – is also established from which the rest of the film can build upon, in terms of introducing a set of victims and killing them, one by one. Although *Halloween* was the progenitor of this technique, with a nod to the 1974 horror film *Black Christmas*, *Friday the 13th* turned this formula into an art form through clever execution and sly misdirection.

In *Halloween,* the film's villain is established in a crisp, sharp, simple way so the film could quickly get onto crafting a thriller. It opens with a six year old boy named Michael Myers who, on Halloween night,

As *Friday the 13th* moved deeper into development, the project drifted further and further away – stylistically – from the model established in *Halloween*. (Photo courtesy of Kim Gottlieb-Walker www.lenswoman.com)

brutally stabs his sister and is institutionalized for fifteen years. Then he escapes and returns to his hometown to continue his rampage. Crisp. Sharp. Simple. From here, the film's off to the races, free to do whatever it wants in terms of shocking and surprising the audience in a multitude of clever, inventive ways.

In examining the story structure of *Friday the 13th,* it's clear the film pauses to consider *Halloween*'s approach for the introduction of its story, but then veers off and establishes its own formula – most popularly known as "the Dead Teenager" genre – which countless post-*Friday the 13th* slasher films released in the early 1980s tried to emulate.

It rests on 13 acres of earth over the very center of hell..!

MARI, SEVENTEEN, IS DYING. EVEN FOR HER THE WORST IS YET TO COME!

SHE LIVED IN THE

LAST HOUSE ON THE LEFT

TO AVOID FAINTING KEEP REPEATING, IT'S ONLY A MOVIE ...ONLY A MOVIE ...ONLY A MOVIE ...ONLY A MOVIE ...ONLY A MOVIE ...ONLY A MOVIE

SEAN S. CUNNINGHAM FILMS LTD. Presents "THE LAST HOUSE ON THE LEFT" Starring: DAVID HESS ● LUCY GRANTHAM ● SANDRA CASSEL ● MARC SHEFFLER ● and introducing ADA WASHINGTON ● Produced by SEAN S. CUNNINGHAM Written and Directed by WES CRAVEN ● COLOR BY MOVIELAB [R] RESTRICTED

Theatrical poster for *Last House on the Left* (AKA *The Last House on the Left*). The number "13" referenced on the poster stayed in Sean Cunningham's mind throughout the 1970s and led to the creation of the *Friday the 13th* logo and title. (Photo courtesy of David A. Szulkin)

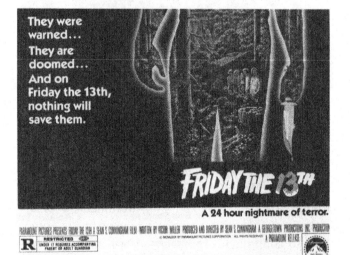

They were warned... They are doomed... And on Friday the 13th, nothing will save them.

FRIDAY THE 13TH

A 24 hour nightmare of terror.

PARAMOUNT PICTURES PRESENTS FROM THE 13TH A SEAN S. CUNNINGHAM FILM WRITTEN BY VICTOR MILLER PRODUCED AND DIRECTED BY SEAN S. CUNNINGHAM A GEORGETOWN PRODUCTIONS INC. PRODUCTION ©MCMLXXX BY PARAMOUNT PICTURES CORPORATION ALL RIGHTS RESERVED A PARAMOUNT RELEASE

[R] RESTRICTED UNDER 17 REQUIRES ACCOMPANYING PARENT OR ADULT GUARDIAN

Paramount Pictures spent an estimated $4 Million in the marketing and promotion of *Friday the 13th* over the course of the film's theatrical run in 1980. (Photo courtesy of Matt Hankinson)

When *Friday the 13th*'s killer is shown in the film's denouement and revealed to be a middle-aged woman, it represents a sharp contrast to the typical male identity present in virtually all other horror (or horror-slasher) films. This device – the appearance of a female killer – was, of course, immortalized in the

film *Psycho* (1960) but was also later copied by several other horror-slasher films, most notably *Happy Birthday to Me* (1981) and *Sleepaway Camp* (1983).

It's in *Friday the 13th*'s third act where the motive and reasoning behind the killer's murderous actions is embodied in the form of the killer's disfigured, mongoloid son, the iconic Jason Voorhees. The introduction of this secondary villain was a concept that further distanced the film from *Halloween* and ultimately established *Friday the 13th* to be the most influential horror-slasher film, in terms of both execution and story construction, of its era. Jason hadn't been seen before.

Friday the 13th's influence in this regard is most evident when comparing it to its genre contemporaries, the films that also sought to capitalize on the success of *Halloween*. The most notable example was *Prom Night* (1980) which, ironically, was filmed

If you're not back by midnight... you won't be coming home!

PROM NIGHT

A SIMCOM PRODUCTION LESLIE NIELSEN · JAMIE LEE CURTIS in "PROM NIGHT" SCREENPLAY by WILLIAM GRAY · STORY by ROBERT GUZA, JR. PRODUCED by PETER SIMPSON · DIRECTED by PAUL LYNCH AVCO EMBASSY PICTURES Release [R]

The slasher film *Prom Night* – in which *Halloween* star Jamie Lee Curtis was the lead - was filmed almost simultaneous to *Friday the 13th* in 1979 and was a much more blatant copy of *Halloween* than was *Friday the 13th*. (Photo courtesy of Peter Simpson)

almost simultaneous to *Friday the 13th* in 1979. Intended as a blatant copy of *Halloween*, much more transparently so than *Friday the 13th*, *Prom Night* opens with an accidental death. This establishes a motive for the killer whose identity is kept a mystery until the end of the film, much like *Friday the 13th*.

The titular setting of *Prom Night* mirrors the apple pie "Americana" of *Friday the 13th*'s summer camp setting, but while *Prom Night* is shackled by its transparent debt to *Halloween*, *Friday the 13th* was clearly able to escape *Halloween*'s influence and establish its own template that proved to be even more influential, and copied.

None of this is to suggest that *Friday the 13th* doesn't represent the distillation and synthesis of various horror influences, but rather that Sean Cunningham was clever and savvy enough to mold these in-

This is the last scene in the film in which all of these characters are all present together, and all still alive. All of these characters – (from left to right) Brenda (Laurie Bartram), Marcie (Jeannine Taylor), Steve Christy (Peter Brouwer), Bill (Harry Crosby), Jack (Kevin Bacon), Ned (Mark Nelson) – are killed in the film. (Photo courtesy of Henri Guibaud)

fluences into a story that has proved iconic in its own right. To put it bluntly, Cunningham knew how to 'borrow' without leaving too many fingerprints. Tom Savini was the magician who made this illusion seamless.

The story elements of *Friday the 13th* have become such an imprimatur inside the horror film universe so as to render the film's many sources irrelevant. This is a testament to Cunningham and his colleagues, primarily Savini, who took a story that essentially functions as a crude roadmap, a skeleton, and infused it with visceral energy, flesh and blood.

Author's Note: The following synopsis, including grammar and errors, of Friday the 13th is taken from the Friday the 13th Pressbook, which was released by Paramount Pictures in 1980, in advance of Friday the 13th's theatrical release.

Friday the 13th begins at Camp Crystal Lake, an East Coast campground area which has been shuttered down for over twenty years, after the brutal murders of two camp counselors back in 1958 which have remained unsolved. A young owner, Steve Christy (Peter Brouwer), has taken control of the property and plans to reopen the camp, having hired seven young people to be counselors.

Annie (Robbi Morgan), a pretty student on summer vacation, is hitchhiking to Camp Crystal Lake, to begin her new job as cook for the camp. Asking for directions, she encounters a friendly truck driver (Rex Everhart) who gives her a lift - and an ominous warning about "that place."

The truck must turn into another route, Annie looks for another ride, which she quickly finds in a jeep with someone who is headed towards the camp. As they continue down the road, Annie notices that the driver has passed the camp turn-off and does not respond to her queries as to why. Terrified that something terrible might happen, Annie jumps from the moving vehicle. Annie runs into the woods seeking safety, the pursuing car halted by the trees. The driver of the car jumps out and pursues Annie on foot and eventually slashes Annie's throat. There is a terrified scream that comes from the forest.

Meanwhile, six other camp counselors have arrived at Camp Crystal Lake and have started the painting, cleaning and general repair work of the camp. Pitching in to make needed improvements are Alice (Adrienne King), Bill (Harry Crosby), Brenda (Laurie Bartram), Ned (Mark Nelson), Marcie (Jeannine Taylor) and Jack (Kevin Bacon). A local religious fanatic named Crazy Ralph (Walt Gorney) gives them all a scare when he is discovered hiding in the pantry. Ralph warns all the young people that the camp has a "death curse." Then he hurries away.

The camp owner, Steve Christy, leaves town to purchase additional supplies. Night falls, and the full moon brings with it a violent thunderstorm that pelts the camp. Unseen but driven to murder is a sinister prowler who seeks blood. Slowly, methodically, and with savage precision, four of the counselors are murdered, one by one, each meeting a gruesome and bloody end.

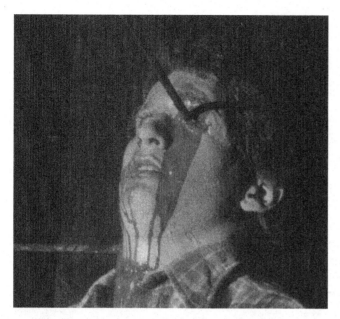

Tom Savini's innovative and shocking effects work in *Friday the 13th* provoked a visceral audience reaction that distinguished *Friday the 13th* from the other horror films – including *Halloween* and its other imitators – in the marketplace. (Photo courtesy of Tom Savini)

The shadowy menace had dispensed them in cruel and bizarre ways: Ned's throat is cut; Jack watches as an arrow explodes out of his throat; Marcie gets an axe in the skull; Brenda is stabbed to death; Steve Christy takes a knife in the stomach while returning to the camp.

Unaware of what has been happening around them, the two remaining counselors, Alice and Bill, begin a search for the others. They begin to realize that something sinister is erupting at the camp, and that they are the next targets. When they find a bloody hatchet in Brenda's bed, they run to the office in an attempt to telephone the police. The line has been cut. Their communication with the outside world has been shut-off. They try to leave the camp by attempting to start the pick-up truck, but it doesn't work.

Relentlessly, the rain pounds away at the camp, washing blood. Alice returns to the cabin as Bill braves the torrential rain to check the camp's generator which has been providing the power for electricity. When Bill doesn't return after a long time, Alice goes to look for him. Alice stumbles through the rain and dark as she makes her way to the generator cabin to look for Bill. There, she sees Bill's corpse, mounted to the door with arrows. Consumed with terror and with panic obliterating her senses, she runs blindly.

Suddenly, a jeep appears outside the cabin that Alice has barricaded herself in, scared beyond belief. Alice runs out and sees an older woman who appears to comfort Alice. This is Mrs. Voorhees (Betsy Palmer), a local resident whose property borders that of Camp Crystal Lake. She attempts to calm the frantic Alice, who has edged past the border into hysteria.

Mrs. Voorhees assures Alice that she'll drive her to safety, and then lapses into a memory during which she recounts how the camp had been closed long ago because her son, Jason, had drowned while his counselors were off on a tryst when they were supposed to have been on duty. As Mrs. Voorhees turns to talk to the long-dead Jason, Alice freezes for a moment as she realizes this is the crazed murderer from whom she must escape. Alice runs, her nerves shattered.

With everyone dead around her, and nowhere to run, Alice senses safety as she reaches a boat at the dock, but the twisted face of Mrs. Voorhees appears as a menacing image in the black water of the lake where she has cornered Alice. A rolling, scratching duel to the death ensues on the dark, wet sand. Alice, enraged and wild, pushed to the limit of her instinct to survive, flies at the madwoman and beheads her. Numbed and conscious of very little around her, Alice saunters into a canoe which silently drifts toward the middle of the lake.

The sun rises, with the rays gently rubbing against the rippling water of the lake. Alice opens her eyes. The nightmare is over. The horror. Suddenly an aquatic demon, the drowned Jason, reaches up from the depths and grabs Alice, pulling her into his watery grave.

Alice abruptly awakes in a hospital room. A policeman (Ronn Carroll) is there to piece together the bizarre events of the long night at Camp Crystal Lake. When Alice mentions the child, Jason, who had

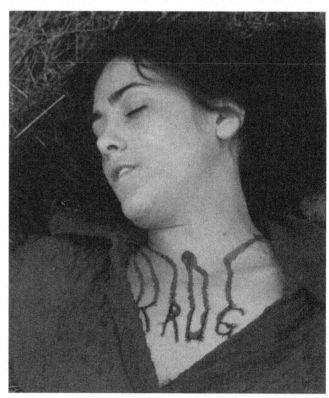

Last House on the Left cemented Sean Cunningham's reputation, for better and worse, as an exploitation filmmaker. (Photo courtesy of David A. Szulkin)

grabbed her and pulled her into the water, she's told that no little boy was found and that no one was in the lake except Alice. Alice murmurs, "Then he's still there."

METHODS OF MAYHEM

The Sean Cunningham who executed and masterminded *Friday the 13th* in 1979 was a much different filmmaker and person than the Sean Cunningham who collaborated with Wes Craven on *Last House on Left*. Filmed in October 1971, *Last House on the Left* laid the foundation for Cunningham's career as a horror filmmaker and all the baggage that came with it. Although *Friday the 13th* wasn't even a dream at this point, the two films are forever intertwined.

Sean Cunningham was twenty-nine years old when he and Wes Craven conceived and filmed *Last House on the Left*. Cunningham considered himself very much an amateur filmmaker at this point, even though he'd already directed the sex documentary film *The Art of Marriage* (1970) and the pseudo-documentary porno film *Together* (1971).

Cunningham brought to *Last House on the Left* the youthful exuberance of someone who was still intoxicated by the novelty of the filmmaking process. "We hardly looked like a film crew," recalled Cunningham about the filming, most of which took place near his home in Westport, Connecticut. "We were, literally, kids running around with a camera."

By summer 1979, this energy and verve had been replaced with a cynical, jaded, wry personality, reflecting a man who'd spent nearly a decade staring at the guts of the film business. However fragile Cunningham's self-esteem was when he approached *Friday the 13th*, his primal motivations were much the same as they'd been when he made *Last House on the Left*: grave financial need and self-preservation.

Both *Friday the 13th* and *Last House on the Left* are representative of the resources and skills Cunningham possessed during the different time periods in which these films were made, and the creative people that Cunningham was surrounded with on each film. *Last House on the Left* had a budget of $90,000. It was filmed on Super 16MM. These two factors went a long way, in spite of the filmmakers' self-proclaimed amateur status, of establishing the film's primitive, raw feel-qualities the film's ardent supporters point to as differentiating it from future slasher films like *Friday the 13th*.

With Wes Craven Cunningham found himself paired with a cerebral, thoughtful filmmaker who brought an effective balance to his own business-like, pragmatic demeanor. *Last House on the Left* also marked Cunningham's professional introduction to Steve (Stephen) Miner, a then-twenty year old filmmaking novice who served as a production assistant and assistant editor on *Last House on the Left*, and eventually grew to be Cunningham's protégé and production partner on *Friday the 13th*.

Last House on the Left was financed by Hallmark Releasing Corporation-- a Boston-based film distribution company born in 1970 and run by partners Robert Barsamian, Stephen (Steve) Minasian and Philip Scuderi. Hallmark was an offshoot of the New England-based theater chain Esquire Theaters of America that the partners had run since the 1960s. *Last House on the Left* represented one of Esquire/Hallmark's first forays into the waters of financing and film production. The three partners, all lawyers, later financed *Friday the 13th* under the banner of Georgetown Productions.

Last House on the Left was originally intended by Craven and Cunningham to be a hardcore film. When it was filmed in 1971, Craven and Cunningham visualized the film as being a harsh rebuke against the sanitized violence present in film and television at that time, while also commenting on the Vietnam War and the dark underbelly of the flower power/hippie generation. Critics argue that such themes are irrelevant and just served as a license for the filmmakers, Craven and Cunningham, to wallow in degradation and depravity.

Friday the 13th had a final production budget of roughly $550,000 (many sources state $500,000), greater than any previous film that Cunningham had ever been involved with. It was filmed in Panavision, with a production crew that was, at least in terms of the

Sean Cunningham and Steve Miner were largely unfazed by the harsh critical reaction unleashed upon *Friday the 13th* given the abuse and scorn they'd received in the wake of *Last House on the Left*'s release. (Photo courtesy of David A. Szulkin)

Tom Savini was the creative engine behind *Friday the 13th* and deserves the most credit for the film's success. (Photo courtesy of Tom Savini)

key technical positions, comprised of mostly capable professionals.

Like *Last House on the Left, Friday the 13th* is reflective of its era: the gloom of the recessionary period that lingered in America in the late 1970s. Both films have a semi-documentary look and feel. In *Last House on the Left*, this is enhanced by the film's use of Super 16MM, the film's micro-budget and the filmmakers' inexperience. Although *Friday the 13th* is also framed in a stark, semi-documentary format, the film's use of Panavision lessens the impact of this.

Friday the 13th and *Last House on the Left* both take place in a wilderness, woodsy setting and use this to play on the fear of isolation. Both films are about the loss of a child and feature parental figures who seek bloody revenge to satisfy the grief and rage they feel over this injustice.

In 1980, just prior to release, Cunningham explained that his intent with *Friday the 13th* was "to psychologically prepare his audience for terror; to show that reality is perhaps the most effective method to present horror, that 'this could happen to me' is what truly scares the wits out of an audience, while they love it." Take away the time period of this statement, and Cunningham could've just as easily have been describing *Last House on the Left*, with the stark exception of the "while they love it" part.

Friday the 13th even carries the specter of Vietnam, but this is visible not in the film's characters or story, but rather in the film's gory effects. Tom Savini had been a combat photographer in Vietnam (cinematographer Barry Abrams had also served as a cameraman in Vietnam) and Savini carried this grim influence into his subsequent film work, especially *Friday the 13th*.

While some critics dismiss the effects in *Friday the 13th* as being outrageous, surreal, and the stuff of fantasy, they were, unlike the bloody images in *Last House on the Left*, largely a representation of the real thing, at least according to Savini. "Yes, I think Vietnam was a lesson in anatomy for me," Savini says. "I'm the only makeup effects artist who's seen the real thing, so my reputation for realism is a result of my Vietnam experience. John Chambers was the makeup effects artist who saw the results of a war on

the individuals and created prosthetic appliances for them, but I was actually there and saw it firsthand."

Even though Cunningham's involvement with *Last House on the Left,* and the film's enduring reputation, was integral in helping Cunningham bring *Friday the 13th* to fruition, Cunningham sees few similarities between the two films. "If you examine it, *Last House on the Left* has a sort of cynical edge to it," Cunning-

Last House on the Left's connection with *Friday the 13th* was highlighted upon *Last House on the Left*'s home video release in the 1980s. (Photo courtesy of David A. Szulkin)

ham said. "It seems to say, 'You want horror? Well, here's real horror.' *Friday the 13th*, on the other hand, is a roller-coaster ride, a funhouse sort of thing."

"The woodsy locations and overall low-budget quality of *Friday the 13th* remind me of *Last House*," says journalist David A. Szulkin, a *Last House on the Left* scholar and the author of the book *Wes Craven's Last House on the Left: The Making of a Cult Classic*. "Both are vulgar movies that pander to certain low appetites in an audience. *Last House* had a hippie/freak sensibility that was gone by the time of *Friday the 13th*. I think it's interesting to look at the two movies in terms of the changing times, the changing youth culture."

IT'S A WHOLE NEW BALL GAME!
They're down by 39 runs in the last inning...
BUT THEY'VE NOT YET BEGUN TO FIGHT!

HERE COME THE TIGERS
...and there goes the League.

A SEAN S. CUNNINGHAM FILMS LTD. PRODUCTION
Starring RICHARD LINCOLN and JAMES ZVANUT • Also Starring SAMANTHA GREY • MANNY LIEBERMAN • WILLIAM CALDWELL
FRED LINCOLN as Aesop and Introducing XAVIER RODRIGO • Written by ARCH McCOY • Music Composed and Adapted by HARRY MANFREDINI
Director of Photography BARRY ABRAMS • Produced by SEAN S. CUNNINGHAM and STEPHEN C. MINER PG PARENTAL GUIDANCE SUGGESTED
Directed by SEAN S. CUNNINGHAM • Color by Movielab • An American International Release

If non-genre films like *Here Come the Tigers* had been successful it's likely that *Friday the 13th* never would've been made. (Photo courtesy of Barry Abrams)

Aside from some of their similar production elements, *Friday the 13th* and *Last House on the Left* arrive at very different places within the exploitation/horror genre. *Last House on the Left* is an exercise in brutality that almost dares the viewer to not turn away while *Friday the 13th*, in spite of its gory images, is a truly interactive experience between film and viewer whose main goal is to entertain, to jolt, to shock. *Friday the 13th* makes no attempt to mirror reality, in any way that would break the conventions of commercial horror filmmaking, while *Last House on the Left* dares, if not aspires, to offend all classes.

Friday the 13th represents escapism while *Last House on the Left* offers no escape. "The violence in *Friday the 13th* was bizarre, but it wasn't real," Wes Craven said. "It [*Friday the 13th*] was goofy. I was more interested in psychological underpinnings and irony, and I think Sean discovered that he was much more interested in being entertaining rather than assaultive. *Last House* didn't allow you to have fun at all."

If nothing else, *Last House on the Left* provided a training ground in fear filmmaking - what works and what doesn't work - for both Cunningham and Steve Miner. "I think he learned what not to do," says Szulkin. "*Last House* was a learning experience for all of those guys. Sean didn't set out to be a horror filmmaker or a 'schlock-meister.' I think, at this point, Sean's comfortable with being the horror guy, but, particularly after *Last House*, he and Wes really wanted to do other things."

By the end of the 1970s, Cunningham had developed into a competent, efficient, technically-sound filmmaker. It's a skill-set ideally suited to the cold, mechanical work of making commercials, documentaries and industrial films, all of which kept Cunningham financially afloat in the mid to late 1970s.

Cunningham harbors no denial about this - not now and not in the 1970s. Few filmmakers are as honest and self-aware of their own capabilities and limitations. "I've always approached filmmaking from a business sense, not an artistic sense," Cunningham says. "The bottom line is: can you sell the movie for more than it cost to make? That's a job. That was always my main goal."

Friday the 13th was Cunningham's lone vision in his career, his bolt of lightning. Whether driven by desperation or pure greed, or both, Cunningham's vision, paired with luck and timing, carried *Friday the 13th* from the planning stages all the way through to the film's massive commercial success.

Friday the 13th began as a marketing gimmick and then Cunningham went in search of a film to support it. There was a logo. There was a title. There was a strategy. No characters. No plot. No setting. Although Cunningham's direction of *Friday the 13th* proved to be very assured and crisp, his canny planning and salesmanship was integral to the film's success. "I'd done the two kids' movies [*Here Come the Tigers* (1978) and *Manny's Orphans* (1978)] before *Friday the 13th*, and I was looking for another idea and the *Friday the 13th* title just hit me," Cunningham recalls. "This was before we had a script, or a concept, although I knew I wanted to do a horror film that took place at some kind of isolated location. All I could see was the title *Friday the 13th*."

This vision, or belief, infused Cunningham's direction of *Friday the 13th* with an energy and zeal, not present in his work before or since. In spite of the base commercial motives that inspired *Friday the 13th*, the film represents, within the constraints of Cunningham's abilities, a joy of filmmaking and in scaring the audience.

Although the making of *Friday the 13th* was a chaotic, stressful process for Cunningham, directing was fun. He proved adept at the art of manipulating and toying with the audience's sensibilities. "The scary things in the script came about by sitting down and asking ourselves, 'What would be fun?'" Cunningham said. "You'd think of all the situations that frightened you as a child. There's a boogeyman some place. Your mother would come into the room and assure you that there's no one in the closet, and she'd turn out the light and eventually you'd go to sleep. We tried to do a switch on that. We dedicated the film to the idea that there's really something under the bed or in the closet, that there's a hostile force trying to get you. Part of the business of growing up is learning to ignore that there's a hostile force out there trying to do you in. It's playing on that fear. What I wanted

9

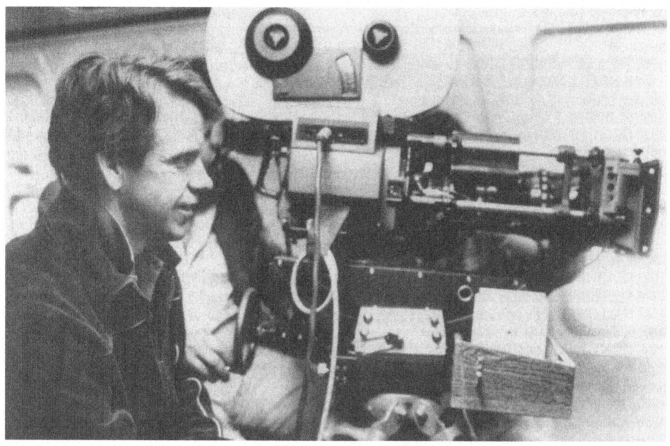

Despite his background in theatrical production, Sean Cunningham emerged throughout the 1970s as someone who took a wholly businesslike approach to filmmaking. (Photo courtesy of Sean Cunningham)

to do is create a frightening, funhouse atmosphere."

Just as the infamy and notoriety - if not mainstream commercial success - of *Last House on the Left* followed Cunningham like a bad cold throughout the 1970s, the success of *Friday the 13th* further stigmatized his filmmaking career on a much larger, transformative level.

Certainly *Friday the 13th* established Cunningham as an influential filmmaker in the horror genre, a legacy, good or bad, that he's never escaped. "After *Friday*, I was like the new kid in the whorehouse, and everyone wanted to take a crack at me," says Cunningham. "In many ways, *Friday the 13th* was my sample reel to show Hollywood in terms of what I could do. I was ready and excited to do other films, but I was trapped by *Friday the 13th*."

Within the horror genre, *Friday the 13th* established a cottage industry comprised of endless copycats, numerous sequels, a television series, a 2009 remake.

Comic books. Toys. Despised by film critics, most notably the late Roger Ebert and Gene Siskel, but loved by fans, *Friday the 13th*, the original film, remains one of the most influential and visited landmarks in horror cinema.

The first film is usually the best, as they say, and almost certainly the most influential. That applies to the *Friday the 13th* franchise and the countless horror films that *Friday the 13th*'s success gave birth to. A cult phenomenon buried within the mainstream public consciousness, an independent blockbuster, the progenitor of a filmmaking industry, a vanguard in the world of modern horror filmmaking, *Friday the 13th* warrants a closer examination than it's ever been given before.

CHAPTER 2

STRAIGHT OUTTA WESTPORT:
THE SEEDS OF SPLATTER

*"You don't have to pass a bar exam
to become a movie producer. You just
have to buy some stationery."*

– Sean Cunningham

*"I always looked at Sean as being more
of a businessman than a filmmaker."*

– Production designer Virginia Field

The origin of *Friday the 13th* is tied to the life of its founder, Sean Sexton Cunningham, the son of first-generation Irish immigrants. He spent the first six years of his life in New York, living in a Fifth Avenue apartment with his family, which later included two younger brothers. The Cunninghams relocated to Westport, Connecticut in 1948 and it was this setting that defined Cunningham's destiny, especially the direction and tone of his filmmaking career that eventually spawned *Friday the 13th*.

Cunningham flourished in academics as an adolescent and seemed poised to enter a professional vocation that matched his prim, respectable upbringing. As the 1950s drew to a close, Sean, who turned eighteen on New Year's Eve 1959, enrolled at Franklin and Marshall College in Lancaster, Pennsylvania. He aspired to pursue a medical career, but this turned out to be a misguided pursuit. Realizing his heart didn't reside within the staid world of academia, Cunningham quickly gravitated to the school's theater program, and an unlikely show business career was born.

Sean Cunningham's career had been at a standstill prior to *Friday the 13th*. (Photo courtesy of Barry Abrams)

This picture of Sean Cunningham was taken in early 1980, just prior to when Paramount Pictures and Warner Bros. acquired the distribution rights to *Friday the 13th*. (Photo courtesy of Barry Abrams)

"I became interested in the theater there, and spent all my time at it," Cunningham said. "I also realized I had wanted to become a doctor for all the wrong reasons; that I wanted the status, and that I wasn't really equipped to deal with a scientific discipline, but more with a creative discipline. I thoroughly enjoyed my enormous involvement in theater in college, and didn't enjoy at all the scientific discipline of memorization." In addition to helping mount various theatrical productions at Franklin and Marshall, Cunningham also acted in various plays produced at the school. This fostered short-lived dreams of a career as a leading man. By the time Cunningham earned a Master's degree in Drama and Film at Stanford, he realized his calling was behind the scenes or, more precisely, behind the camera.

"I went to grad school for film and drama at Stanford, and decided I didn't want to act anymore, but wanted to direct," Cunningham recalled. "Next, I got one of those lucky breaks, in a way. A friend of mine involved at the Lincoln Center called me and asked if I wanted a job. I had great visions of being tapped as a leading man, and found the job was as a dresser. I befriended the stage manager and really learned the craft."

From the mid to late 1960s, Cunningham lived a nomadic existence, managing stage productions that travelled right across the United States. Along with New York's Lincoln Center, where he served as stage manager for a well-received production of *The Merry Widow*, Cunningham helped mount stage productions at the Oregon Shakespeare Festival and at the Mineola Playhouse on Long Island where Cunningham ended up producing revivals of *The Front Page* and *Our Town*.

Still, as the 1960s drew to a close, Cunningham, though busy and productive, had grown weary of the theater model, both the art form and the business itself.

In the fall of 1969, Cunningham, with the support of his wife, Susan (the couple, who'd been married for about four years at this point, had an infant son, Noel), decided it was time to make a career change and move from theater to the world of feature filmmaking.

"Theater is an anachronism – it doesn't last," Cunningham said. "Film is a lasting statement. I had raised some money for theatrical projects, and that didn't seem like a very good financial investment. I figured maybe I could raise some money for movies, and figure out how to make them as I went along. It seemed like fun, so that's what I tried to do."

Cunningham's time in the theater represented the last time in his professional career he was ever involved in an enterprise entirely driven by creative, innocent motives. Although the theatrical world was, is, very competitive and ruthless, the world of theater, in retrospect, was like a panacea compared to the abyss that Cunningham found himself entangled in throughout the 1970s.

Cunningham's fateful decision, in the twilight of 1969, to move into the filmmaking arena marked the beginning of his transformation from energetic, optimistic, upper-crust New England boy to the brash, cynical, self-effacing, wholly businesslike figure that emerged throughout the 1970s.

Together was a surprising box office success and marked the beginning of Sean Cunningham's relationship with Hallmark Releasing Corporation, the newly-formed distribution company in Boston – run by Robert Barsamian, Stephen Minasian and Philip Scuderi – for whom *Together* was one of the first titles they distributed. Cunningham only received a tiny portion of the film's profits. (Photo courtesy of David A. Szulkin)

"I lived like a gypsy in the 1970s," Cunningham says. "I had a passion for the theater, but I didn't approach film with any sense of artistry. I looked at the prospect of making films as being a fun job and I was hoping I could make enough off the movies so that I didn't have to get a real job. That was my goal."

With a budget of $3500, gathered from donations Cunningham sought from family and friends, he officially entered the film business in the fall of 1969 when he directed, produced and wrote a sex documentary – or "white coater" as it would come to be known – called *The Art of Marriage*.

A complete novice in the rituals of low budget filmmaking, Cunningham only brought three crew members with him for the making of *The Art of Marriage*. Whether it was beginner's luck, or blissful ignorance, *The Art of Marriage* was a modest success when the film was released in a handful of theaters in 1970.

"At the time, we had [referring to the film] what were called 'white coaters,'" Cunningham said. "They allowed you to get away with showing hardcore XXX-rated movies as long as they were under the guise of freedom of speech. You billed it as an 'educational' or 'medical' movie. At the beginning, someone would come out and say, 'We're now going to show you marriage practices in Denmark and these are the ways you can improve your marital bliss.' Then for the next 80 minutes you saw people fucking like crazy."

For Cunningham, who has always measured the success of a film through the prism of a cost-to-revenue ratio, *The Art of Marriage* served its purpose by giving him some degree of financial breathing room, as well as invaluable filmmaking experience. "I was in completely uncharted waters," Cunningham said. "As dreadful as *The Art of Marriage* was, I had to find a theater that would make some sort of deal with me to play it. *The Art of Marriage* was first released at the Brant Theater on 42nd Street in Manhattan, and it played for twenty-seven weeks! We probably got over $100,000, so I had what most people in the film business never had: a hit movie."

Aside from being his first film, *The Art of Marriage* was most significant because it marked Cunningham's introduction to Wes Craven, a fellow struggling filmmaker who would collaborate with Cunningham on *Last House on the Left*. With the proceeds from *The Art of Marriage*, and another $50,000 in "donations" from family and friends, Cunningham set-up shop in New York - under the banner of Sean S. Cunningham Films - by renting a one-room office in the West 45th Street building. This is the place where Craven and Cunningham collaborated on Cunningham's second directorial outing, and where Craven and Cunningham eventually conceived *Last House on the Left*.

GETTING HIS ACT TOGETHER

It was the spring of 1970 and Sean Cunningham was now a real filmmaker, complete with business cards and office space. In fact, Cunningham paid the bills during these lean first months by using the editing equipment he'd set-up in the West 45th Street office to shoot commercials, short films, anything to keep himself busy, and eating. "We were trying to do anything to keep the lights on,

Together's unlikely commercial success established Sean Cunningham as a canny marketer and promoter. (Photo courtesy of David A. Szulkin)

essentially," Cunningham said. "We had purchased some Steenbeck editing equipment, along with some sound transfer equipment and as a result we could effectively do post-production. We would go out and shoot little hand-held commercials, or testimonials, that kind of stuff. It was very informal; we were just trying to figure it all out."

Cunningham's next film, his second feature, was a soft-core pseudo-documentary film entitled *Together*. The film starred future porn Goddess Marilyn Chambers, who had dated one of Sean Cunningham's brothers, and was then best known, at that time, for her television appearances in Ivory Snow laundry detergent commercials. Cunningham began filming *Together* in May 1970, and continued until July when the money –obtained from family, friends, and even the Cunningham family doctor - ran out.

The filming of *Together* resumed in September, and crawled through December, with no clear end in sight. Enter Wes Craven, hired by Cunningham to synchronize dailies for the film. Craven's work eventually earned him an "associate producer" credit and Cunningham's faith and trust. Craven even made his directorial debut on *Together*, when he shot additional footage in Puerto Rico during a particularly chaotic period.

Cunningham's partner on *Together*, and in the office, was Roger Murphy who served as *Together's* cinematographer and editor. The volatile relationship that existed between Cunningham and Murphy tightened the bond between Craven and Cunningham. Cunningham began to rely on Craven, more and more, to help him cut and edit the film, especially when Cunningham and Murphy reached the point when they were no longer on speaking terms.

THE BOSTON CONNECTION

When *Together* was finally completed, Cunningham went out and sought a distribution deal, and was met with universal rejection. Desperate, he brought the film to Esquire Theaters of America, the theater chain operated out of Boston by partners Robert Barsamian, Stephen (Steve) Minasian and Philip Scuderi.

Esquire controlled a chain of movie theaters throughout New England and upstate New York that represented a mix of urban movie houses, multiplexes, drive-ins and porno houses, the last two sectors of which the company were most identified with. By the fall of 1970, Esquire had expanded its operations to include film distribution, under the banner of Hallmark Releasing Corporation.

Together was one of Hallmark's very first releases as a distribution arm, and also technically marked the company's first entry into film production, since partner Stephen Minasian received a token producer credit - as Steve Minasian - on the released film, even though he had no creative involvement with the film itself.

The partnership with Hallmark, later renamed Georgetown Productions, on *Together* marked the beginning of a decade-long working relationship – a very one-sided, stormy and often unhealthy relationship driven by desperation and greed - that would eventually– under the Georgetown moniker – spawn *Friday the 13th*.

Sean Cunningham and Steve Miner cut their teeth in horror filmmaking while making *Last House on the Left*. (Photo courtesy of David A. Szulkin)

Hallmark's headquarters were located inside a very unassuming-looking two-story building on Church Street, an area of Boston regarded as the "Boston film district" back in the 1970s for its colorful assortment of distributors and theaters. Hallmark - which was named after a Boston suburb - was ideally-suited to this modest setting where the company's three partners conducted business with little attention and fanfare.

Robert Barsamian, Stephen Minasian and Philip Scuderi entered the film business as lawyers, and their three very different personalities made for a very chaotic, volatile business structure. Philip Scuderi (b. November 16, 1929 – d. November 23, 1995) was the frontman. He was a bombastic, charismatic showman who brought great passion, and a sometimes outrageous zeal, to the films he distributed, screened, financed and produced throughout the 1970s and into the 1980s.

Like Scuderi, Stephen Minasian (b. January 28, 1925) was also a creative force, but Minasian's personality was much more low-key and reserved. Robert Barsamian (b. September 20, 1928) was Stephen Minasian's brother-in-law and maintained a quiet business role in the company.

"Phil Scuderi was a handsome, charismatic, firecracker of a guy," recalls George Mansour, a Hallmark booking agent in the 1970s. "He was a smart, tenacious, terrific person, but he had lots of affairs, and had lots of mistresses, including a secretary who worked in the office. Steve Minasian was a stolid guy, very smart, but conservative, low-key and a real family man. There were no fireworks with Steve, unlike Phil who was married but had a mistress and ended up dying much too young from a heart attack. Robert was Steve's brother-in-law and he loved to play practical jokes, and always joked with people. He wasn't involved with the film business that much. They didn't put their names on *Friday the 13th* or the other films because they didn't want to be associated with the films because they wanted to keep as low of a profile as possible."

The business itself operated like a rollercoaster throughout the 1970s, full of ups and downs, and unexpected developments. Basically, when the theaters were doing well, the money flowed, fairly efficiently, and everything operated smoothly. But when the theater business was sluggish, everything would grind to a halt. Payrolls would be missed, Hollywood studios sued over nonpayment of royalties, and the later film productions that Hallmark invested in, beginning with *Together*, would run out of money. "Sometimes checks would bounce and I'd go to the porn houses, which always did well, and I'd take money out of the receipts," Mansour recalls. "I'd leave the bad checks, which didn't go over well with the bosses. Other than that, it was a pretty normal office of business, with a payroll clerk, accountant, secretary, and the three bosses."

Last House on the Left was a financial success for Wes Craven and Sean Cunningham but both men struggled to develop subsequent film projects outside the genres of exploitation and porn. (Photo courtesy of David A. Szulkin)

Whether it was Boston's virulent reputation as a mob city, particularly in the 1970s, or the lurid aspects of Hallmark's theater business, or the garish, over-the-top wise-guy attire that Scuderi and his partners would often wear in public, the company was dogged by reputed ties to organized crime. This reputation was emboldened by the fact that Hallmark, and the names of its partners, showed-up in various federal investigations into organized crime, most involving the alleged smuggling of film prints, of pornographic films (a genre known to be a hotbed for money laundering throughout the 1970s) from Europe. Although Esquire/Hallmark, in fact, released films of every genre, from dramas to kids' movies, the company's ties to - and its passion for - exploitation, horror, and pornographic films would always represent its identity and legacy.

This was the wonderful world that Sean Cunningham entered into when he drove (there have been some reports that Cunningham took a bus to Boston) – unable, or unwilling, to finance the cost of a plane ticket - from New York to Boston and met with Scuderi about acquiring *Together*, which carried a total production cost of $70,000, for distribution. This marked the beginning of a bizarre relationship that would take on a predictable pattern over the subsequent decade.

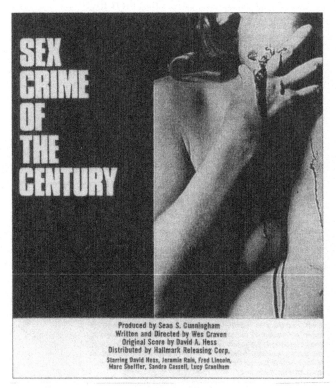

Advertisement for *Sex Crime of the Century*, one of the alternate titles that *Last House on the Left* was released as. (Photo courtesy of David A. Szulkin)

Cunningham, who, as mentioned, struggled even to finance this initial trip to Boston, was desperate, had nowhere else to go, and was prepared to take any deal that Scuderi threw his way. Wes Craven, who also had many experiences with Scuderi and his partners, would later, half-jokingly, describe the basic relationship between Cunningham and Scuderi as a "bullets over Broadway" type of situation, a tongue-in-cheek reference to Hallmark's alleged ties to the Boston mafia.

Cunningham and Scuderi screened *Together* at a local Boston cinema, after which Scuderi offered to pay Cunningham $15,000 for the distribution rights. Cun-

ningham grudgingly accepted this and Hallmark took over the film. *Together*'s theatrical premiere took place on August 8, 1971, at the Four Seasons multiplex in Providence, Rhode Island. "Phil [Philip Scuderi] saw what I saw," Cunningham said. "If you marketed this right, it could play in suburban theatres. We'd take out big ads in local papers that read, 'What can your children teach you about S-E-X? Find out Tuesday – Special Screening at 10:00 AM. Free!' Who's going to come at ten o'clock in the morning? The buzz was off the charts. We just did phenomenal business. People were literally lining-up around the block to see it. It was 1971 – before *Deep Throat*. 'Porn chic' happened later."

Benefiting greatly from the fact that it was less explicit than most of its X-rated counterparts in the marketplace, not to mention hardcore titans like *Deep Throat* (1972) and *The Devil in Miss Jones* (1973) which soon followed, *Together* appealed to middle-of-the-road couples looking for a hot little movie to snuggle up to, minus the guilt and shame associated with the hardcore genre. "There was a scene where a girl, I think it was Marilyn Chambers, takes a yellow flower and uses it to caress this large, flaccid black penis, and as she's caressing it, it gradually becomes erect," George Mansour recalled. "That was the big scene, the one unusual thing in the film. Hallmark's rationale for the success of *Together* was the fact that there was a vast audience who had never seen an erect black penis."

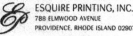

LAST HOUSE ON THE LEFT

presented by

SEAN S. CUNNINGHAM FILMS LTD.

starring

DAVID HESS • LUCY GRANTHAM • SANDRA CASSEL • MARC SHEFFLER • and introducing ADA WASHINGTON

Written and directed by .... WES CRAVEN
Produced by .... SEAN S. CUNNINGHAM
COLOR BY MOVIELAB • Running Time 91 mins.

• • • • •

PRODUCER'S STATEMENT

Since the opening of the motion picture "Last House On The Left," municipal officials, film reviewers, and theatergoers have deluged the theaters with complaints about the film, and requested that its exhibition be terminated immediately.
The thrust of the criticism is that the film is too violent.
The critics have completely failed to understand this film. It is one of the finest anti-violence films ever made. Here, at last, is a film which puts violence in its proper perspective, as so few films have in the past.
In this film, unlike so many recent, successful motion pictures, violence is not glorified, nor the violators romanticized. All is shown as ugly and as debauched as it is in real life. For example, we have all seen recently motion pictures in which upwards of 50 and 60 people are killed before the last reel. It is all done in an atmosphere where real people do not die, do not bleed, or do not suffer.
In this film, prior to the last couple of minutes, only two persons have been killed — but they are shown in the true nature of what homicide is, real people dying tragically.

In past films, criminals are made glamourous and heroic. We identify with them in a happy and pleasant manner. In "Last House On The Left" the criminals are shown for what they really are, mean and horrible.
Nor does the film make any attempt to minimize or make pleasurable experimentation with drugs. This is risky business which can only produce consequences as shown in the film.
This, then, is a moral film. A film which has become all the more gripping because we have become so unused to seeing how wicked and unforgivable violence and killing are.
For as long as records for numbers of homicide are broken each week in our urban centers, and the evening news brings us new tales of violence and burning, and we continue to treat these horrors in a nonchalant manner, it will be necessary for films like "Last House On The Left" to bring the true measure of violence to the consciousness of us all.
It is indeed ironic that the criticism which this film has received is because the worth of its message has been improperly assessed. The large numbers of parents now bringing their children to the theater is perhaps illustrative that the true meaning of this film is now being properly received. The film is rated "R" in the best sense of that rating.

— ORDER ALL ACCESSORIES FROM —

ESQUIRE PRINTING, INC.
788 ELMWOOD AVENUE
PROVIDENCE, RHODE ISLAND 02907
(401) 781-0900

TRAILERS • 1-SHEETS

STILLS • RADIO SPOTS

PRESS • MATS

The partners at Esquire/Hallmark were notorious for outrageous promotional gimmicks. (Photo courtesy of David A. Szulkin)

Expanding into mainstream movie houses and multiplexes, *Together* became a surprise underground hit that eventually piqued the interest of national distributor American International Pictures (AIP), with whom Minasian and Scuderi had a very chummy, close relationship. AIP, who'd never previously handled an X-rated film, agreed to give *Together* national distribution. By February of 1972, *Together* had cleared $1 Million at the North American box office, and by 1977, the film had accumulated rentals - the amount returned to the central film distributor - of $4 Million. "After that [*Together*'s release], Hallmark said, 'Well, what do you want to do?'" Cunningham recalled. "Wes and I said, 'Something else. If you guys will write us a check, let's figure out another movie.'"

Unfortunately, for Cunningham, his share of the profits from *Together* was relatively-miniscule, having sold the distribution rights for a pitiful $15,000. "Phil bought *Together* from Sean, and released it, and it was a big hit because of the 'Ivory Snow' Marilyn Chambers," Mansour recalls. "Sean was angry about this arrangement, and Phil, as payback, agreed to put up the money for Sean's next film, which turned out to be *The Last House on the Left*."

LAST STOP AT THE LAST HOUSE

Last House on the Left was born in the summer of 1971 – while the success of *Together* was still building - when Hallmark approached Cunningham about doing a scary, violent movie. "It was almost instant," said Cunningham, regarding the project's birth. "I imagine that we raised the money to do *Last House* over the summer, just a few months before we started shooting. It was one of those things that, when you start out, seems so easy and obvious. Everybody had made a lot of money on that little *Together* movie, so the natural enough thing for the distributors to do was to ask us, 'Well, you wanna do something else?' And Wes and I said, 'Uh, yeah! We'll make a regular movie where people talk!' So Hallmark put-up the initial money for us to do *Last House*."

Cunningham says that the inspiration for *Last House on the Left* resulted from a discussion he had with Wes Craven, about the role of violence in cinema which Cunningham felt, by 1971, existed on the level of cartoonish fantasy. "We resisted doing a conventional horror movie," Cunningham said. "At that time, that meant Vincent Price walking around in a castle, and the young groom saying, 'You stay here, honey, I'm gonna go for help!' Around this time came the advent of Clint Eastwood, which meant a whole bunch of 'Bang, bang, you're dead' movies. The Vietnam War was grinding down. Wes and I came from a pacifist, peace-and-love kind of background. We knew that somebody dying can be re-

Friday the 13th's popularity brought a new audience to *Last House on the Left*. (Photo courtesy of David A. Szulkin)

ally horrifying. 'Bang, bang, you're dead' didn't really deal with that. So we set up a situation where a couple of girls die, and it's a total mind-fuck! To this day, I find that film [*Last House on the Left*] absolutely unnerving."

Last House on the Left began filming on October 2, 1971, near Cunningham's home in Westport, Connecticut, with a budget of $90,000. Shortly after the start of filming, Craven and Cunningham were approached by Steve Miner, a twenty-year-old Westport native and filmmaking novice, who viewed the arrival of Craven, Cunningham, and their ragtag production crew, as a godsend.

Miner's mother was a film librarian, and this influence sparked Miner's interest in film. "My mother would always bring home movies for us to watch," Miner recalls. "I'd see a lot of 16MM films and that's when I really started to fall in love with cinema and when I started to think about it in terms of a career. Living in Connecticut, it seemed really far away at the time."

Miner had recently been drifting around the ski slopes of Colorado, in search of direction, before re-

Although *Last House on the Left* has enjoyed a strong cult following over the years, the film's popularity, and genre influence, pales in comparison to that of *Friday the 13th*. (Photo courtesy of David A. Szulkin)

far ahead of him because everyone who worked on *Last House* still had a lot to learn about the craft of filmmaking."

Last House on the Left had its initial release, at two theaters, on August 23, 1972 in Hartford, Connecticut. Even this small screening sample provoked a harsh reaction, as evidenced by an editorial in the September 3, 1972 edition of the *Hartford Courant* newspaper that labeled *Last House on the Left* "...a horrible, sick film."

Expanding to the rest of the East Coast, *Last House on the Left* found enthusiastic business and widespread repugnance from film critics, including the famed, late Gene Siskel of the *Chicago Tribune* newspaper who labeled *Last House on the Left* "the sickest film of 1972".

Ironically, film critic Roger Ebert of the *Chicago Sun-Times* newspaper, and Siskel's future co-host, emerged as *Last House on the Left's* most ardent and influential critical supporter when he called the film "a tough, bitter little sleeper of a movie that's about four times as good as you'd expect..." in his three-and-a-half star review that was published in the *Chicago Sun-Times* on October 26, 1972.

Although *Last House on the Left* represented a de-

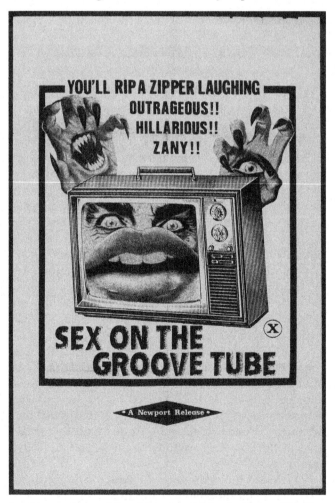

Sean Cunningham and Steve Miner reunited for the filming of *The Case of the Smiling Stiffs (AKA Sex on the Groove Tube)*, but the experience proved disastrous. (Photo courtesy of Matt Hankinson)

turning to Westport in the hopes of finding some entry into the world of filmmaking, whether it be in commercials, industrial films or a low budget exploitation-horror film like *Last House on the Left*. "When I heard that Sean and Wes were doing *Last House* in Connecticut, near my home, I begged them for a job," Miner says. "I spent a lot of time making coffee for the actors and the crew, but I also learned so much about filmmaking."

With Miner, Cunningham found both a true apprentice and a future close collaborator who eventually proved to be his closest ally during the entire process of *Friday the 13th*. "He was full of energy and enthusiasm and I could see he had a lot of talent," Cunningham says of Miner during the filming of *Last House on the Left* that saw Miner work twenty hour days, carrying a boom mike and lights, doing assistant camerawork, anything that had to be done. "Steve went about learning every aspect of filmmaking during the making of *Last House*, and by the time we finished the film, I realized that I couldn't live without him. Looking back, I don't think the rest of us were that

Australian video cover for *The Case of the Smiling Stiffs*. *The Case of the Smiling Stiffs* was an unlikely hit in Australia where the film retains a strong cult following. (Photo courtesy of David A. Szulkin)

Here Come the Tigers was the first of two children's films that Sean Cunningham filmed in and around his home-base of Westport, Connecticut, the second being *Manny's Orphans (AKA Kick)*. (Photo courtesy of Barry Abrams)

parture from porn, it heralded the beginning of what Cunningham would describe as the "puke in a bucket" era of his career, an ignoble title that later crystallized with the arrival of *Friday the 13th.* "*Last House* became kind of a double-edged sword," Cunningham said. "Since it was very cheap and exploitative, and successful at its own level, people thought of me with the notion that, 'If you want to get puke in a bucket – and get it cheap – boy, I've got just the guy for you!' And I just didn't want to do that."

By February 1973, *Last House on the Left* had grossed just over $1.5 Million, according to the national box office charts. This figure doesn't represent the totality of the box office returns which continued to accrue, largely through drive-in screenings, throughout the 1970s and well past *Friday the 13th*'s 1980s release. Both Craven and Cunningham made a nice sum of cash from the film, and continued to see returns for years afterwards. Even so, money woes plagued Craven and Cunningham throughout the rest of the

1970s, eventually driving Cunningham back to the horror genre and towards the creation of *Friday the 13th.*

For Cunningham, the businessman, *Last House on the Left* represented a successful venture, especially relative to the financial screwing he'd endured with *Together.* Regardless, Cunningham wasn't at all anxious to reunite with Philip Scuderi – if he could avoid it. "Wes and I were striking off in slightly different directions," Cunningham said. "Steve Miner had been working for me and he was trying to cut some NHL [National Hockey League] film. We were all just learning. I was trying to do documentary films and commercials. I also did not want to deal any longer with Phil and the folks in Boston. They were, and continue to be, very difficult people to deal with. In a perfect world, you wouldn't have to deal with people who cause you problems, so after *Last House*, Wes and I decided to stay away from them. We were friendly, and I didn't want to quite close the door, but I didn't particularly want to work with them again."

BACK TO PORN

In the period following *Last House on the Left*'s 1972 release, Craven and Cunningham made determined, valiant attempts to develop projects outside of the exploitation and horror genres, or at least as far away as they could get. "Wes and I made a lot of money from *Last House*, especially considering that he was driving a cab and I was working in a theater," Cunningham said. "My career wasn't progressing at that point, anyway, but the backlash against *Last House* had no effect on me. The truth is, all anyone in the movie business cares about is whether or not your picture makes money. They don't care why; if you can get people into theater seats, then you're a desirable commodity."

The first film project that Cunningham developed after the release of *Last House on the Left* was an action film project called *Frog*. The story followed a black action hero not very dissimilar from the titular character from the film *Shaft* (1971). Cunningham approached basketball star Walt "Clyde" Frazier to play the title role, but the project went nowhere.

Cunningham also developed a dramatic script about the relationship between a divorced father and his child. Wes Craven also tried to jumpstart several wildly ambitious projects during this period, but none of the non-horror projects Craven and Cunningham developed between 1972 and 1975 gained serious traction.

With his dreams of mainstream respectability on ice, Cunningham accepted an offer from producer, and friend, Bruce "Brud" Talbot to travel down to Miami, Florida and assist him with a soft-core comedy project that was set to commence filming. Cunningham accepted the offer after Talbot assured him that solid financing was in place. This wasn't the case.

Enlisting now close friend Steve Miner-- who was in the midst of achieving an art degree and starting up his own editing business-- to help him with the film, Cunningham and Miner traveled to Miami to begin work on the project that was filmed under the title *Silver C*, short for *Silver Cock*. "It's the kind of film I'd never made before, not even with *Together*, and which I'll never make again," says Cunningham with a laugh. "It was a disaster."

The film, which was eventually released in the fall of 1973 as *The Case of the Smiling Stiffs* (later as *Case of the Full Moon Murders*), was a sex parody of the *Dragnet* television show. It followed two amorous detectives who have to track down a horny vampire. Porn superstar Harry Reems starred in the film which also featured future *Friday the 13th* co-star Ron Millkie. Cunningham was supposed to co-direct and co-produce the film with Talbot. Miner was assisting with editing and the filming of additional insert sequences. When the money for the film evaporated during filming, Cunningham was forced to take the film over completely.

"That wasn't a movie that I really had much to do with, except that I was aware of it," Cunningham said. "Yeah, there was a friend, Brud Talbot, who wanted to do this goofy sex movie about a failed female vampire. The premise was that she would go around and give guys head, and so much so that they would almost die, but only on a full moon, and they would almost die with the biggest smile on their face. He [Talbot] asked me to become kind of a line producer on it, and on *Last House* and *Together* we had bought some editing equipment, camera equipment, sound equipment and he [Talbot] was using all this stuff and, anyway, we went down to the set and he shot it. It came back, and the picture was a mess, and he couldn't finish it and he couldn't pay any of his bills. So now I had all these bills with all this money that was owed

to me, so I had to find a way to re-cut it or cut it in such a way that it might be sold. We put together a version of it and I believe we did get to sell it but, boy, that was a mess."

"It was not really an X-rated film like *Deep Throat* or *Behind the Green Door* but a witty and clever sex comedy, a parody of the old TV series, *Dragnet*," Ron Millkie recalls. "There was certainly no sexual parts exhibited and the sexy scenes were done tastefully! (including my classic line from *Dragnet*, 'Joe, I told you, she's clean.') This particular film sequence sent our AD [assistant director], Steve Miner, into such convulsive laughter that I thought we were going to have to call an ambulance. There were other lines that I still remember, like the one at a widows' cocktail party at which a gentleman bragged, 'I got AT&T at 60' and the widow replied, 'Well, that's nothing. I got syphilis at 60!' I remember Sean's energy and lightness of spirit and his humor. I am not proud, but certainly not sorry, for doing *Case of the Full Moon Murders*. Without that chance that I took in my early days as an actor, I never would have met Sean Cunningham and I never would have been part of the *Friday the 13th* legend. It was a smash hit in Sydney, Australia. It played for five years in the same theater. I was also offered to do the sequel in Sydney and declined the offer. The American premiere was held in my home city of Hartford, Connecticut and they used my real name in the final credits. I wasn't too happy about that."

"It was a bizarre experience," recalled Miner who briefly landed in jail during filming, for reasons that are more peculiar than anything in the finished

Several members of *Friday the 13th*'s eventual crew worked on *Here Come the Tigers*, most notably cinematographer Barry Abrams. (Photo courtesy of Barry Abrams)

film. "I got a call at the last minute to go down there, and I worked on the film for three weeks or however long we shot. It was a real mess, and I think I ended up cutting it when we got it back to the editing room. It was supposed to be a comedy, but it wasn't funny... it was just stupid. It was the first time I directed anything though. I shot a bunch of insert scenes back in

Connecticut, with the two cops. It got some limited release in the U.S., but I've heard that it was a big hit in Australia. They thought it was hilarious down there."

The awful experience in Miami foretold an abyss in Cunningham's career that lingered between 1974 and 1976. Anxious to move on from *Case of the Full Moon Murders*, Cunningham agreed to join Wes Craven on the hardcore film *The Fireworks Woman*. Cunningham produced the film which Craven co-wrote and directed under the pseudonym Abe Snake, one of many Craven used between 1974 and 1975 for the various X-rated film titles he worked on. Cunningham kept his name off the film altogether.

Released in 1975, *The Fireworks Woman* marked the end of Cunningham's porn career and his one and only acting appearance (Cunningham can be seen pushing a lawnmower in one scene). No matter what, Cunningham was done with porn.

Needing a change of scenery, as well as time to reassess his career goals, Cunningham – who also tried, without success, to develop a children's fantasy film project based on the *Hansel and Gretel* fairytale – next moved to Spain where he set-up a tax shelter corporation. There, he served as an un-credited co-producer on the obscure Spanish tax shelter film *The People who own the Dark* (AKA *Planeta Ciego*) which was released into total obscurity in 1976.

The time in Spain, and the surrounding period, represented the most tumultuous period in Cunningham's life. His personal demons took hold of him during this time and embodied themselves in a bout with alcoholism-- a byproduct of the dauntless career pressures and struggles. "In Spain, they have siesta, so I was getting drunk twice a day," Cunningham said. "Plus, I didn't have too many responsibilities, so I could get drunk as much as I wanted to, and I had two alcoholic parents, so I knew a lot about booze. I thought I had decided that I wasn't going to become a drunk like my parents, and I didn't. I became a drunk unlike my parents."

Returning to the United States after this, to his East Coast stomping grounds, Cunningham spent most of the period between 1975 and 1976 in the anonymous, quiet, utterly respectable setting of industrial/technical filmmaking, a realm in which he proved extremely adept. "When I came home, my wife had had it," Cunningham recalled. "I went to AA [Alcoholics' Anonymous] on Mondays to get her off my back. As it turned out, I was one of those fortunate guys. I discovered sobriety. That's when my life changed dramatically. Sobriety brings with it very different perspectives. I no longer had interest in the 'naughty factor.' I just wasn't going to do that anymore."

Meanwhile, Steve Miner went out to Los Angeles, following the example of Wes Craven who'd relocated there, to do editing work and make contacts. "Wes was a great example because he'd taken the initiative and gone to Hollywood and gotten an agent and done it," Miner says. "I wanted to follow Wes's example because I could tell he was headed for bigger and better things."

Cunningham largely stayed in Westport throughout 1976, travelling to New York when needed, but kept in regular contact with Craven and Miner. Cunningham also maintained a relationship with the partners at Boston-based Hallmark Releasing, primarily Philip Scuderi.

Having spent the 1970s working solely in porn, exploitation and horror, often in various combinations, it was completely unpredictable, by the summer of 1976, that Cunningham's next exploitation target would be located within the kids' movie genre.

THE KIDS' MOVIES ARE JUST ALRIGHT

In the summer of 1976, Cunningham emerged from his feature filmmaking sabbatical. He and Steve Miner began work on *Here Come the Tigers*, a children's comedy film shot in and around Cunningham's home-base of Westport, Connecticut. Budgeted at $250,000, Cunningham's largest budget to date, *Here Come the Tigers* was directly-inspired by the box office success of the 1976 film *The Bad News Bears*, which starred Tatum O'Neal and Walter Matthau and followed the wacky adventures of a little league baseball team and their dysfunctional coach.

Here Come the Tigers attempted, within the resources of Cunningham and Miner, to copy *The Bad News Bears* model, as sort of a *Bad News Bears* on the East Coast. "I thought it would be fun to make children's movies," said Cunningham of the inspiration that was partly born out of his aborted *Hansel and Gretel* project. "There's a feeling that you get, especially when you're making "snuff" movies. Do I have to do this? Can't I do anything else?"

The Bad News Bears had been a solid hit, grossing more than $40 Million at the North American box office and returning nearly $25 Million in rentals to its distribu-

Sean Cunningham was inspired to make *Here Come the Tigers* by the modest box office success of the film *The Bad News Bears*. (Photo courtesy of Barry Abrams)

Boston-based investors Robert Barsamian, Stephen Minasian and Philip Scuderi monitored the filming of *Here Come the Tigers* and did the same on *Friday the 13th*. Although *Here Come the Tigers* was regarded as a failure by Sean Cunningham and his team, Scuderi and his partners at Hallmark Releasing Corporation (later to be known as Georgetown Productions) actually made a tidy profit from the film. (Photo courtesy of Barry Abrams)

tor, Paramount Pictures. In truth, *The Bad News Bears* had been more of a cultural phenomenon than a commercial one. The 1976 film, which later spawned two sequels and a 2005 remake, would ultimately be regarded most as a scathing satire of sports competition in America, but Cunningham wasn't interested in attempting satire or social commentary, nor would he have been suited to the task.

For Cunningham, *Here Come the Tigers* was an obvious, transparent move to hit on a commercial formula. Cunningham would follow *Here Come the Tigers* with another formula kids' movie, *Manny's Orphans*, which was shot in the summer of 1977 and centered around the wacky adventures of a kids' soccer team. "They were formula pictures and I had fun doing them," Cunningham says. "I knew they weren't going to be masterpieces. We had a theory at the time and the theory was that America was looking for some good old-fashioned family fare. That's where we made the mistake."

If Cunningham's theory had been correct, *Friday the 13th* probably never would've been attempted. *Here Come the Tigers* and *Manny's Orphans* represented a stab at respectability. Cunningham's failure in this led him back to the horror genre. The greatest significance of *Here Come the Tigers* and *Manny's Orphans* is that the films were populated by most of the crew that would later march to Blairstown with Cunningham to make *Friday the 13th*.

Here Come the Tigers also sent Cunningham back into Philip Scuderi's clutches. The principals of Esquire/Hallmark financed *Here Come the Tigers* and *Manny's Orphans*. This was a time when Scuderi and his partners were focusing more and more on film production and away from the theater business which was showing signs of stagnation.

By 1977, the Esquire theater chain, which had once totaled over 100 screens throughout New England and the Northeastern section of the United States, had dwindled to a reported twenty screens. It was during this period that Universal Pictures sued Esquire for the alleged nonpayment of film rentals in the amount of $82,000, a lawsuit related to receipts taken from early 1970s blockbuster films like *American Graffiti* (1973) and *The Sting* (1973).

Like many fringe/regional film companies, Esquire/Hallmark was a direct victim of the blockbuster mentality seeping through the film business, slowly but surely, throughout the 1970s. Whereas the Esquire theater chain had once grossed upwards of $20 Million a year at its height, the company was, by 1977, in financial straits. *Here Come the Tigers* represented the beginning of the company's eventual permanent shift away from distribution and releasing, toward a focus on the financing and producing of feature films.

Here Come the Tigers marked Sean Cunningham's first film collaboration with writer Victor Miller who wrote the script for *Here Come the Tigers* under the pseudonym Arch McCoy. (Photo courtesy of Barry Abrams)

Scuderi saw film production as the company's future. He also felt that Cunningham was a good bet, given how profitable their previous ventures had been. *Here Come the Tigers* was an easy sell for Cunningham. "My conversation with the producers probably went something like, 'Did you ever see *Bad News Bears*?'" Cunningham recalled. "'Yeah,' and then, 'Do you think you can make a movie like that?' 'Well, sure.' 'But can you make it now?' 'Yeah, I can make it.'"

For partners Robert Barsamian, Stephen Minasian and Philip Scuderi, the company's increased emphasis toward feature film production necessitated the three men supervising their investments personally. Cunningham and the rest of the cast and crew on *Here Come the Tigers*, *Manny's Orphans*, and especially *Friday the 13th* learned this firsthand.

The making of *Here Come the Tigers* was also notable for marking the addition of two more key *Friday the 13th* principals: cinematographer Barry Abrams and screenwriter Victor Miller. Both men brought interesting and varied life experiences to Sean Cunningham's production unit, especially Abrams.

The Abrams-Cunningham relationship was a marriage of opposites that nonetheless clicked. Just as Cunningham's formal Westport matched his straightforward filmmaking approach, Abrams' fiery stance was the product of an adventurous past.

Born in Amarillo, Texas, in 1944, Abrams was a 1966 graduate of the University of Nebraska. His professional career began in December 1966 when he arrived in Saigon, Vietnam, and was assigned to the Armed Forces Vietnam Network (AFVN). Abrams served as a cameraman and director for AFVN, who provided American soldiers with radio and television programs during the Vietnam War. "I was one of the first two directors of the television and radio station in Saigon, which featured Adrian Cronauer who was later immortalized in the movie *Good Morning, Vietnam*," recalled Abrams. "It was an exciting, dangerous time. After work, me and my friends would go up to the top of buildings where we could hear and see all of the explosions, mortars and rockets. We'd ride motorbikes around to different places, lived in an apartment, ate great meals and I would have serious discussions with friends about the war. I never carried a gun or rifle when I was in Vietnam." In 1970, after a three-year tour in Vietnam, Abrams headed to Tokyo where he worked as a cameraman for ABC News, a job he held for a year. This led him to New York where he served as a cameraman on the film *Hi, Mom!* (1970), notable for being one of filmmaker Brian De Palma's earliest efforts, as well as marking an early leading role for a young Robert De Niro. Abrams found a home at Firehouse Films, a production house in New York City, where he spent the next phase of his career shooting commercials and documentaries. Abrams would continue to work there into the 1990s, most-

Here Come the Tigers embodied the cynical nature of Sean Cunningham's filmmaking career throughout the 1970s. (Photo courtesy of Barry Abrams)

ly in the shooting of toy commercials, Abrams' financial beachhead throughout much of his later career.

Abrams only found sporadic film work throughout the 1970s, shooting the documentary film *Hollywood on Trial* (1976) and providing additional photography for the Larry Cohen-directed film *The Private Files of J. Edgar Hoover* (1977). Despite his sparse pre-*Friday the 13th* feature film credits, he was a revered figure in the New York filmmaking community.

By the mid 1970s, Abrams was firmly settled in Greenwich Village, his base of operations, along with his first wife and young son. It was here that Abrams surrounded himself with a loyal and worshipping technical film crew, namely James Bekiaris, Max Kalmanowicz, Braden Lutz, Richard Murphy, Tad Page, Carl Peterson and Robert Shulman. All of these people, with the fateful exception of Max Kalmanowicz, later joined Abrams to form the guts of *Friday the 13th*'s camera and technical crew.

After graduating from the University of Nebraska in 1966, Barry Abrams was sent to Vietnam. Abrams was stationed in Saigon where Abrams served as a cameraman and director for the Armed Forces Vietnam Network (AFVN) which was later immortalized in the film Good Morning, Vietnam. (Photo courtesy of Nalani Clark)

Here Come the Tigers, which commenced filming in the fall of 1976, marked the beginning of a close friendship between Abrams and Cunningham. On a personal level, Cunningham's feisty, witty nature was a good match for Abrams' exuberance and passion.

On a professional level, Abrams' creative flair made for an effective counterpoint to Cunningham's often mechanical, static sensibilities. Like Cunningham, Abrams didn't suffer fools well, and could exhibit a hair trigger temper from underneath his usually gregarious demeanor. This usually surfaced when Abrams was under the influence of alcohol, a not uncommon occurrence for him and the rest of his crew during this period. Like Cunningham, Abrams was desperate for mainstream recognition, something which eluded him throughout his career.

"I met Barry in 1974 when we made this independent film that was made by a woman and was about how she'd grown up with terrible parents who'd messed up her life," recalls Max Kalmanowicz, the soundman on *Here Come the Tigers*. "Then we made *The Private Files of J. Edgar Hoover*, but that film didn't have the impact or success that we'd hoped for and it didn't lead to more film work. I got back in touch with Barry when I was hired to do the sound on *Here Come the Tigers*, and that's when I believe Barry and Sean first met. We were excited about making this film because we thought it was a step-up from our previous film work, and Barry was really excited about shooting his first feature as a DP (director of photography) and getting to make what we thought was our first real movie. Barry and Sean had mutual respect. Barry had tremendous self-confidence, and although Barry had studied photography, this was his first film getting to shoot action and getting to work with lots of exteriors since most of the film took place on a baseball diamond."

"Barry and Sean seemed to have a very good and intuitive working relationship," recalls *Here Come the Tigers*' co-star Abigail Lewis, a friend of Abrams'. "Sean was mostly upbeat and had massive amounts of energy, bouncing around and usually smiling. He wasn't really an actor's director, but he was a good action director. Barry was always an intense guy, lots of energy, and was more volatile in those days. We were all staying in the same hotels and spent probably far too much time together. One moment I particularly remember with Barry, not on the set, was when he was going on about something and I asked him if he couldn't choose some other word in the English language besides constantly using 'fuck' and he launched a tirade at me, basically telling me 'Fuck you, shut the fuck up,' and he would say whatever the fuck he wanted. Whew!"

1967 or 1968, and he was a real renaissance man. We all lived around Greenwich Village back in the old days, and we all hung around at the Buffalo Road restaurant bar, which had an amazing clientele. Barry was a nice guy, and could be very gentle, but he had no patience for nonsense and stupid people, and was very quick on the trigger. I remember on one film there was a projectionist who wasn't maintaining a clear focus and Barry just tore his head off. He could kill you if you weren't doing your job properly."

"Sean was a nice guy and I'd describe him as being very 'wired' during the filming of *Here Come the Tigers*, in terms of his energy and zeal," says Robert Shulman, who served as a key grip on *Here Come the Tigers* and later *Friday the 13th*. "With *Here Come the Tigers*, *Manny's Orphans*, and then *Friday the 13th*, we were really just a bunch of friends who were having fun together, partying too hard, and learning how to make movies together."

"The relationship between Barry and Sean, in terms of the filmmaking process, was that Barry was the creative person and Sean was the producer," Kalmanowicz says. "Sean directed every movie he did, really directed them, in every sense of what a director does. Sean controlled everything and he planned everything. Barry would listen to Sean and then bring the creative part of it to life. *Here Come the Tigers* was well put together, given its budget, and we were excited because we thought it was going to get a major release because we had a distributor in AIP. We felt like we were part of a film that looked like it might go in terms of getting seen by a wide audience and being successful. *Here Come the Tigers* was a very happy, smooth shoot."

Braden Lutz jokingly chokes Richard Murphy. Lutz served as camera operator on *Friday the 13th*, and played the killer in many scenes, while Murphy was soundman. In the years that followed *Friday the 13th*'s release, Lutz struggled with personal demons and later died from water poisoning. (Photo courtesy of Nalani Clark)

Barry Abrams never carried a gun while serving as a cameraman in Vietnam. (Photo courtesy of Nalani Clark)

"Sean had grown up in Westport, where we shot *Here Come the Tigers*, and he very much seemed like a guy who was hustling to make movies, while Barry had spent several tours in Vietnam," recalls Richard Murphy, the boom operator on *Here Come the Tigers*. "I met Barry in

"There were lots of long days on the baseball field but everyone stayed pretty even and professional while shooting," Abigail Lewis recalls. "There was one day we were shooting an interior in a kitchen, supposedly mine and the coach's, and in the scene I was fixing eggs for breakfast and I don't know how it started but we all got the giggles. I'll never forget my line: 'Eggs will be ready in a minute.' I'd compose myself and try again but just could not stop laughing, which was of course contagious. Finally, either Barry or Sean wisely decided we needed to take a break, which we did, then resumed shooting. It was all good fun, no tempers or annoyance. There was very good camaraderie on the set. Sean's wife was also around a lot, as I recall. Most of the crew knew each other fairly well and had worked together and socialized together for years. It was a good group of people."

The harmonious mood on the set of *Here Come the Tigers* was briefly disrupted when Robert Barsamian, Stephen Minasian and Philip Scuderi made their way to the Westport filming location to keep tabs on Cunningham and their investment. Clad in their trademark black and white wise-guy attire, the trio was humorously nicknamed "The Hats" by the cast and crew because

After departing Vietnam in 1970, Barry Abrams worked as a cameraman for ABC News, based in Tokyo, covering events in Southeast Asia. Abrams quickly settled in New York where he worked throughout the 1970s, leading up to Abrams' eventual collaborations with Sean Cunningham. (Photo courtesy of Nalani Clark)

of their appearance, originally coined by boom operator Richard Murphy. "The Hats, the Boston investors," Max Kalmanowicz recalls. "We called them the Penguin Theater chain because of the way they dressed in black. We called them The Hats. They financed *Here Come the Tigers* and then *Manny's Orphans*. They thought they could make money by doing a copy of *The Bad News Bears*. All we cared about was trying to make a living."

"The three Armenians, Barsamian, Minasian and Scuderi," Richard Murphy recalls with a laugh. "They were dressed like wise-guys, mob guys, and it was so over-the-top that it was funny. Scuderi was clearly the leader, the front-man, and he was there to make sure things went smoothly. Sean had convinced them that he was a viable commodity in terms of making money and making movies that would make money. They would talk to Sean and Steve behind closed doors, especially Phil Scuderi,

and we didn't know what went on behind closed doors, but it was obvious something was going on, although Sean always had this ability to be positive and project this feeling that nothing was wrong. I think Steve Miner was a lot more scared of those guys than Sean was."

Unlike Barry Abrams, screenwriter Victor Miller, who wrote *Here Come the Tigers* under the pseudonym Arch McCoy, was a product of the same preppie, New England upbringing as Cunningham. A Yale graduate, majoring in English, Miller had spent the early 1970s as a largely non-descript author of detective novels, most notably novelizations of the *Kojak* television series. By 1975, Miller turned his attentions to screenwriting. It was during this period that Miller was introduced to Cunningham through mutual friends Saul Swimmer and Bruce "Brud" Talbot.

As fate would have it, Cunningham and Miller lived in close proximity to each other in Westport, and would spend a great deal of time together, from the mid to late 1970s, in each other's kitchens, brainstorming feature film ideas. "Sean and I were in constant contact, in and out of each other's homes, about five years previous to *Friday the 13th*," recalls Miller. "I wrote *Here Come the Tigers* for Sean, which was about a screwed-up baseball team, and then *Manny's Orphans*, which was about a screwed-up soccer team. We believed that America was looking for G-rated family fare, and that we would fill that need in the marketplace, but it turned out we were completely wrong."

Yale graduate Victor Miller was a novelist before making the transition to screenwriting. (Photo courtesy of Victor Miller)

Along with Abrams, his film crew, and Victor Miller, *Here Come the Tigers* also marked Cunningham's first teaming with composer Harry Manfredini who ended-up crafting *Friday the 13th*'s iconic musical score. "I met Sean through a director named Gary Templeton, for whom I did a number of very successful children's short films," recalls Manfredini who has ended-up being Cunningham's most enduring collaborator over the years. "One of his partners knew Steve Miner and he knew that Steve and Sean were working on a children's feature film, so that's how I got introduced. I got my very first feature film, *Here Come the Tigers*, from that, and then another, and then, of course, *Friday the 13th*. How's that for some really great luck in a career?"

Here Come the Tigers was released, tentatively, in April of 1978. The film did very little business, at least according to the North American box office charts where *Here Come the Tigers* didn't even make a ripple. Moreover, it completely failed to thrust Cunningham and Miner onto the Hollywood and New York filmmaking radar, and establish them as filmmakers capable of making money outside the exploitation genre. "We were a bunch of losers making movies out of a garage in Westport," Miner says. "At that point, it seemed like we were a million miles away from being successful mainstream filmmakers."

Here Come the Tigers was a complete flop to most of the cast and crew. But for Philip Scuderi, and Hallmark Releasing, it was a different story. Booking the film into his dwindling chain of theaters, and selling the ancillary rights, Scuderi, Hallmark, realized a nice little profit out of *Here Come the Tigers*, unbeknownst to virtually everyone who'd worked on the film. Better yet, for Hallmark, the film's modest success was completely under the national radar, which is exactly what Scuderi and his partners, in keeping with their veil of secrecy, had envisioned.

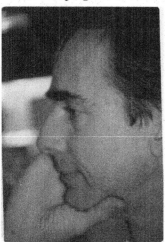

Victor Miller and Sean Cunningham had collaborated together for several years before they began developing *Friday the 13th*. (Photo courtesy of Victor Miller)

"*Here Come the Tigers* did make money," Max Kalmanowicz says. "The same financiers came back to Sean right away and wanted to do another movie, with the same crew. We didn't know it was successful because it wasn't a big mainstream success, but it did very well for the financiers. Otherwise, they wouldn't have wanted to invest in another movie with the same production team. *Here Come the Tigers* was made for about $300,000 and the goal of the financiers was to just make a little bit of money and stay under the radar. It was a product that they could program into their New England theater chain and sell the ancillary rights and make even more money, which they did."

In the summer of 1977, Cunningham, Miner, along with most of the *Here Come the Tigers'* production team, began filming *Manny's Orphans* (AKA *Kick!*) with an increased budget of $400,000. As the multiple titles establish, the film follows a ramshackle group of soccer-playing orphans, although no one involved with the project had any illusions that the story was anything other than *Here Come the Tigers* with soccer cleats.

The increased budget of *Manny's Orphans*, the largest Cunningham had ever worked with, reflected a production quality a notch above *Here Come the Tigers*. This was most notable in the casting of veteran character actor Malachy McCourt, the first actor of any prestige that Cunningham had ever worked with. Moreover, Abrams, Cunningham, Miner and the rest of the crew had gelled. It helped that Abrams' and his crew from New York were already very close

Victor Miller drew upon many of his own life experiences when developing the script for *Friday the 13th*, primarily in relation to the character of Pamela Voorhees whose twisted relationship with Jason was based, in part, on Miller's own troubled childhood. (Photo courtesy of Victor Miller)

friends. This was a good harbinger for *Friday the 13th*.

Cunningham's prior collaborator, Wes Craven, was a frequent visitor on the set of *Manny's Orphans*, where he provided counsel and mentorship, much in the way Cunningham did with Miner. "The soccer movie was a step-up for us," Kalmanowicz says. "It had more money and more solid elements in place. The film had a name star in Malachy McCourt, and a better script. It was a better production in every way. It wasn't as derivative as *Here Come the Tigers*, even though it was financed by the same Boston investors. It was a cute film that had heart."

Manny's Orphans introduced two more additions that would figure prominently in the making of *Friday the 13th*. The first was Ari Lehman, a thirteen year old kid who had a sizable supporting role in *Manny's Orphans*. Lehman and his parents, who didn't know Cunningham at the time, lived in Westport, not far from Cunningham who eventually tapped Lehman to portray a young (and deformed) Jason Voorhees in *Friday the 13th*.

The more significant addition to Cunningham's production team was the appearance of production designer Virginia Field who would combine with Abrams, Cunningham and Miner to comprise the leadership of *Friday the 13th*'s production unit, not to mention the forming of a close – if not enduring – friendship.

Like Barry Abrams, Field took an adventurous, circuitous route to a film career, and to the company of her *Friday the 13th* colleagues. "I spent the 1970s wandering around the world for four or five years, with no particular destination in mind," Field recalls. "I was a flower child, a gypsy, and I would travel around the world, farming and picking grapes in places like France, Greece and

Italy. Eventually, I returned to New York, where I'm from, and took night school drafting classes. I had no degree of any kind, nothing, and I lived in East Harlem. I spent a lot of time at the Lincoln Center Library, at the art exhibit, even though I didn't know shit. Then, one day, I was able to visit a film set, and I was hooked right away."

After studying film design at a specialized school in New York, Field was accepted into the designers' union, and then began searching for film work. In 1977, after hearing about *Manny's Orphans*, Field met Cunningham and Miner in Westport to discuss her working on the film, and a partnership was born. "I could see that Sean and Steve were partners," Field recalls of her first meeting with Cunningham and Miner. "Sean was Steve's teacher and mentor. I was very comfortable with Sean who viewed film as a product rather than an art form, which was okay with me because Sean was very honest and open about this. Sean understood film as a product, which I think was one of his strengths, and his whole interest was business. Sean also impressed me as a family man who'd figured out how to do things well, both as a director and as a person, and was very loyal to his crews."

"She [Field] was my weird friend Mel's weird kid sister who was tiny and played the harp," recalls Robert Shulman of growing up with Field in New York. "I may have met her in a coffee house after I graduated and moved to New York. Then she resurfaced on *Friday the 13th*."

Virginia Field joined Sean Cunningham's production unit for the filming of *Manny's Orphans*. (Photo courtesy of Tony Marshall)

Unlike *Here Come the Tigers*, *Manny's Orphans* failed to find theatrical distribution and was eventually released in 1978 in the form of a handful of phantom screenings, an ominous foretelling of the film's legacy as being the most obscure and little-seen film of Cunningham's directing career. This was especially bad news for Cunningham who, despite Hallmark's financial participation in *Manny's Orphans*, had much of his own capital, aside from his blood and sweat, in the film.

Luckily, United Artists eventually stepped in, after all of the other studios Cunningham had approached had passed, and offered Cunningham a lifeline in the form of a one year option - along with a token payment of $25000 - for the purpose of developing *Manny's Orphans* as a pilot for a prospective television series.

Neither the pilot nor the series ever came to pass but the $25000 Cunningham received from United Artists allowed him to remain somewhat financially-solvent during a period that otherwise represented a standstill in his career. Contrary to his hopes, and cynical calculations, *Here Come the Tigers* and *Manny's Orphans* hadn't advanced his career beyond his Westport, Connecticut fiefdom.

Still, *Here Come the Tigers* and *Manny's Orphans* yielded unexpected fruit, certainly related to the evolution of *Friday the 13th*. First, the kids' films had allowed the production crew, the crew that would get back together for the filming of *Friday the 13th*, the opportunity to bond and gel. Second, the indifferent response in the marketplace to *Here Come the Tigers* and *Manny's Orphans* compelled Cunningham to realize that his illusions of respectability were just that and his filmmaking destiny was inescapably tied to the genres of exploitation and horror, and more likely both mixed together.

"I'd made two nice family films that didn't do very well, but had just kept me afloat," Cunningham recalls. "Eventually, I realized the only movie I could get the money for was a scary movie. That was the beginning of how *Friday the 13th* was born."

CHAPTER 3

PLANNING A *LONG NIGHT* AT CAMP BLOOD

"I'm sitting around thinking about titles and I think, if I had something called Friday the 13th, I could sell that...and it just sort of stuck in my mind."
– Sean Cunningham

"Sequel? Sean and I had put out two films already that had barely covered their costs. I could not think further than how my wife and two kids would get through the next month without going on welfare."
– writer Victor Miller

The creation of *Friday the 13th*, from concept to story, took place between the fall of 1978 and the spring of 1979. This evolution was driven by several factors related to Sean Cunningham's career and the overall marketplace.

Three key factors led Cunningham and writer Victor Miller, along with the later invaluable support of Steve Miner, to create *Friday the 13th*. The first motivating factor was the release of the independent horror film *Halloween* in October of 1978. Unlike the inspiration of *The Bad News Bears*, Cunningham knew how to make a horror film.

The second was Cunningham's own bleak career prospects by the fall of 1978, highlighted by the lackluster commercial response to his kids' films *Here Come the Tigers* and *Manny's Orphans*. The third and much understated had to do with Cunningham's futile attempts to secure theatrical distribution for *Manny's Orphans*. The release of *Halloween* influenced Cunningham not so much by its commercial success, which was gradual and would take many months to be fully understood, but more in the blueprint the film established.

The artistry and technique that John Carpenter displayed in *Halloween* was beyond Sean Cunningham's grasp as a filmmaker. (Photo courtesy of Kim Gottlieb-Walker www.lenswoman.com)

By October of 1978, with *Manny's Orphans* languishing in purgatory, Cunningham realized his only means of business and filmmaking survival was to retreat back to the primitive style of exploitation/horror filmmaking that had given him his only taste of real success. He wasn't made for porn, despite the surprise success of *Together*, and he certainly wasn't cut-out to make kids' films, but Cunningham had a knack for exploitation and horror. "You have to understand that I had all of my money tied-up in the children's film," said Cunningham, referring to *Manny's Orphans*. "I couldn't figure out what else I had to sell. The only thing I had was my track record; the films I had done earlier, which were all kind of dark and gothic."

While the kids' movie genre was alien to him, Cunningham could relate to the success of *Halloween*, and the impact of John Carpenter's film, and, in particular, how and why *Halloween* worked so well. "I think the influence of *Halloween* has been overstated in that the two

films themselves are very different," Cunningham says. "I was very influenced by the structure of Carpenter's film, and why it worked so well, the formula, whereas the story and technique were of little interest to me."

In the fall of 1978, Cunningham reached out to colleagues and friends with his desire to make a horror film out of *Halloween*'s model. Some of these people had worked with Cunningham on *Here Come the Tigers* and *Manny's Orphans*, and were under the distinct impression that Cunningham was ready to abandon filmmaking altogether and enter a less frustrating profession somewhere in the business world. "After we did the last kids' movie, I knew that Sean wasn't going to continue making films that didn't make money," Virginia Field says. "Sean wasn't passionate about that."

The first person Cunningham reached out to was Wes Craven,, his one true filmmaking mentor. Despite the fact that Craven's only two years older than Cunningham, Craven was very much the teacher and Cunningham the student in their relationship. Cunningham had leaned on Craven's advice and counsel throughout the making of *Here Come the Tigers* and *Manny's Orphans*. Sensing this was a crucial juncture in his career, Cunningham was especially open to Craven's guidance; he knew this might be the last stop.

Craven saw *Halloween* and appreciated and understood the artistry and technique in John Carpenter's film far more than Cunningham did. The two friends had several discussions throughout the fall of 1978. None of these discussions involved the possibility of Craven directing said horror film. This project, whatever it was going to be, was Cunningham's baby. "Sean was good friends with Wes Craven and they talked a lot about *Halloween*

Sean Cunningham took his own inspiration for the Pamela Voorhees character from the Evelyn Draper character played by actress Jessica Walter in the thriller film *Play Misty for Me*. (Photo courtesy of Jason Pepin)

before we all got involved with *Friday the 13th*," Virginia Field recalls. "I had no idea we copied *Halloween* until I saw *Halloween* later and saw the similarities in *Friday the 13th*."

Cunningham next approached Victor Miller who'd become his go-to writer, indeed the only writer in his small circle. He instructed Miller to see *Halloween*, study it, and create the foundation for a horror script they could develop together. "We had already tried to give America what it said it wanted – nice G-rated movies – but our two previous (*Here Come the Tigers* and *Manny's Orphans*) G-rated attempts were not horribly successful," laughs Miller. "We were in constant contact – in and out of each other's houses - the previous five years. Our expectations in the beginning were certainly tempered by the fact that our previous outings had not done all that well in spite of their low budgets. This was, at least, something different, a real roller-coaster, as Sean kept referring to it."

Prior to his collaboration with Cunningham on *Friday the 13th*, Miller was a complete neophyte to the horror genre, although he had written a thriller novel called *Hide the Children* (Ballantine Books, September 1978), to little fanfare. The story of *Hide the Children* involved a busload of kidnapped school-kids, a harbinger of a real-life incident that occurred six months after Miller had completed the novel. "The only films we actively discussed were his *Last House on the Left* with Wes and *Psycho* and *Halloween*," says Miller of his initial discussions with Cunningham. "I would mention *Diabolique* every once in awhile. I do know that we settled early on with the decision to keep ghosts and the supernatural out of the mix."

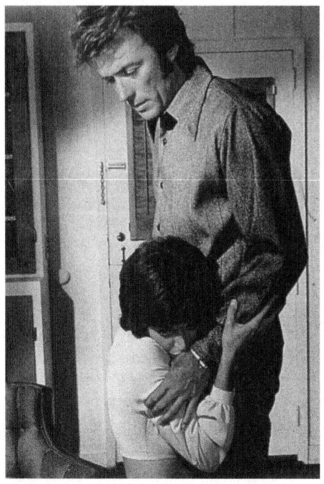

Sean Cunningham was close friends with screenwriter Dean Riesner who received co-writing credit on the Clint Eastwood-directed film *Play Misty for Me.* Cunningham later adopted Jessica Walter's butch appearance in *Play Misty for Me* when conceptualizing – and casting – the Pamela Voorhees' role. (Photo courtesy of Jason Pepin)

Despite his non-horror pedigree, Miller felt he had a good handle on what made *Halloween* tick, and what Cunningham was looking to take from that film. "I saw *Halloween* and figured out the genre, the structure of that film, pretty quickly," says Miller. "It was simple. You start with a historical evil, and some event in the past that shadows the present day action. Then you create a setting where teenagers or college-aged kids are isolated and beyond the help of adults. The last part was that you kill anyone who has premarital sex. Those are the truths I learned from watching *Halloween*."

Throughout Christmas 1978 and early 1979, Cunningham and Miller went back and forth, in each other's kitchens, dissecting *Halloween* for the purpose of crafting their own horror film. "I laid-out the structure of what I had learned from John Carpenter and Debra Hill's *Halloween* and I began trying out different ideas that could work," Miller recalls. "Some of the ideas were god-awful but the good ones stuck. Over the years of our friendship, Sean and I had developed shorthand for talking plot and concepts in his kitchen and mine and during lulls in the volleyball games at his house in Westport. I had written a couple of other scripts for Sean that never saw the light of day – they were vehicles for somebody like Clint Eastwood, etc. – that Sean and I thought might fly. It really was loose, easy, and exciting. We always laughed a lot. I would come in with ideas and we'd wrestle them back and forth."

One of the key decisions Cunningham and Miller grappled with during their many conferences was the choice of an isolated location for their horror film. After mulling around such venues as an apartment building, an amusement park funhouse, and an isolated island, Cunningham and Miller finally settled on the summer camp locale that has become so synonymous with the horror film genre. "I made up a list of venues for teenagers to be isolated in that included "summer camp" about midway down the page," Miller recalls. "We both finally agreed that was it. It took longer than you might have thought, but hindsight makes it seem kind of obvious now."

As for other genre influences, Miller denies any discussion or knowledge of legendary Italian filmmaker Mario Bava and his 1971 film *Twitch of the Death Nerve* (AKA *Bay of Blood*, *The Bay of Blood*). Although many horror film historians have cited the influence of Bava's film in *Friday the 13th*, Miller pleads ignorance to this. "Sean certainly never mentioned him to me," Miller says. "Bava was not anyone I knew about. Credit should've gone to Carpenter and Hill for being my inspiration, and *Carrie*, *Diabolique* and *The Haunting* – *Carrie* for the chair jumper at the end."

Next, Cunningham and Miller discussed the kinds of bizarre deaths they wanted to feature in the story, and for this purpose, Cunningham and Miller referenced classic childhood fears, as well as fairytale mythology and religious iconography. "Harry Crosby's death on the generator door came right out of the pictures I'd seen of Catholic martyred saints," Miller says. "Religions do horror much better than I ever could. As for gory scenes to make it more commercial, Sean and I were wedded to the concept that tension trumps gore every time. Gore can be indicated when you pop the tension, but we were making a rollercoaster, not an abattoir. Gore seems to rule these days but *Friday* (the first) is remarkably short on long gory shots with icky screams and torture."

Cunningham himself had no aspirations, originally, of making an especially gory film. "I was more like a naughty kid trying to scare his friends, saying 'Boo' from behind the bushes," Cunningham recalled. "It's not any fun to gross people out. I was trying to create a rollercoaster with hills and valleys. The metaphor works, especially when you watch a film with an audience. Like with a rollercoaster, it's a social experience. If you see a horror film in an empty theater, it's just ugly and grim; there's no fun. But if you go with

Sean Cunningham based his vision of the Alice character on Jamie Lee Curtis' tomboyish Laurie Strode character in *Halloween*. (Photo courtesy of Kim Gottlieb-Walker www.lenswoman.com)

400 kids laughing and screaming, it's a different experience. There's also that whole date thing going on; the guy has his arm around the girl, who is hiding her face."

The Kevin Bacon 'Throat Scene' was born out of a combination of Miller's childhood nightmares and a twisted biological perspective, as were other murders in the story. "Specifically, as a kid, I always looked under my bed every night to make sure there were no molesters or monsters lurking," Miller says. "I never found a real one until I let Kevin Bacon have it in such a biologically-impossible manner. The axe-in-the-face [referring to the

Marcie character's death scene] was the farthest I could go with a fear I had of being bashed in the face. The corpse in the upper bunk tickled my fancy because I loved the idea of having two randy kids making love while a gory body is lying eighteen inches away. I just conjoined a peeping tom and mayhem showing the Alpha and Omega of biology. You see that happening all the time in *CSI*-type procedurals on TV today. So many of them begin with two horny twenty-something characters looking for a forest glade in which to screw and wind-up, inadvertently, kneeling down on the pelvis of a dead body nearby."

The idea of having a female killer in the story came to Miller, with Cunningham's encouragement. "Mrs. Voorhees came as soon as I came up with the camp location," says Miller who derived the name Pamela Voorhees from a girl he'd known in high school named Van Voorhees. "I certainly didn't even consider a male villain after I had seen Michael Myers in *Halloween*. I was already borrowing quite enough from the very talented Carpenter and Hill. I didn't want to make it look too obvious. I also had a subtext to my choice of a mother avenging the death of her son on a serial basis."

Cunningham liked the idea of having a "madwoman" serve as *Friday the 13th*'s killer, further inspired by the 1971 thriller film *Play Misty for Me* which featured

The first photographic version of the original *Friday the 13th* logo. This was used as the basis for the first advertisement that appeared in the July 4, 1979 edition of the entertainment trade publication *Variety*. (Photo courtesy of Richard Illy/Illy Lighting)

Jessica Walter as a demented female stalker, named Evelyn Draper, who terrorizes Clint Eastwood (the film's director and star) throughout the film. Cunningham was close friends with screenwriter Dean Riesner, the co-writer of *Play Misty for Me*, and Cunningham especially felt that Walter's butch, masculine appearance in *Play Misty for Me*, as seen in Evelyn Draper's cropped hairstyle and sideburns, was an effective model to emulate for creating *Friday the 13th*'s female killer.

Miller denies having any knowledge of the *Play Misty for Me* influence. He based the motivations of the Pamela Voorhees character, and her murderous rage, on his own troubled relationship with his mother. "My own mother was not exactly trustworthy," Miller says. "I never knew when she would have my back or attack me, so Mrs. Voorhees was my subconscious attempt to have the Mom I never had – albeit psychotic, but, hey, you can't have everything. Imagine having a mom who would kill because you had not been taken care of properly. (I was raised by nannies and a governess until I was eight or nine, so the stuff of horror is all there.) The fact that Mrs. Voorhees couldn't possibly have lifted Harry Crosby up onto a wooden door passed my mind from time to time, but I didn't give a damn. Why spoil a great picture with logic, especially if you pace it so quickly no one has the chance to ask, 'Hey, how did that lady do all that heavy lifting and throw bodies through the window?' I only wish they had had time and money enough to do one of my final tableaux which was to have all the dead counselors hanging 'like Easter eggs' from the tree outside."

The Jason Voorhees character, from which the long-term commercial future of the *Friday the 13th* franchise was derived, was much less defined during Miller's initial outline. Named after Miller's two sons, Ian and Josh, the original incarnation of Jason Voorhees that was developed portrayed Jason as a fairly normal, entirely human kid who had drowned during the summer previous to the story's events. This one element, more than any other, would be radically enhanced and redrawn during pre-production and even extending into the last days of *Friday the 13th*'s filming in Blairstown, New Jersey. Much more clearly realized by Miller, in relation to the finished film, was the persona of *Friday the 13th*'s heroine, Alice, and *Friday the 13th*'s resident voice of doom, Crazy Ralph.

In retrospect, the Alice character looks like a knockoff of actress Jamie Lee Curtis's Laurie Strode heroine in *Halloween*, a notion enhanced by actress Adrienne King's own tomboyish appearance in *Friday the 13th*. According to Miller, the similarities were purely coincidental. "Alice fit the role of the single white female who survives," Miller says. "She could've been Alan, but who wants to see a madwoman chase a nineteen year old boy around the woods? I dined on *Halloween*'s structure more than its individual plot elements. With Crazy Ralph, or Ralphie the Rat Boy as Sean and I referred to him during our story discussions, Sean and I envisioned him as one

of those crazy characters you'd see in a film like *Deliverance*; a character who knows the truth, who gives you the sense that something bad is going to happen, and looks crazy but turns out to be closer to reality than most of the 'normal' people."

THE MOST TERRIFYING FILM EVER MADE!

By the end of March 1979, Victor Miller was knee-deep into the writing of a first draft script entitled *Long Night at Camp Blood* (AKA *A Long Night at Camp Blood*). Cunningham and Miller worked through several drafts through the spring and early summer of 1979.

Cunningham gave Miller constant encouragement and careful notes, just as he'd done several years earlier. "Sean would edit each draft with phrases like 'Keep it relentless,'" Miller recalls. "Sean came up with the title *Friday the 13th* after I had already written a first draft called, infelicitously, *Long Night at Camp Blood*."

Cunningham claims it was during the desperate search for an alternate title for *Manny's Orphans* that

The advertisement that was published in *Variety*. This advertisement also appeared in the *International Variety* version. (Photo courtesy of Richard Illy/Illy Lighting)

the bolt of lightning that was *Friday the 13th* – title and logo – struck him. "I was trying to get support for *Manny's Orphans*, but I guess it was too soft and too sweet and too nice," Cunningham recalled. "This was the movie I thought was going to be my ticket to the big-time. I was trying to figure out a campaign for that movie when they [distributors] told me, 'The title's no good. *Manny* is too ethnic. *Orphan* sounds too sad. We should have another title!' At that moment, I thought of *Friday the 13th*. If I had a movie called *Friday the 13th*, I could sell that. I couldn't sell *Manny's Orphans*."

The moment when *Friday the 13th* was truly born, the moment it became a tangible concept beyond words on paper, occurred shortly after this when Cunningham stood in his Westport home with a single red brick in his hand. He took a piece of chalk and scribbled the words *Friday the 13th* on the brick, envisioning a logo. "I got an idea for an ad – the letters *Friday the 13th* breaking through a bunch of glass," Cunningham said. "'The most terrifying film ever made,' I envisioned it to say. Now that could sell tickets! If only I had a movie to go with the ad, I would really have something!"

Cunningham's specific vision for the *Friday the 13th* logo was for the brick to be photographed as it exploded through the glass, ideally at a 90 degree angle. Cunningham felt this brick-through-glass concept would make for a compelling advertisement.

Cunningham took his concept for the *Friday the 13th* logo to a friend and a local ad agency art director named Michael Morris. He liked Cunningham's idea, but suggested the concept would be enhanced by making the brick bigger for the purpose of creating three-dimensional letters that would "pop out." Cunningham stressed to Morris, during these discussions, his belief that the block of letters should be photographed when "the block" formed a 90 degree angle upon breaking through the glass. Morris agreed and then hired a local photographer named Richard Illy to photograph the block design that Morris had created and bring *Friday the 13th* to life, or at least something Cunningham could promote.

Morris instructed Illy to incorporate the 3-D concept into the photograph, in order to maximize the logo's visual impact. "Mike told me that he had suggested the 3-D block to Sean, explaining that it would be a bigger, bolder sell of the movie title in the poorest photo medium: a newspaper," Illy recalls. "Basically a more dynamic graphic. When I picked up 'the block' from Mike he said, 'Remember the 90s.' 'Right,' I replied. 90 degree hole in the glass and 90 percent through the pane. That's what Mike and Sean wanted. Mike then told me, 'Just don't wreck it. It cost a fortune.'"

Illy was a struggling artist and aspiring professional film gaffer. He had no idea his photograph would ever become such an iconic piece of pop culture history. Although, as fate would have it, Illy was, by the spring of 1979, dating Denise Pinckley. She, as a secretary working in Cunningham's Westport office, (located at his Long

Lots Road home address in Westport, over his garage) eventually ended-up running *Friday the 13th*'s production office in Blairstown, New Jersey. "I was a starving artist living in a small house with wood-framed storm windows," Illy recalls of the period when he photographed the original *Friday the 13th* logo. "I took one off the house. It was divided into two large panes of glass. I scored the obligatory 90 degree angle in the glass with a glass cutter and almost all of the glass fell out of the frame. Before I wrecked the other pane, I went to a glass shop where I learned how to cut properly, with pressure under the pane. They also let me collect shards of broken glass. I went for pieces that looked dangerous. A friend of mine, who was the art director for *Boating Magazine*, lent me her old four-by-five Speed Graphic camera to take the shot."

Paper version of the *Variety* advertisement. **(Photo courtesy of Richard Illy/Illy Lighting)**

Getting the perfect shot, bringing the *Friday the 13th* insignia to life, required much more effort than a simple point and click technique. "Because of the camera's fixed lens, and my low ceiling, I was unable to get far enough away from my own floor to get the shot I needed!" Illy recalls. "I built an incline plane out of plywood so I could back-up the camera. The plywood stage was covered in black felt, and the storm window was clamped to milk crates on each side. The hole in the glass turned out well with both smooth and jagged lines, using the cutter and pliers. I propped 'the block' up in the hole with two chopsticks from the bottom. Next I arranged the glass in, on and around 'the block' until I liked it. I was going for what this would look like if it was actually thrown through the glass and I froze it 90 percent through with a strobe. I lit the scene with hot lights. The back of my head was on the ceiling for focus. Then I made four exposures for Michael. The end."

Besides the image that appeared in the *Variety* advertisement, Illy's photographic concept was used in a secondary advertisement, unreleased, that was used to attract interest from distributors in the spring of 1980. The *Variety* advertisement would feature the headline FROM THE PRODUCER OF *LAST HOUSE ON THE LEFT* COMES THE MOST TERRIFYING FILM EVER MADE! The other unreleased advertisement featured the tagline THE PERFECT DAY FOR TERROR and announced a February 1980 release date for *Friday the 13th*.

This was wishful thinking.

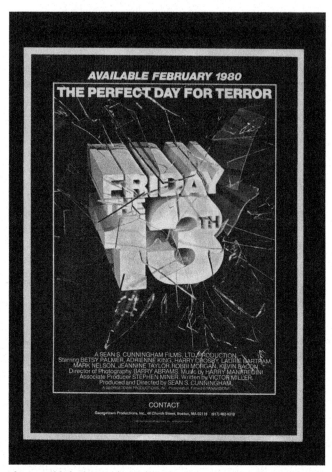

This unpublished secondary advertisement was eventually used for the purpose of attracting potential distributors in the spring of 1980. The Georgetown Productions company address is at the bottom of this advertisement, beneath the cast and crew credits. (Photo courtesy of Richard Illy/Illy Lighting)

FRIDAY THE 13TH MAKES VARIETY

Armed with a fully-realized visual concept for *Friday the 13th*, Sean Cunningham took the audacious, bold step of placing the aforementioned advertisement in the entertainment trade paper *Variety*. The advertisement ran on July 4, 1979, and also appeared in the *International Variety* format. It also pronounced that *Friday the 13th* was "currently in production" and the film would be "available November 1979."

None of this, of course, contained a shred of truth, most especially the November 1979 release date. But Cunningham's main purpose was to stir interest in the marketplace, evoke a reaction and attract financing to the project. "I ran the ad in the summer, around the Fourth of July, in weekly *Variety*, a big full-page ad, and the phones started ringing off the hook," Cunningham recalled. "Everybody wanted this film. I said, 'Shit, I better make this film.' So we scampered around and tried to write a script and get a cast to do it all."

Cunningham's boasts that he "got incredible response from brokers all over the world" and that he was deluged with telegrams and telexes related to financial offers for *Friday the 13th*, following the publication of the *Variety* advertisement, aren't borne-out by the circumstances and events related to this time period. The reality is that Cunningham received no firm financial offers regarding *Friday the 13th* throughout July 1979.

He did, however, hear from actors, crew members, and technicians, inquiring if there were any jobs available-- whatever the project was, whenever it started filming. Most of these people had worked on Cunningham's previous films, *Here Come the Tigers* and *Manny's Orphans*, and had heard about *Friday the 13th* through the *Variety* advertisement.

Then there was Philip Scuderi to reckon with. By summer 1979, Hallmark Releasing had morphed into Georgetown Productions – also named after a Boston suburb - for the express purpose of financing and producing films. After financing *Here Come the Tigers* and *Manny's Orphans*, Scuderi financed the puerile comedy film *King Frat*, a blatant *Animal House* rip-off that was scarcely released in July of 1979. The Scuderi people flooded Cunningham's office as well. "I do recall sending my resume to Connecticut when the first of the *Friday the 13th* films was being produced, with no response," recalls Reuben Trane, the producer of *King Frat* who later worked with Scuderi on the horror-slasher film *Eyes of a Stranger* (1981). "I never had a handle on Scuderi. I always felt he was using cash from his many screens to finance his film ventures. It seems we had money on Monday after a good weekend and no money after a rainy weekend."

If Cunningham could've found any way to avoid doing business with Scuderi and his partners again, he would've taken the opportunity. It just wasn't there. Cunningham took a second mortgage out on his Westport home with the thought of producing *Friday the 13th* as a guerilla project. The second mortgage was also an attempt to gain some sort of independence, and leverage with Scuderi, should he have been Cunningham's only option.

If the *Variety* advertisement ultimately failed in its main purpose to secure mainstream financing for *Friday the 13th*, the Richard Illy photograph made for great wallpaper at Cunningham's Westport home office. "I was dating Denise Pinckley at the time who'd become a temp for Sean in Connecticut, and started working for Georgetown, and I couldn't believe it when she told me that the office was wallpapered with my shot," Illy recalls. "Then I met this woman who told me she'd been working as a temp at this ad agency and that the ad agency was papered with the images of the *Friday the 13th* logo, which I found very ironic."

Another oft-repeated mantra on Cunningham's part over the years, and this goes hand-in-hand with the advertisement in *Variety,* is the notion that the *Friday the 13th* project had no money, no outline, no script, and basically just had the *Friday the 13th* title at the time of the *Variety* advertisement. While the money part is certainly true, the fact is that the story elements were well in place, at least in terms of Cunningham and Miller's approval, even though Miller's script still bore the title *Long Night at Camp Blood* instead of *Friday the 13th.*

Victor Miller's version of the *Friday the 13th* script was nearly complete by the time of the *Variety* ad's appearance, after which Cunningham and Miller spent two more weeks working on it. While it's true that Cunningham didn't have a completed script by the time of the ad's publication, the bones were certainly in place.

"I worked on the screenplay that eventually became *Friday the 13th* during the spring/summer of 1979," says Miller, setting the record straight. "After I began my efforts, he went about securing financing. The newspaper ad came later."

THE OTHER FRIDAY THE 13TH

Sean Cunningham had a secondary motive for taking out the advertisement in *Variety.* He wanted to stake a claim to the *Friday the 13th* title because he was aware another producer was mounting a *Friday the 13th* film project. Cunningham even gave brief thought to changing the project's title to *Friday 13,* removing "the" from the title.

Cunningham had expressed concern about the *Friday the 13th* title to friend Michael Morris when he commissioned the logo. "Sean took the ad in *Variety* because he'd heard that another producer was going to be using the *Friday the 13th* title for another movie and Sean wanted to lockup the title and stake his claim to the *Friday the 13th* title before the other *Friday the 13th* proj-

ect went into production or was released," Richard Illy recalls. "Sean had heard a rumor that there was another *Friday the 13th* out there and it made him very motivated to get the concept out there. I think he was waiting to see if there'd be a backlash from this other production he'd heard about. Back then, there was no internet, obviously, and it was like the pony express in terms of news spreading in the film business, but it spread pretty quickly."

This "other" *Friday the 13th* film project was *Friday the 13th: The Orphan,* a psychological-horror film inspired by a short story, *Sredni Vashtar,* from British

Contrary to popular belief, the producer of *The Orphan* (AKA *Friday the 13th: The Orphan*), Sondra Gilman, denies that Sean Cunningham or Georgetown Productions provided any financial settlement for the free use of the *Friday the 13th* title. (Photo courtesy of Sondra Gilman)

writer Saki (AKA Hector Hugh Munro). The story portrayed a disturbed young man plagued by nightmarish visions that compelled him to commit gruesome murders.

Written for the screen and directed by John Ballard, the film's chaotic production history began in 1977 – when the project was first known as *Betrayal* – and was eventually completed in 1978. The film premiered at the 1978 Miami Film Festival and was eventually released theatrically in November of 1979 to scant notice.

It was during this period that the film's title changed, in chronological order, from *Betrayal* to *Fri-*

day the 13th (without *The Orphan* in the title) to *Friday the 13th: The Orphan* and then finally to *The Orphan*.

In comparing Cunningham's film with *The Orphan*, there's no suggestion, from all parties involved, that the two films have anything aesthetically in common. The contention is entirely based on the title and the chronological time-line of how both projects used *Friday the 13th*. In terms of *The Orphan*, this ties in directly with Sondra Gilman and Louise Westergaard, the producers who eventually took over Ballard's film, and subsequently interjected the *Friday the 13th* title on their own accord.

"John Ballard had been shooting a movie called *Betrayal* and brought it to us," Sondra Gilman recalls. "We felt there was a lot of value in it but we felt it had to go in a different direction. We kept some footage and shot additional scenes. I believe the new filming was done in 1978. We were invited to show the movie at the Miami Film Festival in 1978. The distributor and Louise and I felt the title *Betrayal* no longer applied to the finished product and changed the name to *Friday the 13th*. The plot was based on a Saki short story."

Clearly, Gilman and Westergaard – and the project itself – staked a claim to the *Friday the 13th* title

George Mansour served as Hallmark Releasing's booking agent in the 1970s. (Photo courtesy of George Mansour)

well before Cunningham claims he got his inspiration.

For his part, Ballard, who wasn't on speaking terms with Gilman and Westergaard by the time *The Orphan* was readied for commercial release, denies any involvement with or knowledge of the *Friday the 13th* title. "The *Friday the 13th* title wasn't my idea at all, although we were actually ahead of the other production," Ballard recalls. "They put in these clunky-looking block lettering titles. I thought *The Orphan* was fine, and then they wanted to do *Friday the 13th: The Orphan*. They wanted a gimmick, a hook, and they just imposed it on the film. They put in these dates, captions, you know, and then the last date was *Friday the 13th*."

The most explosive charge regarding the two films concerns the widely-accepted legend that the producers of *The Orphan* threatened Sean Cunningham and Georgetown Productions with a lawsuit. The legend follows that Cunningham and Georgetown Productions reached a financial settlement with the producers and distributor of *The Orphan* in exchange for free use of the *Friday the 13th* title. "Not clear if there any legal steps taken, but I do recall a lot of back and forth between World Northal [the distributor] and 'the other' production," Ballard recalls. "I never met Sean Cunningham or Phil Scuderi, never heard of them, and I never heard about the ad in *Variety*."

This long-held urban legend was fueled by George Mansour, Philip Scuderi's former associate and booker, who gave weight to this story several years ago with the following recollection: "There was a movie before ours called *Friday the 13th: The Orphan*. Moderately-successful, but someone still threatened to sue. I don't know whether Phil Scuderi paid them off, but it was finally resolved."

Today, Mansour denies saying this, denies any memory of *The Orphan*, or of any financial settlement. The truth is that the only people who would know about this are Sondra Gilman and Louise Westergaard, along with the distributor, World Northal. Since Westergaard and World Northal are deceased, and Ballard was absent from this process, that leaves Gilman. She denies having had any contact throughout 1979 – or at any other period - with Cunningham and Scuderi, and denies that there was any type of financial settlement for the purpose of turning *Friday the 13th: The Orphan* into *The Orphan*. "Yes, we saw the ad in *Variety* and while we were upset that our title had been used by someone else, we figured that was life and he [Cunningham] jumped the gun on us," Gilman says. "We then changed our title to *Friday the 13th: The Orphan*. We had no contact with Sean Cunningham and we had no settlement. We dropped the title *Friday the 13th* and only went with *The Orphan* to eliminate any confusion between the two films."

In retrospect, it doesn't seem that the title controversy had much of a negative effect on *The Orphan*. If anything, *Friday the 13th*'s enormous success has engendered it more attention and relevance than the film otherwise would've received had the film not crossed paths with Cunningham's film. "I think the change of title did have an adverse effect on the movie but that's business," Gilman says. "We probably came up with it before they did, but we weren't clever enough to stake our claim. I am thrilled for any success a producer has with a product and we all try to achieve the most with our work."

GEORGETOWN

Gaining a monopoly over the *Friday the 13th* title was a relief for Cunningham who was fearful of potential legal action from the other production. While the title controversy turned out to be a false alarm for Cunningham, his dealings with Philip Scuderi in July and August were very acrimonious. *Friday the 13th* marked the first credited production for the newly-christened Georgetown Productions banner, but the dynamic of the Cunningham-Scuderi relationship was the same.

The transition from Hallmark Releasing to Georgetown Productions represented a differentiation without a change in how business was conducted. It was the same two-story building on Church Street, the same payroll clerk, secretary, and, most certainly, the company was still controlled by the same three Boston lawyers-turned-exploitation movie moguls: Robert Barsamian, Stephen Minasian and the flamboyant Scuderi.

Just like with Cunningham's previous collabora-

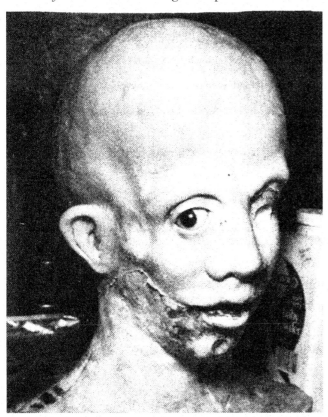

The "mongoloid" Jason concept evolved during the scripting process and throughout pre-production. (Photo courtesy of Tom Savini)

tions with Hallmark, Scuderi was the point-man at Georgetown and certainly the point-man for *Friday the 13th*. "They were theater owners with a substantial cash flow, so numbers didn't intimidate them," said Cunningham, referring to the period when he first approached Georgetown with *Friday the 13th*. "It's the same kind of gamble that people make when they invest in a Broadway show or in wildcat oil. It's a highly speculative investment. If it pays off, it's terrific. You've got to be a little crazy to do it."

Cunningham felt he needed approximately $500,000 to "comfortably" produce *Friday the 13th*, although he had privately let it be known that he was prepared to go the ultra-low budget route and shoot *Friday the 13th* for between $70,000 and $100,000---a budget range that the second mortgage on Cunningham's Westport home would support, in tandem with Cun-

An overview of Blairstown, New Jersey as it appears today. (Photo courtesy of Robert Armin www.brettmcbean.com)

ningham's life savings. In other words, Cunningham was prepared to make *Friday the 13th* in the vein of *Last House on the Left*, at least in terms of format and scope.

By the summer of 1979, the relationship between Cunningham and Scuderi was well-defined: Cunningham's films, with the exception of *Manny's Orphans*, had made money for Scuderi and his partners. Yet Scuderi was keenly aware that he was Cunningham's last resort, thus giving Georgetown a great deal of leverage over Cunningham, or so it seemed at this point. "I had gone away from the investors in Boston, but after I placed the ad, they called and said they would like a piece of it," Cunningham recalled. "I was trying to syndicate it for $500,000, and they came in with an initial offer of $125,000. It was a good start."

The $500,000 figure represented a large investment for Georgetown Productions who were on wobbly financial legs by 1979, and at pretty much every other juncture from the mid to late 1970s. The number also represented a milestone for Cunningham, whose most expensive film prior to *Friday the 13th* had cost $400,000 and proved to be his least successful film. "They [Georgetown] came back to me after we had an early draft of the script and they said that they changed their mind," Cunningham recalled. "They wanted to invest the entire $500,000. They really wanted to control it."

In this situation, it didn't hurt that Cunningham was approaching Georgetown with a horror film, given that his previous horror effort, *Last House on the Left*, was still playing the drive-in circuit by 1979 and generating consistent revenues. This combined with the eye-popping *Variety* advertisement made for a very attractive package to Scuderi.

Cunningham approached Scuderi with everything he had to offer at this point, namely the *Friday the 13th* title, his previous track record, and a screenplay by Victor Miller. To most of this, Scuderi responded with great enthusiasm. He loved the title, loved the idea of a summer camp horror movie, and believed that Cunningham was the man who could pull it off, even though Scuderi was extremely aware of how desperate Cunningham was. The only element that Scuderi didn't like was Miller's script.

From the middle of July through August 1979, Cunningham and Scuderi went back and forth, grappling with each other over money, and the conditions Scuderi sought to attach to any investment in *Friday the 13th*.

The relationship between Cunningham and Scuderi is, arguably, the most important in the legend of *Friday the 13th*. "We tried to negotiate the deal in a certain way that I thought I could live with, but they wouldn't cave on a few points that I considered to be crucial, like who gets the money and when, and cash flow," Cunningham recalled. "Finally, one night I was having a phone conversation with Phil Scuderi. I said, 'No, I just can't do it" and I hung up on him. It wasn't the wrong thing to do. It was the right thing to do. On the one hand, they're putting up all the money, so we get to make the movie, but on the other hand, it was just going to be like signing up for a root canal. It was a way to go forward, but it was another way to go backwards."

Although the perception left over from the Cunningham-Scuderi relationship is probably of Cunningham groveling in front of Scuderi and his partners

A wide shot of the arches that Annie walks through in the film. (Photo courtesy of Brett McBean www.brettmcbean.com)

for financing, this only reflects the state of Cunningham's career prospects prior to – and during - the development of *Friday the 13th*. "That was a very troubled night," recalled Cunningham of the same phone conservation with Philip Scuderi. "I spent the night tossing and turning, and I got up early in the morning and went jogging. I thought, 'It's not the deal you want, but it's not the movie you want either.' I come back to the house, it's 6:45 a.m., and the kids had just gotten up. I called Phil at home and said, 'I thought about our conversation last night, and I changed my mind. I'm willing to do it on the terms you suggest,' and he said, 'I'm glad you called because I was just leaving the house.' He was about to go take the money and invest it in a shopping center.' That's how we got to make *Friday the 13th*."

To everyone but Craven, Miner, and his family, Cunningham had seemed the picture of calm during this stressful period. Even before Cunningham secured financing from Scuderi, Cunningham had assured his closest collaborators, through the spring and early summer months of 1979, that *Friday the 13th* was going to be made, and be made for $500,000. Cunningham also knew that Scuderi's pledge was hardly concrete and could wither at any moment. Still, there were no outward signs of panic. "It was directly after the two kids' films that Sean had me in the kitchen at his home and said, more or less, the following: I am going to make a film called *Friday the 13th* and it is going to be the scariest film ever, and you are going to score it," Harry Manfredini recalls. "He never said it was going to make or break anyone. I

A close-up shot of the arches in Blairstown. (Photo courtesy of Brett McBean www.brettmcbean.com)

think if it did not work, and was not such a hit, we would have just kept going, onto another project. There was never that kind of 'make or break' feeling or thought."

Ultimately, Cunningham wrested much of the creative control, and a large degree of leverage, over *Friday the 13th* from Scuderi and his partners, without them even knowing it. This would happen during the filming in Blairstown, and then during *Friday the 13th*'s post-production phase. But by the end of July of 1979, Scuderi was calling all the shots. Cunningham was at Scuderi's mercy, and they both knew it. The decisions Scuderi made during this period, in the summer months of 1979, especially in relation to Victor Miller's script, firmly established Scuderi's creative influence – his imprint - upon *Friday the 13th*.

FRIDAY THE 13TH VERSION 2.0

Unhappy with Victor Miller's *Friday the 13th* script, Philip Scuderi contacted Ron Kurz, a novelist and fledgling screen-writer, to make changes he felt were vital to *Friday the 13th*. As Cunningham was made aware, these changes were also a condition of Georgetown's financing of *Friday the 13th*.

Like Cunningham, Kurz had a decade-long relationship with Scuderi prior to his involvement with *Friday the 13th*. The Kurz-Scuderi relationship was born out of the time Kurz spent as a theater manager in Baltimore in the early 1970s. Prior to *Friday the 13th*, Scuderi had contracted Kurz to perform scripting duties on the Scuderi-financed *King Frat*, which Kurz worked on under the pseudonym Mark Jackson. Despite these connections, Kurz would have no direct contact with Cunningham or Miller throughout his substantial involvement with *Friday the 13th*. Just as Miller answered

Main Street in Blairstown. (Photo courtesy of Brett McBean www. brettmcbean.com)

directly to Cunningham, Kurz answered only to Scuderi.

Philip Scuderi was enamored with Kurz as a writer, seeing him as his kind of writer for his kind of films. Kurz subsequently became Georgetown's go-to writer, beginning with *King Frat* and *Friday the 13th* and extending into the early 1980s with titles like *Friday the 13th Part 2*, *Eyes of a Stranger*, and *Off the Wall*. "Phil, who's since died, was quite a force," Kurz says. "Try and picture a cross between Michael Corleone and Roger Corman. You'll never see his name on anything, but he was hands-on involved with lots of films. He basically

gave Wes Craven, Sean Cunningham and Steve Miner their starts in the business. Phil was more than just a financier type: he was a creative force in his own right, often coming up with wild scenes, usually acted out in restaurants. All I had to do was write them down the next day. Phil and I had a great working relationship."

After Sean Cunningham had approached him with *Friday the 13th*, Scuderi immediately contacted Kurz regarding the reworking of Victor Miller's script. "After I'd written a couple of movies for Phil, I heard

A reverse shot of Main Street. (Photo courtesy of Brett McBean www. brettmcbean.com)

Main Street in Blairstown doubled for fictional Crystal Lake in the film. (Photo courtesy of Brett McBean www.brettmcbean.com)

through the grapevine that he'd been approached by a down-and-out producer named Sean Cunningham," Kurz recalls. "All Sean had was a great-sounding title: *Friday the 13th*. Actually, he had something else: an awful, tepid script that had been written by Victor Miller, a soap opera writer and a Guild member who had been working under the umbrella of Sean's production company. Phil liked the idea, but he hated the script. He demanded changes in the script before he'd put up any serious money. He brought me in to revise the script. He wanted me to add humor, my strength, and give it something. He didn't know what, but something."

One of Kurz's major contributions to the *Friday the 13th* script, and ultimately to pop culture, was his reimagining of the Jason Voorhees character who existed in Victor's Miller's script as a fairly normal – if a bit strange – kind of kid who drowns. Kurz sought to give Jason Voorhees a much more gruesome persona and to feature the Jason character in a surprise ending that would serve as a "chair-jumper" for the audience. "In Victor Miller's script, Jason was merely a normal kid who had drowned the season before," Kurz says. "Everything centered on the unseen Mrs. Voorhees and her revenge. In rewriting it, I came up with the idea of making Jason 'different' – read mongoloid – and having him leap out of the lake at the end once the audience is lulled into thinking closing credits are about to roll."

This key addition to the *Friday the 13th* script

A side-angle shot of the main cabin. (Photo courtesy of Brett McBean www.brettmcbean.com)

The diner that Steve Christy visits in the film. (Photo courtesy of Brett McBean www.brettmcbean.com)

thrilled Scuderi, and, in retrospect, went a long way to both securing the financing for *Friday the 13th* and determining *Friday the 13th*'s destiny as a sustainable film franchise. "I remember being out to dinner in Boston with Phil and his secretary on the night I told him of my Jason idea," Kurz recalls. "He listened for a minute, then got up without a word and left the table to go out into the lobby where we saw him pacing around. His secretary looked at me and said, 'Wow, you got him good with that one.'"

Cunningham and Scuderi kept in touch throughout Kurz's rewriting of the *Friday the 13th* script, with Cunningham being fully aware of, and generally supporting, the changes Kurz made, especially the Jason con-

cept. Cunningham was also loyal to Miller who gradually became aware of the changes that were being made to his original script on the urging of Scuderi (with whom Miller didn't have a very warm relationship). "I had no perspective because Sean didn't mention him [Ron Kurz] to me until he told me that Phil wanted a scene in the movie that I would probably hate – the motorcycle cop scene – and that Phil had a writer he liked who had written it," Miller says. "He didn't show me the scene on paper. I told him [Cunningham] that it would seriously work against the concept that the kids were out of reach of help by the cops, the National Guard or grownups, but Sean told me that Phil was paying for the movie and what he wanted would go in. Phil had done that before when he backed *Here Come the Tigers* and wanted pink fart clouds to come out from the players in the dugout. By the time of *Friday*, Phil didn't much care for me because I kept arguing against most, if not all, of his ideas on *Tigers* and another screenplay I wrote for him that was supposed

The entrance to Camp No-Be-Bo-Sco, the real-life campsite that doubled for Camp Crystal Lake in the film. (Photo courtesy of Brett McBean www.brettmcbean.com)

to be an *Animal House* rip-off [referring to *King Frat*]."

"I learned later that, as I was writing new scenes or revising old ones, Victor Miller was down in Connecticut with Sean and was putting them into a draft under his own name," Kurz says. "I really don't blame him. He was working, legitimately, through Sean and the Guild and I was breaking every Guild rule on paper for Phil, not even using my own name. In Victor Miller's second draft, 45 of the 97 pages are either new scenes of mine or revised earlier scenes. Ah, the movie business! You gotta love it!"

THE PERFECT SUMMER CAMP

In July of 1979, while Sean Cunningham was in the process of haggling with Philip Scuderi over the creative direction and financing of *Friday the 13th*, Cunningham and Steve Miner enlisted production designer Virginia Field (from *Manny's Orphans*) to scour the East Coast for a summer camp location that would be suitable for *Friday the 13th*. "Sean wasn't passionate about the visual aspect of filmmaking and so he gave me the freedom with my visual work and my design," Virginia Field says. "Sean gave me a lot of freedom in terms of picking a summer camp location and designing the look of it."

With only an incomplete version of the *Friday the 13th* script to study at this point, and no experience in horror filmmaking, Field listened to Cunningham's detailed description of the *Friday the 13th*

A shot of the main cabin. (Photo courtesy of Brett McBean www.brettmcbean.com)

outline and story in order to visualize the kind of summer camp location that would be a good fit for an unprecedented horror film sub-genre. No pressure.

Cynically, the always cash-conscious Cunningham was also hoping Field would find a summer camp with a wealth of cabin space that could double as cheap lodgings for the *Friday the 13th* crew. "I felt that we needed a camp that had a strong sense of history, and had a real physicality about it in terms of the layout," Field says. "I felt that the movie needed a camp that looked like it had been around for many years, rather than a camp that looked like it had just been opened a few years ago. This camp had to be old. In terms of the physicality of the layout, I felt that the lake had to always be present in the story, and also that nature had to be present and visible throughout. I didn't want a location where you had to walk a long way to get to the lake."

For this purpose, Field contacted friend and scenic artist Robert Topol. "I called Robert Topol, a good friend of a mine and a great scenic artist, and told him I was looking for a summer camp for this movie I was doing," Field recalls. "Robert lived in Connecticut, about 40 minutes from Blairstown, and he knew the area and was familiar with the camps on the East Coast. He found Blairstown, and the boy scouts camp that we ended up shooting the movie at."

"I went to a design class in New York with Virginia Field who went on to do *The Adams Chronicles* on television, while I did theater," recalls Topol who served as *Friday the 13th*'s un-credited art director. "We were friends, and when she called me and asked about a location for

Friday the 13th, I thought of Blairstown. I also thought of a camp in the Poconos, which also would've been good, but my brother had gone to No-Be-Bo-Sco and I knew that area really well. When Virginia told me about the movie, I thought of the classic summer camp horror tale I'd grown up with where there's a monster named Cropsy on the other side of the lake. We didn't have that 'other side of the lake' in *Friday the 13th*, which we did have when I worked on *Friday the 13th Part 2* in Connecticut, but I

The location upon which production designer Virginia Field and her team constructed the pantry that appears in the film. (Photo courtesy of Brett McBean www.brettmcbean.com)

knew that Blairstown would be a good fit for the film."

Blairstown was, is, Blairstown, New Jersey, a township nestled in the surrounding Warren County. The period between 1970 and 1979 represented the biggest jump in population - from nearly 2200 people in 1970 to just over 4000 as of 1979 - in the township's history (Blairstown was incorporated as a township in 1845). Otherwise Blairstown was, by the end of the summer in 1979, very much a microcosm of the bleak economic conditions and malaise that defined the Jimmy Carter presidency in the late 1970s, a period in which small towns like Blairstown were especially hard-hit and had sunk into a recession-driven gloom.

The summer camp that Topol had in mind was Camp No-Be-Bo-Sco (North Bergen Boy Scouts), a Boy Scouts of America summer camp that opened in 1927 and operated - and continues to operate to this day - every summer from the beginning of July to the middle of August.

The spacious location had all the amenities that *Friday the 13th* required, namely an idyllic lake, known as the Sand Pond, cabins sprinkled throughout the location, and a vast area of forest which serves as a starting point for hikes along the fabled Appalachian Trail. Having been in operation since 1927, the place also had a palpable sense of age and history, both elements of which added considerable atmosphere and flavor to *Friday the 13th*.

For the purpose of filming *Friday the 13th*, and the set pieces that would be required to bring the story to life, Camp No-Be-Bo-Sco was perfect. Moreover, Blairstown was in a great strategic location. It was a smooth 80 mile drive away from New York City,

Camp No-Be-Bo-Sco's main office. (Photo courtesy of Brett McBean www.brettmcbean.com)

where Barry Abrams and his crew were based, a 40 minute drive from Connecticut, and just a stone's throw, a handful of miles, from Pennsylvania which connects to Blairstown through the Delaware Water Gap.

"It was a very depressed area," Field recalls of her first visit to Blairstown in July 1979. "It was far from New York, more in terms of sophistication than the distance. Two months before filming, me and my small design team went to Blairstown to look at the camp."

Outside the front of the main cabin, looking towards the lake. (Photo courtesy of Brett McBean www.brettmcbean.com)

In July 1979, Field, along with her ragtag design team that would join her for the filming of *Friday the 13th*, descended on Blairstown, on Camp No-Be-Bo-Sco, to survey the location and make whatever alternations were needed, within Field's miniscule budget, to get the camp ready for filming. Making this more complicated was the fact that the camp was, throughout July, well into its summer session and so it was crawling with kids upon this initial location scouting visit. "There were kids when I went there on the first visit and obviously no kids when we started filming," Field recalls. "We stayed in cabins during that first trip, although Robert Topol's parents lived nearby."

"Blairstown was a country town with lots of open space," Topol recalls. "Camp No-Be-Bo-Sco was a very remote location from town. The camp was located very deep in the woods and you had to go down a long dirt road to get to the end and arrive there. The location certainly was as isolated and remote as it appears in the film. No one could hear you scream!"

Greeted by Robert Topol upon her arrival in Blairstown, Field and Topol immediately got to work transforming Camp No-Be-Bo-Sco into the Camp Crystal Lake location that Sean Cunningham and Steve Miner had impressed upon Field. "We built an entire building for the crew to work out of during filming," Field recalls. "We built all of the toilets that are seen in the film by putting in latrines, although we had to replace those later when the kids used them. Later on, one of my poor assistants had to clean the toilets

Beautiful Crystal Lake. (Photo courtesy of Brett McBean www.brettmcbean.com)

used in the film because we had so little money. Talk about a thankless task! We built the sink and shower stall used in the film. We built the pantry used in the film. We built an addition to the main cabin that Adrienne King hides in during the climactic scenes of the film."

"We were very excited and nervous in the weeks leading up to the filming," Steve Miner recalls. "There was a lot to do. We had to find a suitable location for the camp, and we knew that a lot of the summer camps were going to freak out when they found we were making a slasher film, which they did. We didn't need a lot of things from the campsite, but our needs were very specific. You know, we needed an archery range, some cabins, a certain feeling of isolation and, of course, a lake for young Jason to jump out of."

Virginia Field and her design team were the first of the *Friday the 13th* crewmembers to visit Blairstown. (Photo courtesy of Tony Marshall)

"One of the first things we did after we arrived at the camp was to make an addition to the latrine cabin by rigging breakaway walls to the latrine cabin, and making the floors come out," Topol recalls. "In one of the cabins, we went down under the bed so they could film under the bed, which was used for the Kevin Bacon scene. We built the dock seen in the film, and we also built the camp entrance that appears in the film, along with the split fences and the archway. We also built some of the furniture used in the film. We also built the archery range."

Field and Topol, along with Field's tireless support team, also worked to give Camp No-Be-Bo-Sco a sense of history and personality, more than the place already possessed, and to bolster the illusion that Camp Crystal Lake had really been in business for many decades. "We built the town signs that appeared in the film and we also built signs that reflected Native-American traditions," Field recalls. "We worked twenty hours a day before filming. I probably made the Welcome to Camp Crystal lake sign, but I don't remember. I do remem-

Blairstown in 1979 was a portrait of small town America. (Photo courtesy of Tony Marshall)

ber that we built areas in the main cabin with the markings of Indian tribes, to show the history of the place."

Daniel Mahon, who was Field and Topol's chief assistant in Blairstown, recalls that the Welcome to Camp Crystal Lake sign was created through the application of block plywood letters upon an existing square sign which served as a framing square template for the now infamous logo. "Thinking back, I believe I laid-out the letters with a framing square on Luan (1/4" plywood)," Mahon recalls.

Withering downtown Blairstown as it appeared prior to the start of *Friday the 13th*'s filming. (Photo courtesy of Tony Marshall)

"I did the best I could, not being a professional sign-maker."

"I think that Virginia and I created that sign [the Welcome to Camp Crystal Lake sign] based on the look of everything that we saw around the camp area, which was mostly clad in yellow," Topol recalls. "We used native carvings to give the place a sense of history, and we also put kids' graffiti in the cabins. We used worn wood in our construction to make it seem like the camp had a long history."

While Field, Topol and their minions were renovating Camp No-Be-Bo-Sco, Sean Cunningham was, as mentioned, still in the midst of a back and forth, tug of war negotiation with Philip Scuderi and Georgetown Productions over the $500,000 in financing.

The Camp No-Be-Bo-Sco location was suggested to Virginia Field by friend Robert Topol, who served as *Friday the 13th*'s art director. (Photo courtesy of Tony Marshall)

It was in July of 1979, while Field was in Blairstown, that the tense negotiations between Cunningham and Scuderi reached an impasse and it seemed like *Friday the 13th* was dead, at least in terms of the $500,000 model that Cunningham was looking for. This may have been because Cunningham and Scuderi couldn't agree on terms. Maybe Scuderi was unable to come-up with the $500,000. Maybe the specter of the title controversy gave lawyer Scuderi pause. The only certain fact is that Cunningham, having taking a second mortgage out on his Westport home, was virtually broke.

Whatever was the case, Cunningham called Field while she was in Blairstown and told her that *Friday the 13th* was, effectively, dead. "Sean called me and said he'd run out of money and we had to come back," Field recalls. "One month later, we were back on with the money, but discovered that the toilets we'd built at the camp had been used. "

"After we finished the work at the camp, we then waited for Sean Cunningham and the DP [director of photography] Barry [Barry Abrams], a great guy, to show up and give their approval," Topol recalls. "They came by prior to filming to give their approval of the work we'd done, and I was very nervous, but they were happy with what we'd done with the camp."

By August, Field and Topol had seen a virtually complete copy of the *Friday the 13th* script – although not the absolute final draft which would be dated August 21, 1979 – to itemize their design requirements for Camp

No-Be-Bo-Sco. Upon reading the script, neither was terribly enthusiastic. "There are three reasons for me to do a movie, and they have to do with whether I love the script, whether the film could make lots of money, and whether I love the people I'm working with," Field says. "With *Friday the 13th*, I didn't like the script, and I didn't think it would make any money, but I loved the people who I was going to be working with, and that's why I did the movie."

"I read the script and thought it was a real dog," recalls Daniel Mahon who served as an assistant art di-

The Welcome to Camp Crystal Lake sign was the result of a collaboration between Virginia Field, Daniel Mahon and Robert Topol. (Photo courtesy of Daniel Mahon)

rector and a scenic artist on *Friday the 13th*, and was a key member of Field's team. "I think we all thought the script was pretty schlocky and that it was very unlikely that a successful film could be made out of such a script."

The grappling between Cunningham and Scuderi over *Friday the 13th*'s financing continued well into August. By this time Cunningham was undaunted and prepared to bring *Friday the 13th* to life by any means necessary, either as the $500,000 model he envisioned, or in an altogether more threadbare form.

Ever the cool and unflappable salesman, Cunningham continued to assure his colleagues that he had the $500,000 in place to make a horror film. If there was one unfailing part of Cunningham's personality, it was that he'd always kept his word.

Despite only a fragile financial commitment from Philip Scuderi and Georgetown, Cunningham fearlessly moved forward with *Friday the 13th*. In late July 1979, in the aftermath of the *Variety* advertisement, Cunningham began to assemble, and in many cases reassemble, the cast and crew that would eventually march to Blairstown and make film history.

CHAPTER 4

HAPPY CAMPERS: THE CAST AND CREW OF *FRIDAY THE 13TH*

"Shortly before we began filming on Friday the 13th, Sean [Cunningham] and Steve [Miner] approached me and offered me a piece of the film instead of a salary. Having shot about ten of these low budget movies up to that point, and having worked with Sean and Steve previously on the kids' movies, I did the smart thing and said, 'No way. I've got a wife and a kid to look after and I need the paycheck.' As it turns out, Friday the 13th ended up making about $90 Million, and I probably would've made about $2 Million from the film, but who's counting?"

– director of photography Barry Abrams

"We weren't looking for the greatest actors in the world. I wanted kids who were somewhat likable, responsible camp counselors, not your typical horror movie geeks. Basically, they had to be reasonably good-looking, and they had to be able to read dialogue fairly well, and they had to work cheap."

– Sean Cunningham

In late July 1979, Sean Cunningham travelled to New York to begin the casting process, even though he didn't have firm financing in place. All he had, at this moment, was the *Friday the 13th* logo from the *Variety* advertisement and the most current draft of Victor Miller's script.

In Cunningham's mind, like Virginia Field's location scouting trip to Blairstown, initiating the casting process meant that *Friday the 13th* was something real and tangible and not just a logo. Cunningham's trip to New York represented a ballsy projection of supreme confidence on Cunningham's part,

1972 Photo of Jeannine Taylor, playing the role of Maggie in the play *Winners* at the London Barn Playhouse in New London, New Hampshire. (Photo courtesy of Jeannine Taylor)

both in terms of *Friday the 13th*, and himself. It also represented a projection of success on Cunningham's part, which belied his own dire circumstances.

As with every other decision in his career, there was also a business motive. By launching the casting of *Friday the 13th*, Cunningham was hoping to generate more publicity for the project and perhaps speed-up the financing process. It worked.

Cunningham viewed the casting as a relatively minor element, certainly in comparison to financing and promotion. He believed that it was entirely ancillary to the film's success and his casual approach to the subject reflects this. Cunningham would worry about casting, in earnest, when he had financing and a completed script. Even then, this wasn't a high priority.

By the middle of July 1979, Cunningham had told so many of his colleagues and friends that he had the $500,000 firmly in place, that he had nearly believed it himself. It was with this belief that Cunningham paid a visit to 1515 Broadway, home

to a suite of offices belonging to T.N.I. (Theater Now, Inc.). This prestigious firm - led by casting directors Julie Hughes and Barry Moss - was also involved with theatrical management and productions.

The austere surroundings were alien to Cunningham who'd never worked with a casting director before. Likewise, Hughes and Moss, a legendary and venerable duo with an illustrious pedigree in the theater world, were in the process of taking baby steps in casting feature films, with *Friday the 13th* being one of their first film projects.

The involvement of Hughes and Moss generated a lot of extra publicity for *Friday the 13th*, in terms of word spreading about the project through various New York-based acting agents.

Friday the 13th was, as such, going to be cast under Screen Actors' Guild (SAG) regula-

Although they moved in some of the same New York acting circles, Kevin Bacon and Jeannine Taylor hadn't known each other prior to being cast in *Friday the 13th*. (Photo courtesy of Harvey Fenton)

tions, the first such project that Cunningham had ever been involved with. "I went from non-SAG to SAG with *Friday the 13th*," Cunningham recalls. "It was a whole other world for me, and a big difference. It was a big learning experience."

It didn't take long for Hughes and Moss, who would later cast several more of Cunningham's films, to see through the cracks of Cunningham's bravado and recognize just how fragile the *Friday the 13th* project was. By the first week of August, Hughes and Moss had a copy of the script and began spreading the word about the film to their contacts in New York. "Sean came into our office with just the *Friday the 13th* logo from *Variety* and no script and said that he wanted to make a movie and wanted us to cast it for him," Barry Moss recalls. "Sean and I hit it off right away and have worked together many times since. The script arrived and we sent breakdowns out to agents who would submit actors and the names of actors they had in mind."

Cunningham's view on *Friday the 13th*'s casting, shared by Hughes and Moss, was that there were no roles requiring established actors, with the exception of Pamela Voorhees.

The character of Alice, *Friday the 13th*'s heroine, consumed the bulk of the rest of the casting energies. For the rest of the roles in the film, primarily the other camp counselor parts, Cunningham had very modest requirements. "I knew there were no star-making parts in the script," Cunningham says. "I think we were just looking for good-looking kids you might see in a Pepsi commercial. We certainly weren't looking for any recognizable actors, nor did I want any."

Of all of the actors cast in *Friday the 13th*, the one that's had the most successful post-*Friday the 13th* career is Kevin Bacon who was cast in the role of Jack.

In 1978, Bacon had thought his film career had taken off with his featured role in the blockbuster comedy film *National Lampoon's Animal House.* However, the film's success had no residual effect. By the summer of 1979, Bacon was a struggling New York actor who had recently appeared on the daytime television soap opera *The Search for Tomorrow,* but also spent much of 1978 and 1979 waiting tables.

Bacon's role in *Animal House* played no role in his casting in *Friday the 13th*. In fact, his was one of the simplest in the film. "We'd cast Kevin Bacon in a movie called *Hero at Large*, which would be released in 1980," Moss recalls. "Kevin had a small part in that film, but we remembered him and thought he'd be good for Jack so we called up his agent who asked what the role in *Friday the 13th* would involve. We basically told the agent that Kevin would get to have sex in the movie. Kevin's agent said that Kevin would like that because he likes sex. It was as simple as that."

One of Bacon's roommates in New York,

prior to them both being cast in *Friday the 13th*, had been Harry Crosby, the son of legendary entertainer Bing Crosby, who passed away in 1977. After his father's passing, Crosby spent the next phase of

As the son of legendary entertainer Bing Crosby, Harry Crosby brought the greatest amount of celebrity to *Friday the 13th*. (Photo courtesy of David Beury)

his life studying drama and music at the London Academy of Music and Dramatic Arts (LAMDA).

Crosby eventually received a Bachelor of Fine Arts degree from LAMDA. He performed and studied in London until the summer of 1979 when he took a two month hiatus and flew to New York. "Kevin and I lived in this flop apartment that was more like a mattress," Crosby recalls with a laugh. "I was supposed to return to England to do a European tour, performing plays around Europe, when I landed the *Friday the 13th* role in New York."

Crosby's modest living conditions in New York were a testament to his determination to go through the same experiences as all other struggling actors and to carve out an acting career without relying on his famous last name and family fortune--a pursuit that Crosby took to extremes.

Conscious about being treated differently

because of his pedigree, Crosby was relieved when he met with Cunningham and Moss for his *Friday the 13th* audition and Cunningham treated him just like any other actor. "I met with Sean and he was very friendly, and he just treated me like any other actor, and not Bing Crosby's son," Crosby recalls. "I just wanted to be treated like any other actor, which is what happened on *Friday the 13th*. I also grew to trust Sean because he told me about his life and the various ups and downs he'd had as a filmmaker prior to *Friday the 13th*."

Mark Nelson honed his acting skills at Princeton University from where he graduated in 1977. Like all of the younger cast members in *Friday the 13th*, save for Kevin Bacon, *Friday the 13th* marked Nelson's feature film debut.(Photo courtesy of Mark Nelson)

Cunningham's growing involvement with the casting of *Friday the 13th* saw him sit in on casting sessions with Hughes and Moss regularly. This was a result of the instant rapport he developed with Moss. People around them during this period thought they were lifelong friends when, in fact, they'd only recently met. "No, Sean and I hadn't met, or gone to school together, before *Friday the 13th* but our personalities just clicked," Moss says. "We laughed at the same jokes, saw eye-to-eye on actors, and we just became instant friends."

Actress Jeannine Taylor's casting as Marcie in *Friday the 13th*, the girlfriend of Bacon's Jack character, marked the first and only feature film the actress would ever appear in, for various reasons. A 1976 graduate of Wheaton College, a liberal arts school in Norton, Massachusetts, Taylor spent the early part of 1979 in rehearsals for the play *Home Again, Home Again*, under the guidance of legendary stage director Gene Saks. She'd hoped it was going to be her Broadway debut.

Jeannine Taylor's 1979 headshot. (Photo courtesy of Jeannine Taylor)

While doing rehearsals during the daytime, the Connecticut-born Taylor performed at night, and on weekends, in a production of *The Umbrellas of Cherbourg* at Joseph Papp's Public Theatre, as well as going to acting classes and rehearsing with scene partners on her dinner and lunch breaks. "And I was married to a fellow actor (whom I rarely got to see!)," Taylor recalls. "The audition for *Friday the 13th* was held sometime in the late spring of 1979. *Home Again* had closed in out-of-town tryouts, and I was back in New York, going on auditions and working with a speech teacher to smooth out my regional accent. (This accent is sometimes referred to as the 'Connecticut squashed A'). I had it bad."

Cunningham and Moss both met with Taylor during her audition, with Cunningham later meeting her alone. "My agents called me with the audition appointment at Hughes-Moss Casting, or Theater Now, Inc. as their company was known at the time, to read for the part of Marcie," Taylor recalls. "They got a script to me ahead of time, and I went in and read for Barry Moss and Sean Cunningham. I remember that Barry called me on the phone prior to my audition and explained that this was going to be an independent, low-budget movie (though it was through SAG), and I seem to recall his mentioning that he knew Sean Cunningham from college days. Anyway, I read for them once and then was called back. Both auditions were held in one of the smaller rooms at TNI. Barry and Sean were both at the first audition, and just Sean at the callback. I remember it as being very low-key and relaxed and basically fun. I think Sean offered me the part at my second audition, but I may not remember this correctly. Anyway, I was free to do it, said yes, and the rest, as they say, is history."

Like all of the performers who appeared in *Friday the 13th*, Taylor had no idea of what *Friday the 13th* was at this point, and certainly no idea of what it would turn out to be. "I thought it would stay under the radar and I could just get some on camera experience," Taylor says. "Period. I was dumbfounded when it became a blockbuster and people started recognizing me on the street. I developed a stock reply to 'Aren't you the girl who...?' I'd say, 'No, no. I'm an attorney.' And at that point, believe me, I wished I was!"

The casting of other roles in *Friday the 13th* was much more casual and transient. An example of this was Mark Nelson, who was cast as Ned, *Friday the 13th*'s practical joker and "third wheel" alongside Bacon and Taylor's relationship in the film. "I'd never done a movie before *Friday the 13th*, having worked entirely in the theater, and was very nervous about doing a movie," Nelson recalls. "My agent asked me if I was interested in auditioning for a movie, so I went into the casting office and I remember that Julie [Julie Hughes] just looked at me and said something like, 'You're the practical joker; you're the wisecrack.'"

Nelson was a 1977 graduate of Princeton, and knew Kevin Bacon, casually, prior to *Friday the 13th*, the two of them having moved in some of the same theatrical circles. Nelson had also spent time at Joseph Papp's Public Theatre, like Jeannine Taylor, but Nelson and Taylor didn't know

Laurie Bartram was the most reluctant member of the *Friday the 13th* cast, given her strong moral and religious beliefs. (Photo courtesy of Harvey Fenton)

each other prior to filming. "I had never met Jeannine Taylor before the movie," Nelson says. "We both worked at the Public Theatre, but not at the same time. I wasn't close friends with Kevin Bacon but I knew him from doing theater and I knew we'd get along well together on the film."

"I'm from the East Coast, New Jersey, and I was in Julie Hughes' office for something else when Julie mentioned *Friday the 13th* to me," recalls Robbi Morgan who was cast as Annie in the middle of August of 1979, just before the start of filming in Blairstown. "She said, 'I'm casting this summer camp movie and I think you'd make a great camp counselor.' She asked me if I could go to the set where they were filming, and so I drove to the set immediately."

Certainly the most reluctant performer in *Friday the 13th* was actress Laurie Bartram, who was cast in the role of Brenda. Bartram was a devout Christian who was, by this time, in the midst of a personal and spiritual metamorphosis-- conflicted between her genuine love of performing and her religious faith. Born and raised in St. Louis, Missouri, Bartram was a trained ballerina who had traveled the world as a dancer from the mid to late 1970s in ballet productions, concerts, operas, and in theatrical revues.

After graduating high school, Bartram travelled to Los Angeles and joined the dance company The June Taylor Dancers. As a member of the fall 1976 season of the Musical Theatre Workshop of the Los Angeles Civic Light Opera, Bartram appeared in a wide range of roles (with the St. Louis Municipal Opera, Bartram appeared in productions of *Take Me Along, Man of La Mancha, Bittersweet, Carousel, Camelot,*

1979 photo of Jeannine Taylor, taken backstage during a Seattle production of the play *A History of the American Film*, in which Taylor played the role of Clara Mortimer. (Photo courtesy of Jeannine Taylor)

Funny Girl, and many others]. Continuing to live in Los Angeles throughout 1977, Bartram took cautious steps towards the pursuit of an acting career, and while she didn't land any film or television roles during this period, Bartram – who'd also appeared

with the Los Angeles Ballet and at the Dance Center in London, England – did form friendships with such show business luminaries as Cher and Vincent Price.

As a performance dancer, Bartram had appeared in Las Vegas, most notably as a featured dancer with the Hudson Brothers at the Riviera Hotel. Although dancing was Bartram's first love, Bartram focused more and more on the pursuit of an acting career in the late 1970s (Some sources have claimed, incorrectly, that Bartram appeared – under the pseudonym Laurie Brighton – in two 1973 episodes of the television series *Emergency!,* but Laurie Brighton was a different actress altogether).

Prior to being cast in *Friday the 13th,* Bartram's filmed acting work consisted of various industrial shows, television commercials and television specials which often featured Bartram dancing. Her most substantial acting role prior to *Friday the 13th* was on the daytime television soap opera series *Another World* where she appeared between 1978 and 1979.

Another World was filmed in New York, where Bartram had relocated in 1978. She attended Manhattan Bible Church, and it was there that she came into contact with a group of travelling Christian missionaries from whom Bartram became acquainted with Lynchburg Baptist College (later renamed Liberty University). She later attended Liberty in the early 1980s. By this time she had left New

Adrienne King was one of the last actresses to audition for the pivotal role of Alice. (Photo courtesy of Harvey Fenton)

York and abandoned her performing career in order to pursue a Christian life in Lynchburg, Virginia. This is where Bartram spent the rest of her life.

The conflict Bartram felt between her performing career and her religious faith festered right through the filming of *Friday the 13th*. In addition to her Christian faith, she had, by the summer of 1979, also given thought to pursuing a career in broadcast journalism.

Bartram's frustration over the glacial state of her acting career, according to her friends in New York, played a role in her eventual decision to leave acting, performance dancing, and New York, a city that she'd unquestionably grown to love by the time of her casting in *Friday the 13th*.

Bartram's casting in *Friday the 13th* was something she viewed entirely as a job, and not one she was thrilled about entering. The filming of *Friday the 13th* actually represented a cathartic passage for Bartram who used the filming period to sort out the direction she wanted to take her life. She eventually embraced *Friday the 13th* with a sense of humor and sharp wit that the cast and crew of *Friday the 13th* would most fondly remember her for. Whether she entirely knew it or not at the time, *Friday the 13th* would be Bartram's final goodbye to her performing life and the beginning of an altogether different life, a million miles removed from the bright lights of New York and the excitement of performing.

Besides the casting for the role of Pamela Voorhees, which turned into a whole process unto itself, Cunningham, Hughes and Moss spent the most amount of care and effort in the casting for the pivotal role of Alice, *Friday the 13th*'s heroine. Cunningham, Hughes and Moss – primarily Cunningham and Moss-- looked at scores of girls before they met with the eventual choice: Adrienne King. "We spent a lot of time on Alice," Moss recalls. "We saw lots of girls before Adrienne, and some of them were good, but they weren't quite right for Sean who was looking for a specific kind of girl to play Alice. Adrienne was one of the last girls we saw for Alice, and Sean liked her immediately."

Born and raised in Oyster Bay, New York, King (who was born in 1955, not 1960 as is commonly stated) made her first acting appearance at the age of six months old when she appeared in an Ivory Soap commercial, followed by more radio and television commercials throughout the 1960s and early 1970s. Her most notable screen appearance during this period was a featured role in a Hallmark Hall of Fame production of *Inherit the Wind,* co-starring Diane Baker and Melvyn Douglas, which aired

in 1965. After high school graduation in 1973, King, an accomplished artist, entered the Fashion Institute of Technology (F.I.T.) in New York on a Fine Arts scholarship. (She would later study with famed acting teacher William Esper at whose studio Jeannine Taylor also trained at prior to being cast in *Friday the 13th*.)

King's background certainly fit the criteria

Sean Cunningham, Adrienne King and Victor Miller deny that the Alice character was modeled after the Laurie Strode character from *Halloween*, despite the obvious similarities. (Photo courtesy of Harvey Fenton)

that Cunningham had been looking for, in terms of commercials and soap opera experience. King had, by the summer of 1979, appeared on the daytime television soap operas *All My Children* and *Another World* and, as a trained dancer, appeared un-credited in the musical films *Saturday Night Fever* (1978) and *Hair* (1979). "In the summer of '79, I heard about this little independent horror film, *Friday the 13th*," recalled King of the period before her first audition. "Barry Moss and Julie Hughes were casting. It was going to be tough getting into the audition since I didn't have a theatrical agent to submit me. My good friend Bill Love's boss's friend, Pam, knew Barry and that's how I got in. Then there was callback after callback, then the screen test."

Upon receiving a copy of the *Friday the 13th* script, a script that contained Ron Kurz's contributions, King overlooked the script's fallibilities and focused on the positives, namely that Alice was the lead role in *Friday the 13th* and the story's only survivor. "What I liked about the script was that my character was not the typical horror film bimbo," said King whose Screen Actors' Guild contract on *Friday the 13th* called for her to be paid $785 per week of filming, the largest amount allotted to any of any of the cast members save for Betsy Palmer. "Alice was strong and tough and had brains. It was also attractive in that I was going to end-up being the film's only survivor."

King's androgynous, tomboyish, unconventional appearance wasn't far removed from Jamie Lee Curtis' persona in *Halloween*, although all parties deny that this was a factor in King's casting, or that King modeled herself, or the Alice character, after Curtis' portrayal in *Halloween*. King's offbeat appearance mirrored her own hard-edged, scrappy personality, along with King's thick Long Island accent which the actress attempted to flatten by the start of *Friday the 13th*'s filming.

Oscar-winning actress Gloria Grahame accepted a flat $1000 offer for the role of Sandy, but withdrew at the last moment. (Photo courtesy of David Beury)

Whether Cunningham, King, or Moss were influenced by thoughts of Jamie Lee Curtis during King's casting or not, there's no disputing that King would ultimately create a scream queen persona that would be quite influential in its own right. "They

brought in every young actress in New York," recalled Cunningham of King's casting. "I liked Adrienne King when I met her. Vulnerable, girl next door. She didn't seem like an actress; she seemed like a kid, which was true for most of the actors in the movie. I wanted a sense of real people who could act and behave naturally, and Adrienne gave me that sense. I liked what she brought to the table. It's one of those things where she just had something."

For her screen test, King read a monologue from the *Friday the 13th* script that would be later spoken by Jeannine Taylor's Marcie character in the film. This is the scene in the film where Marcie and Kevin Bacon's Jack character are outside a cabin and Marcie relates a nightmarish premonition about blood and rain that foretells her grisly death. It's a long monologue, one of the largest blocks of dialogue in the entire film and script, and it was after this reading that Cunningham, won over by King's pluckiness, and intrigued by her offbeat looks, let it be known to Barry Moss that King was the right choice to play Alice. In fact, Cunningham was so enamored with King that he decided to incorporate King's artistry, her love of sketching, into the *Friday the 13th* script. King would turn out to be, arguably, Cunningham's closest confidante throughout *Friday the 13th*'s filming.

Basically, King was no wallflower, and completely unique from the countless other "pretty girls" who went through the Broadway casting office throughout August of 1979. "Originally, they were looking real hard for a name actress to play Alice," King recalled. "They finally realized that even if they could find somebody like that who was willing to do it, they wouldn't be able to afford her, so they decided to go with new talent instead."

The "name actress" that King was thinking about actually had nothing to do with the part of Alice, but was related to several other roles in the film. The most notable, of course, was the Pamela Voorhees role for which Cunningham and Moss, mostly Cunningham, ending up pursuing not one but three different Academy Award-winning actresses throughout August of 1979 and into September.

The most surprising anecdote that developed in New York, before the casting of the Pamela Voorhees' role, had to do with, of all things, the rather innocuous role of Sandy the diner waitress, a character who would only end-up having one scene in the film.

For the role of Sandy, Cunningham and Moss pursued screen legend Gloria Grahame, who'd previously won an Oscar for her performance in the film *The Bad and the Beautiful* (1952) and had received an Oscar nomination for the film *Crossfire* (1947). As with many candidates for the Pamela Voorhees' role, Grahame's once-illustrious career had, by the late 1970s, degenerated into a pattern of exploitation films offset by the occasional token appearance in more mainstream film and television projects.

By the time of *Friday the 13th*'s casting, it

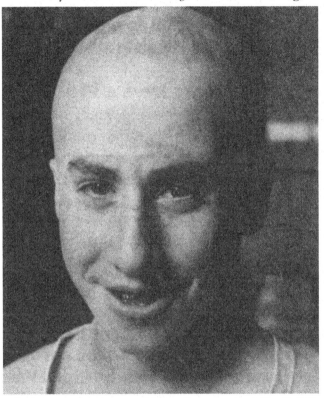

Ari Lehman was fourteen years old when he appeared in *Friday the 13th*, having previously worked with Sean Cunningham on the film *Manny's Orphans*. (Photo courtesy of Tom Savini)

was well-known in the film and television industry that the then 56 year old Grahame, who was diagnosed with stomach cancer in 1980 and died in 1981, was willing to do pretty much anything short of pornography for a paycheck. Still, it was quite a shock for casting director Barry Moss when he contacted Grahame for the role of Sandy and she, fairly quickly, said yes. "We approached Gloria Grahame for the waitress role," Moss recalls. "I asked her to do it and I said that we could pay her 1000 dollars. She was in New York at the time and she told us she would do it. Then she called back, at the last minute, and told us she couldn't do it."

With Grahame out, New York actress Sally

Anne Golden was tapped to play Sandy. The rest of the New York casting consisted of Walt Gorney for the role of Crazy Ralph and Rex Everhart for the role of Enos the truck driver. Willie Adams, who was cast in the role of Barry, was living in New York at the time of his casting. Debra S. Hayes, who was cast in the role of Claudette, was from nearby New Jersey and was also part of the New York casting sessions.

A blonde beauty of the 1950s, Betsy Palmer had largely disappeared from the public eye prior to her casting in *Friday the 13th*. (Photo courtesy of David Beury)

Friday the 13th's SAG designation projected the idea that while it was a low budget film project, it was most definitely not a "super low budget" project by any means. Certainly there were many films made throughout the East Coast between 1979 and 1980 with lesser resources, and many more before and since. Of course, most of these other indigenous film projects were character-based dramas, art-house projects, whereas *Friday the 13th* was a gruesome anomaly that actors, agents, and especially casting directors Hughes and Moss found difficult to categorize.

The rest of *Friday the 13th*'s casting was handled by Cunningham himself out of his base of operations in Westport.

Originally, Cunningham gave thought to casting his son, Noel, for the role of Jason. Both Noel and Cunningham's wife, Susan Cunningham, would join Sean in Blairstown for *Friday the 13th*'s filming where Susan Cunningham, a skilled film editor, edited *Friday the 13th* on location. But this suggestion brought outraged yelps from Mrs. Cunningham.

Louise Lasser was a prime candidate for the Pamela Voorhees role, both in New York and in Blairstown. (Photo courtesy of Jason Pepin)

"He [Noel] thought it would be fun, but when his mother found out, she was having no part of it," Cunningham recalled. "Forget about missing school; there was damn near ice on the lake, and he would have had to get in and stay under the water. So we wound-up hiring the then fourteen-year-old Ari Lehman, who had been in *Manny's Orphans*."

Lehman lived in Westport and he immediately popped into Cunningham's mind for the role of Jason. "A year or so after I'd done the soccer movie with Sean, I got a call from Sean about a new film that he wanted me to be in," Lehman recalls. "When I got to Sean's office, Sean wasn't there, and someone in the office gave me sides to read that were for Kevin Bacon's role. I started reading the part where Kevin's character goes off into the

woods to make-out with a girl and thought 'This is alright,' but then Sean came into the office and says, 'No, that's not the part. You're too young for that. We have another role for you. You're going to play the monster in the movie!' Then Sean asked me if I could swim, and I said yes. That was it for getting the role of Jason. I knew Sean, I was the right age, had the right build, and I was a good swimmer."

Collaborating with Cunningham in the "office" above Cunningham's garage was, of course, Steve Miner, Cunningham's partner in crime and right-hand man. There was also Denise Pinckley who eventually ran *Friday the 13th*'s production office, and who had been dating photographer Richard Illy, the man who helped to bring the *Friday the 13th* logo to life. Another key associate of Cunningham's was Cindy Veazey who'd served as an assistant director on *Here Come the Tigers* and performed various duties in the office.

Veazey had recently gotten married to an actor named Peter Brouwer. He'd previously appeared, from 1976 to 1978, in a soap opera called *Love of Life*. (Although Brouwer later referred to Veazey as being his "girlfriend" at the time of his casting in *Friday the 13th*, the fact is that Brouwer and Veazey were married, at the very least in the common law sense, and remain together today). "I was doing a soap called *Love of Life* and then I was written out of the show and needed work," Brouwer recalls. "I went back to Connecticut to spend time with my girlfriend, Cindy, and look for a job until I could get back to New York for auditions."

Brouwer – who was cast in the role of Steve Christy, Camp Crystal Lake's benefactor and owner - was willing to do anything to be in *Friday the 13th*, whether it meant cutting his long brown hair, trimming his then bushy moustache or donning narrow eye glasses, all of the elements of which combined to create and define the Steve Christy character. "My girlfriend [Cindy Veazey] had gotten a job as an AD [assistant director] on *Friday* and I asked her if there was anything for me," recalls Brouwer who had taken a job on a landscaping crew in the summer of 1979. "They told me that they were looking for big stars, especially for my role, so I thought I was out of luck. I was working on a garden near Sean's home and Sean came by one day to give Cindy a message. He saw me and, a few weeks later, I got the call asking me if I wanted to play the part of Steve Christy."

Actors Ronn Carroll, cast as Sgt. Tierney, and Ron Millkie, cast as Officer Dorf, were both friends with Cunningham and had worked with him previously. "I'd been acting professionally for about twenty years before I'd met Sean and I appeared in some of Sean's commercials and technical films prior to being cast in *Friday the 13th*," Carroll recalls. "All Sean told me was that he was doing a horror film and that he wanted me to play a cop in the film. I met with Sean and he gave me all the script pages that my character, Sgt. Tierney, appears in and nothing more, so I just focused on my dialogue, with no thought as to what Tierney's significance would be in the entire film. Sean told me that I was one of the first people he thought of for the film."

"I'd worked on an industrial film for Sean, and I heard about *Friday the 13th* through the ad in *Variety*," Millkie recalls of his casting that took place in August of 1979, shortly before the start of *Friday the 13th*'s filming. "First I'd had lunch with Sean in New York, and then some time later I called Sean's home number in Connecticut and asked if there was anything for me in the movie. Sean said no, and that he'd already started work on the film, and then he stopped himself and said, 'Wait, wait' and he sent me the sides of the script for the cop character."

SEARCHING FOR MRS. PAMELA VOORHEES

The casting of Pamela Voorhees (AKA Mrs. Voorhees) was one of the most crucial elements in *Friday the 13th*'s eventual success, and was also the most arduous, challenging element of the production as a whole. The process would consume Sean Cunningham's time right through the start of *Friday the 13th*'s filming in September of 1979, and drained the production of energy until it was complete.

It wasn't supposed to be that difficult, especially after Adrienne King had fallen into place for the role of Alice smoothly. Having secured King, and the rest of the main cast who would play Camp Crystal Lake's would-be camp counselors, by the middle of August 1979, Cunningham and Moss turned their attention to the Pamela Voorhees role. Cunningham

had allotted a budget of between ten and fifteen thousand dollars to secure an actress. Given that the role called for an older actress, a woman in her 40s or 50s, Cunningham and Moss didn't envision many problems since most actresses in that age range were, and are, on the endangered species list of the show business food chain, and usually desperate for work.

Following the Gloria Grahame model, Cunningham drew up a list of actresses that he thought would be suitable for the role of Pamela Voorhees. Like Grahame, the list was comprised of actresses who had impressive pedigrees, such as an Academy Award, but who were on the steep downside of opportunity and had grown too old to maintain the interest of Hollywood or New York.

Academy award-winning actress Estelle Parsons was one of the early candidates to take the Pamela Voorhees role. Sean Cunningham thought he had a good chance of landing Parsons for the role, but Parsons eventually declined Cunningham's offer. (Photo courtesy of Jason Pepin)

The model for casting over-the-hill "name" actresses in low budget genre films had been established by academy award-winning actress Joan Crawford. She reinvented herself as a genre actress in the 1960s, beginning with the film *Whatever Hap-*

pened to Baby Jane? (a film that co-starred Bette Davis, another Hollywood screen legend who appeared in several genre films toward the end of her career) (1962) and followed by several more genre entries of increasingly lower quality. Had Crawford not died in 1977, it's very likely that she would've been on Sean Cunningham's list. Pretty much everyone else was.

Basically, Cunningham was looking for faded has-beens with name value that he had a reasonable shot of getting at a modest price. Cunningham's initial list of candidates included - in declining order of Cunningham's level of interest - Shelley Winters, Estelle Parsons, Dorothy Malone and Louise Lasser. Betsy Palmer, the eventual choice, was the fifth name on the list, although Barry Moss had her ranked much higher.

Malone, Parsons and Winters all had Academy Awards on their resumes, two in Winters' case, and, like Grahame, had all found the 1970s difficult in terms of securing quality acting roles outside of B movies. Louise Lasser was best known as a television actress, having previously starred on the short-lived but iconic television series *Mary Hartman, Mary Hartman* from 1976 to 1977. Lasser was also well-known for having been married to filmmaker Woody Allen from 1966 to 1971.

Palmer hadn't appeared in a feature film since *The Long Gray Line* (1959) and was probably best known to the American public from the television quiz show *I've Got a Secret*, in which Palmer had been a panelist from 1959 to 1967. Palmer's recent career, prior to *Friday the 13th*, largely consisted of regional theater. As the least known of the candidates, Cunningham and Moss figured that Palmer would be the most susceptible to their offer, should their top candidates fall through. They were right.

Cunningham told colleagues and friends that his first choice was Shelley Winters, whose recent career had included appearances in such exploitation/horror film titles as *Cleopatra Jones* (1973), *Tentacles* (1977) and *Redneck County Rape* (1979). Even so, Winters was the real long-shot on Cunningham's wish list whereas Parsons, Malone and Lasser would eventually enter into actual negotiations with Cunningham. "I never heard about Shelley Winters for the role of Mrs. Voorhees, or Louise Lasser, but I know that Sean wanted Estelle Parsons and we went into negotiations with her for doing the role of Mrs.

Actress Dorothy Malone, another Oscar winner, remained a strong candidate for the Pamela Voorhees role well into *Friday the 13th's* filming. (Photo courtesy of Jason Pepin)

Voorhees," Moss recalls. "It went on and on before she declined. Dorothy Malone was a major contender for the role, a real sleeper candidate, but that also fell through. Sean had Betsy Palmer on the list and I thought it would be a stroke of brilliance to cast Betsy because the audience would never believe it, when she arrived in the film, that she could be anything but this sweet, nice lady. Unfortunately, Sean decided to dress her like Estelle Parsons, and make her look very butch in the film, with her hair and everything."

"I was disappointed that we didn't get Estelle Parsons because I thought we could get her and I thought she'd be perfect for the role of Mrs. Voorhees," Cunningham says. "She told us that she wanted to do the movie, but then she pulled out at the last minute. It would've been nice to have put 'Academy Award winner' in the advertisements!"

Louise Lasser and Dorothy Malone would remain contenders for the Pamela Voorhees role well into *Friday the 13th's* filming in September of 1979, with Betsy Palmer still being kept in reserve as a backup, last minute option. It's amazing to consider, in retrospect, that Gloria Grahame's near casting in the role of Sandy and Malone's own near casting in the role of Pamela Voorhees could've meant the appearance of two Academy-award winning actresses in *Friday the 13th*.

SUFFER THE CHILDREN

Near the end of July of 1979, about one month before *Friday the 13th* began filming in Blairstown, New Jersey, filming was underway on another independent horror film in an area of New England known as The Berkshires. This was *The Children*, which was directed and co-produced by Max Kalmanowicz, who'd performed sound chores on *Here Come the Tigers* and *Manny's Orphans* and was best friends with *Friday the 13th* cinematographer Barry Abrams.

The relevance of *The Children's* filming to *Friday the 13th* is interesting given that Abrams served as director of photography on *The Children*, and was joined by his loyal technical crew, namely Braden Lutz, Richard Murphy, Tad Page, Carl Peterson and Robert Shulman. This unit formed the bulk of *Friday the 13th*'s technical crew. In many ways, the filming of *The Children* served as a warm-up for the filming of *Friday the 13th*.

Abrams' involvement with *The Children*, and that of his crew, represented both an act of friendship on Abrams' part towards Kalmanowicz and a clear example of the fierce loyalty that the crew felt toward the esteemed cinematographer. For Kalmanowicz *The Children* represented his first shot at directing a feature.

"*The Children* was a film that my best friend was directing, so I wanted to help him out because I knew it was very important to him," Abrams said. "I also thought it would be good exercise for me and my crew to stay busy by working on the film while Sean was still trying to put *Friday the 13th together*."

"Barry had put together a crew who would go wherever he wanted and would do whatever he wanted," says Kalmanowicz who turned down Sean Cunningham's offer to handle sound chores on *Friday the 13th* – a job that fell to Richard Murphy – in

Something terrifying has happened to...

The Children

...pray you never meet them

Albright Films Inc. presents "THE CHILDREN" Starring Martin Shakar • Gil Rogers • Gale Garnett
Produced by Carlton J. Albright • Directed by Max Kalmanowicz
A WORLD NORTHAL FILM   Panavision • Color

Prior to the start of filming on *Friday the 13th*, cinematographer Barry Abrams and his crew worked on the horror film *The Children*. (Photo courtesy of Max Kalmanowicz)

order to focus on *The Children*. "It was considered a badge of honor to be a part of Barry's production crew. He was such a cool, revered guy. He was glib, always positive, and very down to earth."

The Children is a story about children in a small town who are infected by a yellow toxic cloud that transforms them into bloodless zombies with black fingernails who "microwave" every living thing they can get their hands on. The adults in the film, those that have survived, try to stop them.

The Children had a budget of $400,000, a notch under *Friday the 13th*'s eventual budget, and made use of the Panaglide camera, Panavision's version of the Steadicam, a luxury that wouldn't be available to *Friday the 13th*. In addition to the involvement of Abrams and his crew, Jessie (Jesse) Abrams, Barry Abrams' son, had a supporting role in the film, and the film also introduced David Platt to the *Friday the 13th* production team.

Platt, an aspiring actor at the time who had a small part in *The Children*, got his first production job, as the film's un-credited production manager, and would serve as *Friday the 13th*'s boom operator, even though Platt, who would go onto to become a highly successful television director and producer, freely admits that he "didn't know shit about filmmaking" at the time.

Sean Cunningham closely monitored *The Children* with the intention of hiring the crew to work on *Friday the 13th*. (Photo courtesy of Max Kalmanowicz)

"Sean [Cunningham] called me in May or June, before we shot *The Children*, and told me he was going to do a movie called *Friday the 13th* and that he really wanted me to do the sound on the film, but I was getting ready to do *The Children* and get my shot at directing," recalls Kalmanowicz of the period during *The Children's* pre-production which may have actually been in July, given the timing of the *Variety* advertisement. "I thought about doing both, and I really wanted to work with Sean and Barry on the film, but my focus was on my dream of getting to direct my own film. All I knew about *Friday the 13th*, at that time, was that it was a horror film. Barry also mentioned it to me."

Despite the familial relationships that existed amongst Kalmanowicz and his crew, *The Children* was bedeviled by a weak script, poor planning, and countless production problems that led to acrimony and conflict amongst the cast and crew and made the later filming of *Friday the 13th* seem like paradise in comparison.

"*The Children* was a situation where Max wanted to direct a film, and his friends wanted to help him realize that dream, but the script wasn't great," Richard Murphy says. "Max didn't have enough experience and he didn't have someone like Tom Savini to do the effects. There were a lot of fourteen hour days of shooting that would take just a few hours today."

"Barry [Abrams] was a great teacher on *The Children*," recalls David Platt of his time working with cinematographer Barry Abrams during *The Children's* filming. "He knew his business. Barry was an iconoclast. Later on, he left the movie business and directed and produced commercials and then he went to the Virgin Islands with his wife and ran a successful charter business. Then he ended up in Paris. He liked to reinvent himself."

"*The Children* wasn't nearly as much fun as *Here Come the Tigers*," Robert Shulman says. "We all did the film because we loved Max and Barry who had co-produced some commercials and short films together and were very close friends. Carl Albright produced the film with a low budget. There were too many people doing coke on that production to make a good film. As I said it wasn't as much fun as *Here Come the Tigers* and that led to resentments, but we didn't hold these resentments against Barry."

One production anecdote that highlights the problems that plagued *The Children* – and highlights the relative symmetry that existed on *Friday the 13th* - was with the filming of a scene with a dead dog. For the scene, a dog was put to sleep for the filming, but as it dragged on, the dog would continually wake-up and have to be put to sleep again. This went on several times. "The dog was put to sleep and then woken up and put to sleep, over and over again," Richard Murphy recalls. "We opened the closet and the dog was drunk from being put to sleep and woken up so much. It was a disaster. Sean [Cunningham] was much different from Max; much more knowledgeable about filmmaking and the business, especially having grown up with Wes Craven. That

Barry Abrams (behind the camera) oversaw a loyal film crew who would follow him anywhere, including to the filming of *Friday the 13th*. (Photo courtesy of Nalani Clark)

was the big difference, I think. Max didn't have a mentor while Sean had Wes Craven as a mentor."

"*The Children* was a shoestring film," Platt recalls. "I was a struggling actor at the time, and was a production assistant on the film while also having a small role in the film. The production manager was fired and I became the production manager, and then became the boom guy. Richard Murphy was the sound mixer, in a recording studio, and he mentioned that he had this *Friday the 13th* job that would pay us 300 dollars a week, which wasn't a lot even back then. I was very inexperienced, and didn't know a damn thing about what I was supposed to be doing. Richard taught me in a few hours, and when we started work on *Friday the 13th*, I tried my best to just not look stupid and get fired because I really didn't know what I was doing at that point in my career."

While Abrams and the eventual *Friday the 13th* crew were filming *The Children*, Sean Cunningham was also keeping a close eye, as he was still putting the final production pieces of *Friday the 13th* together and had every intention of bringing Abrams and his followers onto *Friday the 13th*. "I remember that Sean was keeping an eye on us while we were filming, and that he would watch dailies of the film," Abrams recalled. "I remember that Sean was fairly happy with the film, so much so that he decided to bring all of us onboard *Friday the 13th* after seeing a rough cut of *The Children*."

That's contrary to the recollection of Kalmanowicz who distinctly recalls getting a decidedly chilly reaction from Cunningham. "Although Sean hired many of our crew members, I could see at the screening that he wasn't happy," Kalmanowicz re-

calls. "After the screening, Sean said, 'I don't know, Max.' Sean was very nonplussed about the movie, and had nothing complimentary or warm to say about the film or my direction. He could've bullshitted me and made me feel good, but there was none of that. It was if, with Sean's reaction to the film, that Sean was telling me that he didn't think *The Children* was up to his level of filmmaking. He could've bullshitted me and at least made me feel good!"

Apart from the fact that *The Children*, which was released June 13, no less, 1980, was filmed roughly a month before the start of *Friday the 13th*'s filming, with much the same crew (*Friday the 13th* composer Harry Manfredini did the musical score for *The Children*), did *The Children* have any other creative influence over *Friday the 13th*?

This doesn't appear to be the case. *The Children* (which was distributed by World Northal) contains no stylistic or tonal resemblance (aside from Manfredini's musical score) to *Friday the 13th* and Cunningham took no inspiration from the film. The biggest influence *The Children* had on *Friday the 13th* was that it kept Abrams and his crew ready and warm

Barry Abrams commanded great respect from his crew, and from Sean Cunningham. (Photo courtesy of Nalani Clark)

for *Friday the 13th*, plain and simple. "I don't think *The Children* had much creative influence over *Friday the 13th*," Kalmanowicz says. "I think of *The Children* as having this strange, four cousins removed, bastard relationship with *Friday the 13th*. The biggest thing was that Barry and his crew got to warm up and get into fighting shape for *Friday the 13th*, so I think the film was very useful in that regard. Barry and his crew cut their chops on *The Children*. They trained for the big fight. *Friday the 13th* was the big fight."

FRIDAY THE 13TH IN 16MM

Sean Cunningham had a backup plan for *Friday the 13th*, should the financing have fallen through, namely to do *Friday the 13th* as an ultra-low budget film, and in 16MM, not far removed from the format of the Super 16MM-lensed *Last House on the Left*.

This is the story that filtered back to New York throughout July and August, to Barry Abrams and other members of the crew, when the crewing on *Friday the 13th* began to take serious shape. "Barry asked me to be assistant cameraman on *Friday the 13th* which was going to be super low budget and shot on 16MM," recalls James Bekiaris, a professional cameraman who served as a Best Boy on *Friday the 13th*. "At that point, I was going to be a cameraman on the film, but then more money came into the production and the film was now going to be shot on 35MM, with Panavision, and I wasn't the assistant cameraman anymore, so I became the Best Boy Electric."

The *Friday the 13th* script that slowly dripped out to the crew throughout August of 1979 seemed, to many of the crew members, to be a perfect match for the primitive, raw nature that 16MM would no doubt have added to the film. "When I read the script, I didn't think this was something that would ever make it to the screen," says Bekiaris who first met Abrams during Bekiaris' days as a student at New York University, from 1976 to 1978, where Abrams and Bekiaris collaborated on a short film that was written by future Hollywood powerhouse Chris Columbus. "None of us thought that when we saw the script. It certainly wasn't a Hitchcock type of thing; it wasn't scary at all in that kind of way. The one thing it did have was visual impact."

THE DAWN OF SAVINI

One of the most important, and smartest, decisions that Sean Cunningham and Steve Miner made during pre-production on *Friday the 13th* was the recruiting of makeup and special effects wizard Tom Savini.

Savini had recently handled the effects on George A. Romero's zombie film masterpiece *Dawn the Dead* which had been released in the United States in April of 1979.

Savini was basking in that film's success by the time Cunningham called him in August. "Sean called me and told me that he'd seen *Dawn of the Dead* and loved the effects work I'd done for that film," Savini recalls. "Sean told me he was doing a movie called *Friday the 13th* and told me he was interested in having me do the effects on his film. I drove to Connecticut and met with Sean and Steve and they told me about their ideas for the film."

Cunningham had been more impressed with the shock and visceral impact that Savini's effects work had generated in *Dawn of the Dead*, rather than the pure gore, and had no interest in having Savini

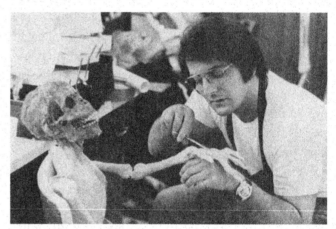

Following his time in Vietnam, Tom Savini began his film career in the early 1970s, without his later trademark moustache. (Photo courtesy of Tom Savini)

– who recalls being given a $17,000 effects budget on *Friday the 13th* – preside over a wall-to-wall gorefest. "When I met with Tom the first time, the first thing that impressed me was his energy and vitality, and I could tell that he was truly a magician with effects who would be able to do magic tricks with our film that otherwise wouldn't have seemed possible," Cunningham says. "With someone as great as Tom, there's a temptation to do more effects than you need, to show more and more, but I didn't want Tom to take a really graphic approach with *Friday the 13th* in terms of non-stop gore. I wanted the effects to be shocking and quick, so you see the shocking image and it's gone, like the shower scene in *Psycho*. It's there, it's shocking, and then it's gone."

Savini, a Pittsburgh native, drove to meet with Cunningham and Miner in August of 1979. "I met with Sean and Steve in Connecticut and they were really excited to meet me because of *Dawn of the Dead*," Savini recalls. "We talked a lot about the film, and not just in terms of the effects, but also in terms of what I could contribute to the story, which really surprised me and impressed me. Specifically, they really didn't have an ending. That's when I came up with the idea of having Jason jump out of the lake at the end of the movie. I'd just seen *Carrie*, which really scared me, especially in the scene at the end where the hand came out of the ground. I thought it would be really spectacular. That was my idea. It really was."

While the authorship of *Friday the 13th*'s climactic lake scene – with the shocking first appearance of Jason Voornees – is a hotly-contested point in the

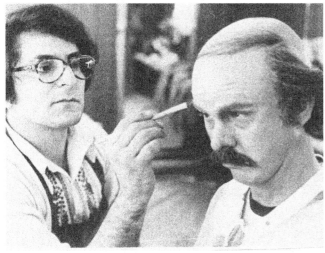

Tom Savini built a fearsome reputation in the early 1970s, providing notable effects work on low-budget horror films like *Deathdream* and *Deranged*. (Photo courtesy of Tom Savini)

history of *Friday the 13th*, there's no question that Savini's creative vision would bring this scene, just like every other scene in the *Friday the 13th* script, to glorious life in a way that Cunningham could never have dreamed. There's also no disputing that Savini's intensity, passion and sublime imagination established him as the dominant creative force on *Friday the 13th*.

The then 32 year old Savini's unique style – the distinct imagery and viscosity present in his effects work – was, in great part, born out of his previous life experiences. The most powerful and shattering of these experiences for Savini was clearly the period between 1967 and 1970 when Savini served in the United States Army, a year of which Savini

spent as a combat photographer in Vietnam. It was during this time in Vietnam that Savini documented and observed the worst horrors of death and disfigurement. These were impossible images to shake and they manifested in Savini's effects work throughout the 1970s, and especially with *Friday the 13th*.

These gory images, the ones related to war, contained a reality that was nothing like the images seen in any feature films, other than the films that Savini worked on. The gory images in *Friday the 13th* are certainly nothing like anything that had been seen in prior genre films, or has been seen since. "Vietnam fucked with me, like everyone else who was there, but it helped my work," Savini says. "When I did *Dawn*, my head was full of images of what I'd seen in Vietnam and it was much of the same with *Friday*. These are the kinds of wounds [referring to the images Savini witnessed in Vietnam] that you don't see in hor-

Tom Savini's groundbreaking effects work on the film *Dawn of the Dead* led to Savini being hired for *Friday the 13th*. (Photo courtesy of Tom Savini)

ror films. That's one of the reasons why audiences were so shocked by what they saw in *Friday the 13th*."

In the early 1970s, Savini attended Carnegie-Mellon University in Pittsburgh, where he majored in journalism, but spent much of his time studying acting and theater. It was here that Savini met Taso Stavrakis who became his best friend, as well as his trusted effects assistant.

In August of 1979, Stavrakis, an accomplished stuntman, joined Savini in the backyard of Steve Miner's Westport home, to help him build the effects that would be required for the filming of *Friday the 13th*. "Prior to the start of filming on *Friday the 13th*, Tom and I built most of the special props for the film behind Steve Miner's house in Connecticut," recalls Stavrakis who's a decade younger than Savini. "Sean and Steve were great to work with because they were very supportive and they gave us a lot of freedom to use our imaginations and try things. It also helped that a lot of the scenes in the script had very plain description and left a lot of room for imagination in terms of creating effects."

Savini and Stavrakis, who hadn't been with Savini during his initial meeting with Cunningham and Miner, worked feverishly in Miner's backyard throughout much of August of 1979, preparing as many of *Friday the 13th*'s required effects as they could, prior to the start of filming in Blairstown. Toward the end of August, Savini and Stavrakis left Miner's house and headed to Blairstown to get a jump on the rest of *Friday the 13th*'s cast and crew and continue preparing effects.

Contrary to previous recollections, including those from Savini himself, Savini and Stavrakis were among the first of the *Friday the 13th* crew to arrive at the filming location, not including Virginia Field's previous trip to Camp No-Be-Bo-Sco. "We prepared the effects in a workspace in Steve Miner's backyard, yes, and then we left for the camp," Savini recalls. "My memory is that we went to Blairstown before the filming and continued to prepare stuff. Then filming began there."

With Tom Savini in place, Cunningham felt he had enough of the production elements solidified to start filming on *Friday the 13th*. Adding to Cunningham's optimism was the deal that he hammered-out with Georgetown Productions that called

for Cunningham, as *Friday the 13th*'s co-creator, director and producer, to receive twenty-five percent of the profits from *Friday the 13th*, and any future *Friday the 13th*-related properties, namely sequels.

This was a shrewd move on Cunningham's part since, by 1979, sequels weren't seen as be-

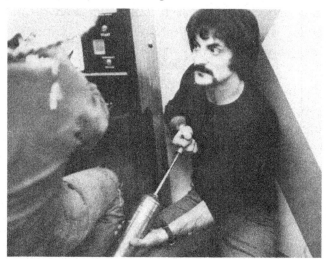

Tom Savini on the set of *Dawn of the Dead*. Sean Cunningham and Steve Miner contacted Savini after seeing his effects work in *Dawn of the Dead*. (Photo courtesy of Tom Savini)

ing the cash cows they would be just a few years later, in no small part due to *Friday the 13th*'s success. The deal also called for Cunningham to wield more creative control than he ever could've imagined, within certain limits that would be clearly defined throughout *Friday the 13th*'s filming.

Of course, the one key element missing from *Friday the 13th* by the end of August 1979 was an actress to play the role of Pamela Voorhees. Ultimately, Cunningham and Miner's inability to cast the Pamela Voorhees role necessitated changes in the shooting schedule, the most obvious being the need to push the filming of the killer's dialogue scenes towards the end of the filming schedule, or whenever Cunningham could find said actress and get her to Blairstown for filming.

By the midway point of the filming schedule, this became such a problem as to inspire, on the part of Cunningham and Miner, an emergency backup plan for completing *Friday the 13th* with no actress in place at all for the Pamela Voorhees role. Thankfully, this never became a reality.

With Camp No-Be-Bo-Sco ending its summer camp session in the middle of August, *Friday the 13th* was supposed to commence filming on August

This shot of the Sand Pond (AKA Crystal Lake) was taken on the first week of September of 1979. (Photo courtesy of Tony Marshall)

20, 1979. Barry Abrams, Sean Cunningham, Virginia Field, Miner, Tom Savini – and a handful of others – were all in place at the campsite at this point. Ultimately, the start date was moved to September 4, 1979 for various reasons, including the evacuation of the camp's staff, the completion of the summer season, the arrival of the rest of the cast and crew in Blairstown, the securing of the first chunk of financing, and finally, the time to cast the Pamela Voorhees role.

From Sean Cunningham's perspective, the time to make *Friday the 13th* was either now or never.

CHAPTER 5

WELCOME TO BLAIRSTOWN:
THE FILMING OF *FRIDAY THE 13TH*

"I was trying to make something that people had to go see. Because I was in the movie 'business,' I wasn't doing high art or anything. I only had a certain amount of money and so anything that I decided to put on screen had to matter."

- Sean Cunningham, referring to his directorial approach on Friday the 13th

Author's note: The following chapters depict the filming of Friday the 13th, based on interviews and recollections of the cast and crew, exhaustive research, and various forms of documentation, such as the advanced shooting schedule that was prepared prior to the start of principal filming which took place on September 4, 1979.

The descriptions of the filming of scenes are organized in chronological order, based on the available evidence that confirms the date of filming of specific scenes. In the cases where the precise date is impossible to confirm, due to conflicting memories and sources, the descriptions of the filming are organized in the chronological order of how they appear in the finished film, or how they appear on the shooting schedule.

The scenes involving the character of Annie, for example, were originally scheduled to be filmed during the fourth and final week of principal filming, over a two day period; they were moved to the beginning of the filming schedule, for logistical and scheduling reasons. As a result, the descriptions related to the filming of these scenes appear in the following chapter that correlates to the first week of filming.

Toward the end of August 1979, the bulk of *Friday the 13th*'s cast and crew, those that weren't

Blairstown as it appeared in 1979. (Photo courtesy of Tony Marshall)

already on location, arrived in Blairstown, New Jersey. They all anticipated the start of principal filming (some additional filming had taken place at the campsite, and around Blairstown, beginning on August 20, 1979, with a partial crew) which commenced on September 4, 1979, the day after Labor Day.

They were greeted by Sean Cunningham and Steve Miner who – along with Barry Abrams, Virginia Field, Tom Savini, and a few other members of the technical crew - had already set-up shop at the main Camp-No-Be-Bo-Sco filming location.

Cunningham and Miner had worked out a deal with the camp's proprietors – involving a modest "rental fee" – that gave the *Friday the 13th* production free run of the place throughout the months of September and October.

Effects expert Savini, along with his assistant and friend Taso Stavrakis, immediately designated one cabin as Savini's makeup cabin to house Savini's effects creations throughout filming, along with Savini's invaluable barbershop chair. Most of *Friday the 13th*'s cast members, those whose characters were killed in the story, would end-up sitting for hours in this chair while Savini worked his effects magic.

Savini also commandeered the camp's cafeteria location for his effects work, particularly the oven which he used to bake his creations. "Me and my small crew stayed at the campsite and we pretty much had the run of the place," Savini recalls. "I set-up a Beta machine in one of my cabins and we'd watch movies when we weren't working. The cast and crew stayed at nearby hotels and motels, but after awhile, a lot of them would hang-out at the cabins with us because we were having so much fun."

Virginia Field set up shop in another cabin, along with her small design unit, for construction and drafting work. "From the day me and my team arrived on location for the start of filming, we started working in the cabin for twenty hours a day, throughout the filming," Field recalls. "I didn't get to watch much of the filming, or party with the rest of the crew, because me and my crew were always working. I spent most of the time drafting designs for materials that we still needed for the film. Chairs, knives, signs, tables, those kinds of things."

The core of *Friday the 13th*'s technical crew – namely Barry Abrams and his crew of followers – had recently come-off of working on the film *The Children*, and they were tired. Some of them had returned to New York – to the village – and then made the 80 mile trip to Blairstown while others had travelled directly in from the Berkshires. Others, like Cecelia and John Verardi, a married couple who lived in Staten Island, walked away from their normal lives completely in order to blindly travel to Blairstown. They wanted to be part of the wacky, uncharted adventure that was the making of *Friday the 13th*.

Cecelia Verardi would perform many tasks on *Friday the 13th* – gofer, hairstylist, liaison between the cast members and the production, makeup effects assistant, makeup girl, production assistant

– while husband John Verardi was a cameraman. "John, my husband, was working at Panavision in New York, and I was going to school to become a lawyer, and had been working at Estee Lauder, when John and I heard about *Friday the 13th*," Cecelia Verardi recalls. "John was offered a management

The weather at Camp No-Be-Bo-Sco was balmy and pleasant at the start of filming. (Photo courtesy of Tony Marshall)

position at Panavision when Barry Abrams called up. We lived in Staten Island, which is about twenty miles from the village where Barry and his crew were based. John called me one day and asked me if I wanted to quit my job, quit school, and go to New Jersey and be a production assistant on this low budget movie. I didn't know what a production assistant was and John told me that I'd basically be a gofer."

While most of the crew came from New York, Cunningham and Miner also brought several crew members in from their Westport base of operations. They included Denise Pinckley, who ran *Friday the 13th*'s modest-looking production office at the campsite, and fourteen year old actor Ari Lehman who was cast as Jason Voorhees. Cunningham's wife, Susan, also made the trip along with their son, Noel. A skilled film editor, Susan E. Cunningham established a makeshift editing bay at the campsite. She worked there throughout the filming, editing the film often simultaneous to the actual filming of scenes.

Miner was originally supposed to edit *Friday the 13th*. But with Susan Cunningham handling the film's editing, Miner was free to devote his energies entirely to his role as *Friday the 13th*'s producer, in tandem with Cunningham. Miner would don many hats throughout filming.

Susan Cunningham's constant presence throughout filming was indicative of the family atmosphere that existed on *Friday the 13th*. Besides Noel and Susan Cunningham's presence, Barry Abrams' son, Jesse Abrams, was also in Blairstown. Wes Craven also appeared in Blairstown, along with his son, Jonathan.

The cast and crew of *Friday the 13th* arrived in Blairstown either by car or vans, but also often by bus, either through a commercial bus service or a chartered company bus that Cunningham secured for the production. Later on, during breaks in filming, Cunningham himself would often drive people – such as cast and crew members - to Blairstown from Connecticut or New York.

Sean Cunningham and Steve Miner met with Blairstown's elders prior to the start of filming in order to foster goodwill between the production and the township. (Photo courtesy of Tony Marshall)

Cunningham's ability to travel to and from Blairstown was a testament to the trust that he placed in Abrams and Miner, especially. There was also the specter of the casting of the Pamela Voorhees' role, a dilemma that festered through the first two weeks of *Friday the 13th*'s filming schedule, and ultimately necessitated Cunningham to have to leave the Blairstown location in order to deal with this issue himself.

If the *Friday the 13th* production wore-out the 80 mile stretch of road from New York City to Blairstown, the arrival of *Friday the 13th*'s cast and crew in Blairstown represented a mini-occupation for the township of roughly 4000 people. After securing an agreement with Camp No-Be-Bo-Sco for use of the campsite prior to filming, Cunningham and Miner also met with the township's leaders in order to foster cooperation and goodwill between the production and Blairstown. "Sean and Steve showed up in town before the start of filming and met with the town elders about the film," recalls Richard Skow who was the Blairstown Fire Chief at the time of *Friday the 13th*'s filming and whose son appeared as one of the sleeping campers in the film's opening pre-credit sequence. "Sean explained that he was making a horror film at the camp and asked if he could use some fire-trucks and police cars for certain scenes in the film. Sean was very friendly, very respectful, and we never had any problems with them during the filming."

Cunningham and Miner were able to secure the use of a fire-truck and several police cars, luxuries they never could've afforded were it not for Cunningham's charm and personal touch. The fire-truck was especially useful for creating rain effects. In addition, Cunningham was granted the free use of Blairstown locations to film around. "Sean was smart enough to arrive in town before filming and schmooze the town elders so they would let him use the town's resources for the film," says art director Robert Topol. "He made friends with the townspeople, and with the cast and crew. Sean had that way about him. He'd shake your hand, and smile at you, and make you feel like you were an important person. He always knew your name, even if he was just introduced to you. He always knew everyone's name."

At the time of *Friday the 13th*'s filming, Camp No-Be-Bo-Sco was under the control of Fred Smith, a local bicycle shop owner who'd served as a Ranger since 1967. Smith, who died in 1985, was an old man at the time of *Friday the 13th*'s filming. He oversaw the land with the help of his young son, and was very protective of both the campsite and its reputation. He was wary at the prospect of a film being shot at the campsite.

Cunningham's charm and personable nature carried the day here in terms of winning over Smith – who was an entertained, happy spectator to much

The layout for Marcie's death scene, as it appeared prior to filming. (Photo courtesy of Tony Marshall)

of *Friday the 13th*'s filming - to the idea of having *Friday the 13th* at the campsite. Smith, however, was never made fully aware of just what kind of film Cunningham and his cast and crew were making.

"It was a very beautiful area, very scenic," Harry Crosby recalls. "It felt like we were isolated from the rest of the world, which I think helped the movie."

"What I remember most about the New Jersey location is the beautiful terrain," Peter Brouwer recalls. "My girlfriend and I would always go hiking along the Appalachian Trail and we loved going into the woods. It wasn't scary at all."

"My fondest memory would probably be when we first started the film and it was still warm and sunny and all of us were together for the first time," said Adrienne King. "Myself, Kevin Bacon, Harry Crosby, Mark Nelson, Jeannine Taylor and the others. We had a great time together; we were all in our twenties and were all so excited about working together. Even though it was such a low-budgeted film and we didn't even know if it would even be completed or not! The sun was still shining and we really got to know each other well and it really felt like being away at summer camp."

"We would drive up from Connecticut to the Delaware Water Gap in New Jersey, and one time I took the bus the whole way there," recalls Ari Lehman. "The countryside is beautiful there, and the camp was situated deep in the woods. Once we arrived, there was convivial, communal working-artist energy. The cast and crew were from NYC, and they would listen to Patti Smith and the Ramones very loudly on their car stereos. It was 1979 and it was fun."

"It was a beautiful location, very tucked away, and very rural," Daniel Mahon recalls. "The camp was closed, obviously, when we arrived and we moved into the barracks while the union crew stayed at the motel. The camp had a very rustic feeling, with log cabins, and the plumbing was Geri-rigged prior to filming. Fred Smith was the manager of the summer camp and basically controlled the physical plant on which the camp was located. Fred was an expatriate and a real character. He kept talking about his neighbor, Lou, and eventually we discovered that the Lou he was talking about was Lou Reed, the famous musician who lived nearby!"

"The camp was cool," soundman Richard Murphy recalls. "Lou Reed had a farm nearby and he would come by during the filming and he played music around us. We got to watch Lou Reed play for free, right in front of us, while we were making the film! He came by the set and we hung around with each other and he was just a really great guy. *Friday the 13th* was all about getting to hang-out in the woods with a bunch of close friends. We were close, close friends sharing our deepest secrets with each other."

"I remember that I took a company bus to the filming location, and that Laurie Bartram and Harry Crosby were on the bus with me," Mark Nelson recalls. "It was a nice trip, very scenic, and the three of us got to know each other a bit which I think helped us during filming in terms of developing some chemistry with each other."

Virginia Field and her design team built the latrine cabin virtually from scratch. (Photo courtesy of Tony Marshall)

"Blairstown was a little rundown at that time," recalls gaffer Tad Page. "There were small farms and people had guns! I loved the camp. The camp was very nice. There were deer running around. We were basically a bunch of city kids, New Yorkers, who were completely out of our element, and looking for action in this isolated place. We were always looking for action after work."

"Blairstown was a very rural place, with lots of hills and valleys, as well as some nice weekend places where people from the city would go," key grip Robert Shulman recalls. "It was a smooth 80 mile drive from Manhattan, the village, where all of us were from. By this point, we'd become this traveling crew, under Barry, so we were ready to go on a moment's notice. We were young, and ready to have a great time making a movie at summer camp!"

The cast and crew of *Friday the 13th* represented wildly varying levels of competence and experience. This was especially visible in the crew which was comprised of both union and non-union members. While the actors in *Friday the 13th* worked under SAG (Screen Actors' Guild) conditions, the film itself was a non-union production. The crew worked on a pay scale that ranged from between 100 to 750 dollars a week.

Abrams and his travelling crew from New York did not divulge to their unions that they were doing *Friday the 13th*. "I never told my union I was doing *Friday the 13th* because I knew they would've punished me for doing a non-union movie like that," recalled Abrams, who had joined the IATSE (International Alliance of Theatrical Stage Employees) camera union prior to *Friday the 13th*, whereas most of the rest of his crew were with the rival NABET (National Association of Broadcast Employees and Technicians) union that Abrams, ever the maverick, had recently left. "None of us told the union we were doing *Friday the 13th* because we knew they would've fined us, especially me since I was in charge of the crew."

The "privileges" that Abrams and his production crew enjoyed on *Friday the 13th* included not only higher paychecks – with Abrams and camera operator Braden Lutz, both of whom oversaw the technical crew, topping out in the $750 dollar a week range – but also with slightly better living conditions.

While most of the junior and non-union crew members joined Savini at the campsite's cabins, Abrams and his group of colleagues and friends stayed at a two-story truck-stop motel in nearby Columbia, New Jersey, about a twenty minute drive from the campsite. At first sight, the motel – called 76 Truck Stop – wasn't much of an attraction, especially since the motel, in keeping with its truck-stop designation, was adjacent to a vast stretch of highway road that was home to an endless stream of big, noisy trucks that rambled up and down the road, back and forth, day and night.

A vestige of the CB radio craze that swept across America in the mid to late 1970s, catapulted by the blockbuster success of the film *Smokey and the Bandit* (1977), the motel (which exists today as a Travel Centers of America location, complete with various amenities) was crawling with CB radios but offered no television for the crew to enjoy. The only luxury

Sean Cunningham modeled Marcie's death scene after the shower scene in *Psycho*. (Photo courtesy of Tony Marshall)

the motel featured was a twenty-four hour luncheonette. Blairstown itself was, as mentioned, a depressed community and scarcely offered the cast and crew of *Friday the 13th* any exciting choices during off-hours.

Against this bland backdrop, Abrams and his crew turned the motel into their own fall version of a spring break party motel, complete with the requisite alcohol, drugs and sex. The sex was in much lower quantities (the males far outnumbering the females on the crew) than the alcohol and drugs the crew would absorb throughout *Friday the 13th*'s filming.

The atmosphere at the motel was rowdy and wild. While Abrams and his crew worked effectively and extremely hard throughout filming, their partying equaled this. Not even an independent production like *Friday the 13th* – in an isolated place like Blairstown – was immune from the alcohol and drug-fueled atmosphere that was pervasive on seemingly all film and television productions throughout the late 1970s and early 1980s. Blairstown's remote location, and a complete lack of supervision, made for an especially toxic atmosphere throughout filming.

The crew of *Friday the 13th* liked to work hard and party hard; they could take it. As much as the motel shenanigans embodied the filmmaking culture in 1979, it was also emblematic of the close friendship that existed amongst Abrams and his crew of friends.

They were young (Abrams was one of the elders on the *Friday the 13th* crew at 35 years old), wild, and full of energy. They were happy to be alive and making a movie, especially together. "We had parties at the motel throughout the filming," Abrams recalled. "We'd drink beer every night, and we just took the place over. It got pretty wild, but we were working hard, and we were all friends. In

those days, we were working out our lighting diagrams for the next day's filming on napkins at the truck-stop where the camera crew ate breakfast after the long nights, although we had done a master plan for the main locations in pre-production."

"The motel was right off the highway and if you walked outside you had to be careful because you could get hit by the trucks that were always flying by," James Bekiaris recalls. "We mostly used the motel to get our meals, drink, party. To get any action around there, we had to go to nearby Strasburg, Pennsylvania."

Musician Lou Reed was Blairstown's most famous resident and visited the set of *Friday the 13th* during filming. (Photo courtesy of Jason Pepin)

"The Martin Sheen drinking scene in *Apocalypse Now* would be a good description of what it was like at the motel during filming," Richard Murphy recalls. "It was a gorgeous area that we were in, but it was a very noisy truck-stop motel with all of the traffic moving around us. We would be partying at six in the morning sometimes. We were a bunch of hard-drinking guys. I recall that Betsy Palmer stayed there when she arrived later on during filming, and that some of the other actors stayed there. Barry and I thought about leaving and moving into the cabins after a couple of weeks, but we all stayed. A lot of the fun we had was a result of the fact that we were all close, close friends. Sean had a young kid and a wife and didn't stay at the motel, and neither did Steve. The actors partied with us, except for Walt Gorney who was at least thirty years older than the rest of us. We didn't really want to hang-out with him."

"We were young and crazy and had wild parties at the motel," Tad Page recalls. "I don't recall the actors ever joining us at the motel for the parties. Most of us stayed at the truck-stop motel right off of Route 80, so that was not as rustic as the rest of Blairstown, but Braden [camera operator Braden Lutz] moved into one of the cabins by the lake at Camp No-Be-Bo-Sco."

"The truck-stop motel was wild," David Platt recalls. "We sat around and drank rum and orange juice and had parties. We'd have beer and eggs in the morning and at night, depending on if we'd been filming at day or night. Usually, it didn't matter. A lot of times we'd wake-up at eleven or twelve in the afternoon, party and then sleep for three or four hours and then go to work. My big thing was trying to learn to operate the Boom mike, without looking incompetent, because I really didn't know the fuck-

The Blairstown Mill as it appears today. (Photo courtesy of Robert Armin www.robertarmin.com)

ing job and I was very much learning on the job."

"Every night we'd all gather in the same room and party," Robert Shulman recalls. "It was about thirty minutes from the motel to the camp location. The truck-stop motel had a twenty-four luncheonette which was great, but the downside was that there were all of these CB radios at the motel which meant

there was no TV. Braden Lutz, who battled alcoholism and substance abuse, decided to stay in a cabin on the other side of the lake. He wasn't the only one who was battling that stuff. Barry was doing a lot of stuff, and so were most of us. Everyone did drugs."

"John [cameraman John Verardi] went ahead to Blairstown and forgot to leave a note at the motel about me so when I arrived at the motel, the manager wouldn't let me in," Cecelia Verardi recalls. "I had to sit there from two in the afternoon until eleven at night before I got into the room. I believe that Laurie [Laurie Bartram] stayed at a hotel and some of the others stayed at the cabins. Actually, I recall that Jeannine [Jeannine Taylor] and Laurie stayed at the cabins initially and then moved to a hotel. I recall that Adrienne [Adrienne King] stayed at a hotel in Connecticut. The unit all stayed together, except for Sean and his family who stayed at Adrienne's hotel. It was a tight circle of friends at the motel. The rest of the production assistants on the film, the production assistant unit, stayed together at the camp where you'd often see them all laid-out on the floor in the cabins."

Cunningham – especially with his family in tow - wanted nothing to do with the shenanigans that existed amongst the crew at the motel. In fact, both Cunningham and Miner recall staying at the campsite, with Savini and the other minions, although Cunningham and Miner also com-

The main street buildings that Annie moved past in the film remain virtually unchanged today. (Photo courtesy of Tony Urban www. tonyurbanphotography.com)

muted to nearby Connecticut during filming. "We were shooting at a Boy Scout camp," Cunningham recalled. "We had no money and we were sleeping, literally, in cabins; cabins with no heat and outdoor plumbing, and it got cold at night."

Braden Lutz grappled with alcohol and drug dependence and settled into one of the cabins for the entirety of filming. He was one of the most underappreciated contributors to *Friday the 13th* and oversaw the crew in tandem with Abrams. Handsome, muscular, tall, and with striking blonde hair, Lutz – who later died of water poisoning - definitely stood apart from the rest of the cast and crew. "Braden was like an albino without the red eyes," recalls Max Kalmanowicz who worked with Lutz on *The Children* and was in New York editing *The Children* – with the help of Barry Abrams' wife Nikki (Abrams met his second wife, film editor Nikki Wessling, between the filming of *Here Come the Tigers* and *Manny's Orphans*, and separated from his first wife after the filming of *Manny's Orphans*) – at the time of *Friday the 13th*'s filming. "He was a strikingly-handsome guy, six-foot-three, with platinum blonde hair, a muscular build, and white skin. Braden was just a big, strong, good-looking guy."

Whatever took place during off-hours, Abrams and Lutz had zero tolerance for incompetence or stupidity. This was evident early in the filming schedule when Camp No-Be-Bo-Sco claimed its first victim. This was cameraman Robert Brady who was terminated during filming. "Robert Brady, a cameraman, was fired by Braden Lutz, with Barry's approval," Tad Page recalls. "Barry and Braden didn't feel he was pulling his weight on the show and they didn't want him around anymore. I think he went into advertising after that!"

Although fun-loving and gregarious, Abrams was also capable of unleashing a very bad temper, especially if he felt that someone, specifically a crew member, wasn't pulling their weight.

The stone bridge Annie crosses over looks just the same today as it did in the film. (Photo courtesy of Tony Urban www.tonyurbanphotography.com)

"Barry was a tough guy," Richard Murphy recalls. "Barry was a cameraman in Vietnam and he never carried a gun. I said, 'Barry, how could you be a cameraman in Vietnam and not carry a gun?' Barry smiled and said, 'I'm a Jew from Texas. I don't need a gun. Nothing scares me.'"

Abrams and his unit understood camerawork, lighting, and all the various subtleties in between, so that they could afford to party in their spare time, and exist without sleep, whereas the rest of the crew was comprised largely of nervous rookies. Of course, in the context of a Sean Cunningham production – recalling the ragtag crew that worked on *Last House on the Left* – this situation was perfectly acceptable. "It was a small crew," recalls cameraman and Best Boy James Bekiaris. "You couldn't do a film nowadays with such a small crew. It was basically me and Bob [key grip Robert Shulman] and Tad [gaffer Tad Page] and Barry and Braden."

"Sean Cunningham had taken a second mortgage out on his house to do this film so he had a lot riding on this, although Sean was very good at never letting people see the stress on him," Daniel Mahon recalls. "We were a very young and inexperienced film crew. I always describe the crew that works on movies as being like carnies with health insurance. That's what we were like on *Friday the 13th*, except that most of us didn't have a warm place to sleep, or much to eat during filming, much less health insurance."

The cast members, the actors and actresses, were spread-out around the territory, with some of the performers staying in the cabins, while others, according to their recollections, stayed at lodgings, hotels and motels, in Connecticut and even Pennsylvania. The performers were, with a few exceptions, distanced from the partying, primarily because of a volatile work schedule that existed for them. With the exception of leading lady Adrienne King, it didn't require the cast members to all be on location throughout the entire filming schedule.

"Motel 96, somewhere in Connecticut," Adrienne King recalled of the lodgings. "It was terrible. The place had no bathtubs. Still, it was a great working situation. From the beginning, everybody, cast and crew, sensed that we were onto something and a special kind of chemistry began to develop. Everybody worked real hard."

"The actors got along great," Tom Savini recalls. "As filming went on, I got to know the actors very well, especially Harry Crosby, who would always hang around me and Taso during the filming, as well as Laurie Bartram, who

The cabin that "The Prowler" moves through during the film's opening pre-credit sequence. The cabin also served as Alice's cabin in the film, in the scene where the snake was killed. (Photo courtesy of Brett McBean www.brettmcbean.com)

I kind of developed a crush on during the filming. They stayed in a motel, while me and most of the rest of the crew stayed at the campsite."

"I think we were in Pennsylvania for a bit," Jeannine Taylor recalls. "Downingtown, PA, I seem to remember, where we stayed at a mom-and-pop sort of motel. There was an open meadow nearby with a lot of deer. I remember going to a country antique-and-collectibles barn with Kevin [Bacon] and Mark [Nelson] and several other people, and we poked around and bought stuff. The place had a lot of old advertising, collectibles – old signs, etc, and jukeboxes. Some enterprising soul had made sets of cufflinks out of old American soda pop bottle-caps. I sent some to a friend in England and he was absolutely thrilled with them."

With the exception of the then 33-year-old Peter Brouwer, the rest of the cast members that arrived in Blairstown pretty much mirrored their college-aged screen counterparts. Age-wise, they were between twenty-one and twenty-five years old, with Adrienne King and Jeannine Taylor falling to the latter end of the spectrum.

Attitude-wise, the cast members were carefree, young, and at the dawn of both their lives and certainly their acting careers. As the start of filming approached, the cast members – like their characters – gave little thought to the on-screen carnage

and mayhem that awaited. "We bonded naturally, as three young actors all making their first movie would," Jeannine Taylor recalls, referring to her on and off-screen relationship with co-stars Kevin Bacon and Mark Nelson. "And the setting in Blairstown at an actual summer camp really did add to that. It was very quiet and isolated, situated on a pristine, crystal-clear lake with little cabins in the surrounding woods. Just driving through the entrance to the camp for the first time under that big Camp No-Be-Bo-Sco sign was a gas! I remember we all burst out laughing and cheered when we saw that sign. Then came the jokes. Mostly from Kevin and Mark. They were both very funny, and I was their helpless-with-laughter audience. If that stuff seems real when you see the movie, it's because it was."

"The young actors arrived at the filming location with great attitudes and lots of energy," Sean Cunningham recalls. "At the time of filming, Harry Crosby was the only recognizable name in the cast, because he was the son of Bing Crosby, and

A close-up shot of the fireplace and main cabin. (Photo courtesy of Brett McBean www.brettmcbean.com)

he was just the nicest, most down-to-earth guy. He was very determined and hard-working and didn't want to be treated differently, just because of his last name. We pretended like we didn't know he was the son of Bing Crosby, which was easy because he was so down-to-earth that you forgot that he had a famous last name. The rest of the cast fit together quite smoothly from the moment they arrived. They were all smart, attractive, could read their dialogue effectively, which was just what I was looking for."

The circumstances – and the culture shock - that the cast and crew of *Friday the 13th* faced upon their arrival and settling in Blairstown, unglamorous as the location and the working conditions were, reflected that this was a film production on the bottom-rung of the filmmaking food chain. For the absolute beginners, *Friday the 13th* represented a chance to simply make a film, even if there was no expectation that it would ever live beyond Blairstown. For the small group of "professionals" amongst the crew, *Friday the 13th* was both an adventure and a low-paying job which carried little expectation of mainstream attention.

The waterfront cabin at Camp No-Be-Bo-Sco doubled for Jack and Marcie's cabin in the film, as well as Brenda's cabin. (Photo courtesy of Brett McBean www.brettmcbean.com)

For Cunningham and Miner – and especially Cunningham who'd put everything he had, emotionally and financially, into it – *Friday the 13th* represented a last chance to show that they could escape their track record of failure and obscurity and maybe get lucky for once. They were certainly lucky in terms of the camaraderie amongst the cast and crew, which was great from the start and would continue right through the end of filming and beyond. "Steve was a very proficient guy, and Sean was a real gem in terms of his personality and the way he treated people," David Platt recalls. "As a filmmaker, Sean was following his passion with *Friday the 13th* – was always looking to find the 'shot' – and there was definitely the sense that this was the last film that Sean was going to make if it wasn't successful. I think Sean was definitely prepared to do something else with his life if *Friday the 13th* hadn't been successful."

Another hopeful sign – it seemed - was the weather. It was usually chilly in Blairstown by the end of August – a reason why the camp season at Camp No-Be-Bo-Sco typically ends in mid August - but was surprisingly balmy and sunny on the eve of filming, a pleasant temperature of 75 degrees.

This changed dramatically during the second half of *Friday the 13th*'s filming schedule when bone-chilling temperatures in the 30 degree range swept over Blairstown and forced Cunningham and his crew to make several adjustments. As well, the shooting schedule and script called for numerous rain effects, under the supervision of atmospheric effects expert Steven Kirshoff, although it would certainly rain plenty enough during the filming, just not when the cast and crew were expecting it. "We used fire hoses for the rain, with the help of the local fire truck in town, and I recall that we used lightning boxes for the thunder," Steven Kirshoff recalls. "It did rain quite a bit during filming, and it got very cold."

The location Steve Christy was when Jack, Marcie and Ned arrived at the campsite. (Photo courtesy of Brett McBean www.brettmcbean.com)

At the dawn of September 1979, on the eve of the start of *Friday the 13th*'s filming, none of this mattered. The summer camp flavor was still palpable at the campsite and the cast and crew were looking forward to a carefree, fun, relatively uncomplicated shoot. "When we started filming, it was 75 degrees and very comfortable," Virginia Field recalls. "The temperature then went down to 35 degrees midway in the filming, through to the end, and we were freezing our asses off!"

"At the start of filming, we were all wearing cut-off pants and open sun shirts," Richard Murphy recalls. "The rain that was used in the film was very loud because Steven Kirshoff couldn't afford pumps and ended up using the fire-trucks. I recall that 750 gallons poured out of the fire-trucks to create the torrential rain in the film, and that created a lot of blowback in terms of my sound recording."

"The weather at the beginning was easily 75 degrees and by the middle – and end – of filming it was down to 25-35 degrees," Tad Page recalls. "It was green at the start of filming and then there were fall colors by the end of the filming, and it was snowing. I remember that we started the job with shirts off in the summer heat and wound-up sweeping snow off the roofs of the cabins so the footage would match. There was a generator at the campsite, the one seen in the film, and I can remember that it was always failing, and at one point I interceded, and along with the soundman - Richie [Richard] Murphy of *Law & Order* fame – we spent a good deal of time hunched over the power-plant in terrible weather and eventually troubleshot a faulty distributor cap."

A shot of Crystal Lake, known as the Sand Pond in real life. (Photo courtesy of Brett McBean www.brettmcbean.com)

Camp No-Be-Bo-Sco's Price Lodge, the location where Marcie is killed in the film. (Photo courtesy of Brett McBean www.brettmcbean.com)

"Freezing weather," Robert Shulman recalls. "As the filming went on, and it got colder and colder, we had these salamander heaters, along with a tent to retreat into after we were done with the filming of a scene. The tent was always full."

Friday the 13th wasn't the only independent horror film in production at this time. While *Friday the 13th* was filming in Blairstown, the slasher film *Prom Night* was filming in Toronto, Ontario, Canada. *Prom Night* had a budget of $1.2 Million and featured *Halloween* star Jamie Lee Curtis as its lead. In addition, the independent horror film *When a Stranger Calls* had been acquired for distribution by Columbia Pictures who were preparing the $1.5 Million film for a late October 1979 release.

The cast and crew of *Friday the 13th* knew nothing of this, or anything else that was going on in the real world. They were completely isolated. There was no escape. There were no rules.

THE SAVINI EFFECT

Although there's some dispute as to whether or not effects expert Tom Savini – who acknowledges a poor memory for chronological detail - was at Camp No-Be-Bo-Sco prior to the first day of filming on *Friday the 13th*, or arrived afterwards, there's no arguing the effect Savini had on *Friday the 13th*'s cast and crew and the eventual film itself.

Calm, intelligent, spiritual and thoughtful in terms of his normal demeanor, Savini's passion for his work tended to bring out the latent

Virginia Field chose Camp No-Be-Bo-Sco as a filming location in large part due to the omnipresent lake. (Photo courtesy of Dean A. Orewiler/ Dean A. Orewiler Portrait Art)

"mad scientist" alter-ego in Savini which was powerfully representative in all of the effects work he did throughout the 1970s and early 1980s.

This had certainly been the case with Savini's work on *Dawn of the Dead*, with its phantasmagoria of effects, but with *Friday the 13th*, Savini set a new bar in terms of inventively-gory images. No one amongst the cast and crew of *Friday the 13th* – not even Sean Cunningham – was prepared for the dynamic force that was Savini. While Savini himself was warmly received by the cast and crew, especially those who would spend many hours in his barber's chair, his crude, unorthodox methods sometimes had a jolting effect on those around him.

"My most vivid memory of Savini is latex," James Bekiaris recalls with a laugh. "He was always working with latex, and always covered in blood. The biggest challenge for the crew, in working with Tom, was filming his effects so they would cut together on film, and that the blood would appear on film in the way Tom intended."

"Tom Savini arrived and he was very disarming, to say the least." cameraman Richard Berger recalls. "Tom liked to introduce himself by pretending to have an accident, or by grasping his neck and having blood spurt out. He also staged a car accident with Taso [Taso Stavrakis] that was really crazy. They were both laying down in front of this car, and they looked like they'd been hit by a car and were dead, but it was all a joke."

shoot that scene, but Tom told me he could make it work and he did. That went on throughout filming, with Tom just creating magic. Tom brought a creativity and imagination to *Friday the 13th* that wasn't in the script, and wasn't anything I ever envisioned. The biggest problem I had with Tom was fighting the temptation to show too many of his effects in the film for too long. Tom's such a genius that you feel like you should use his effects throughout, but that's not what I wanted. I wanted the film to be like a Magic Mountain ride where you get these jolts every once in awhile."

"As soon as Savini arrived, there was lots of blood," Virginia Field says with a laugh. "With the Kevin Bacon scene, I remember that we had to build the bed so that Kevin could rise out of a horizontal position, being under the bed, and slide his head and neck vertically through the bed, while his head rested on the pillow, along with the fake neck that Tom made. I had to work around Tom's effects, and compliment them."

"There was no way we could've anticipated Tom Savini's magic, and what was actually on the page and what was on the screen was incredibly different," Adrienne King said. "You know what they say about one picture equaling a thousand words? In this case it was worth a thousand screams!"

A shot of the lake taken from the woods. (Photo courtesy of Dean A. Orewiler/Dean A. Orewiler Portrait Art)

Boats similar to the type Alice used in the film are stacked beside the Sand Pond which doubled for the lake in the film. (Photo courtesy of Tony Urban www.tonyurbanphotography.com)

"A lot of the effects that were in the script were described in a way that left much to the imagination so that we could do an alternate version in case we couldn't make the effect work," Cunningham recalls. "The Kevin Bacon throat scene was a prime example. I had no idea of how we would

"My impression of Tom was that he had a big ego and was a real showboat during the early stages of filming," Daniel Mahon recalls. "He would always carry around this 'show-book' that was full of images of his work, and I think he did that just to show how important and great he was. That all changed later on when Harry Crosby's eyes got burned, and we thought Harry had been blinded. Tom changed after that."

"Tom had just come off working with [George] Romero on *Dawn of the Dead* where Romero had Tom blow lots of heads off and I think Tom brought that mentality to *Friday the 13th*," Richard Murphy says. "On *Dawn of the Dead*, Tom would stand next to the camera with a shotgun and blow a dummy head to pieces right in front of George. Tom brought that same mentality to our film, like the scene where the girl's standing in front of the archery range and the arrow whizzes by her, and I think it took him some time to adjust and tone it down a bit."

"Tom was a real character," Tad Page recalls. "Taso and Tom staged a car accident where you could see Tom and Taso laying on the road, playing dead, and then they popped up. When we were on the food line, Tom would smash Taso with his tray, and Taso would block it with his hand, parry it, like a wrestler. Everything was a joke for those guys."

Tom Savini's creativity and passion had a jolting effect on the cast and crew. (Photo courtesy of Tom Savini)

"I think the crew had kind of a mixed reaction to Tom at first," Robert Shulman says. "At the same time, I think we were all kind of envious of Tom's great talent, and his ability to work unsupervised, and his ability to create his magic tricks."

"It was a blast!" recalls Jeannine Taylor of working with Savini. "I wish I had taken pictures while Tom was working, or had someone else take them. So interesting, and a little scary when one's eyes and mouth and nose are covered with plaster, with a drinking straw protruding from each nostril so you can breathe. (Like, you think, 'What if my nose gets stuffed up?') Definitely a strange, deliciously-creepy experience, and then seeing a perfect replica of your own face staring back at you. Quite weird and wonderful."

"I was awestruck by Tom and Taso," recalls Cecelia Verardi who served, along with Taso Stavra-kis, as Savini's makeup effects assistant. "I spent a lot of time with them when they were casting Betsy Palmer's head. They were mad scientists. Tom had a mad look in his eyes. He loved creating horrors that would shock and amaze people. Taso was very artistic and creative, mellow, sweet. Taso complimented Tom who really was a mad scientist."

DROWNING JASON

The filming of the first major scene for *Friday the 13th* took place in the last week of August, just before the bulk of the cast and crew arrived. This was the drowning sequence where young Jason, played by Ari Lehman, is seen flailing in the waters of Camp Crystal Lake in Pamela Voorhees' dream.

Only Barry Abrams, Sean Cunningham, Ari Lehman, Tom Savini, Taso Stavrakis and a handful of others were present on location at this point. Lehman would later reappear in Blairstown at the end of the filming schedule for the filming of the climactic lake scene. "In fact, I was on the set three different times," Lehman recalls. "The first two times were in the summer, when we shot the drowning sequence seen in Pamela's flashback. The first time we shot the sequence, Sean Cunningham did not like the way the makeup looked onscreen; he felt it was too scary. He asked Tom Savini to make young Jason more pathetic and less repulsive. The second time worked. Only Tom and Taso and Sean and the crew were there at that time in the summer. Sean wanted to be sure the effect worked right so he had us start to work on the drowning scene as early as possible in case changes needed to be made, which they did. It ended up to be a good plan, especially when Sean decided on the surprise ending, which became easier to do now that we had done the other scene first. The rest is history."

Lehman recalls it was around this period, the filming of the drowning scene, that Sean Cunningham, Victor Miller and Tom Savini ultimately devised the climactic lake scene where Jason rises from the lake and attacks the Alice character. While Ron Kurz, Miller and Savini have all claimed authorship of this concept, in varying degrees, Miller and

Savini have also cited the climactic scene in the 1976 horror film *Carrie* as a key inspiration. Cunningham has always claimed that he'd never seen the Brian DePalma-directed film until after *Friday the 13th* was completed. "After that [the filming of the drowning sequence], I thought I was done, based on the script," Lehman says. "However, after Sean Cunningham saw the surprise ending in *Carrie*, he added a surprise ending to *Friday the 13th*. He, Victor Miller, and Tom Savini devised a dream sequence where Young Jason emerges from Crystal Lake. I returned to the set in October to film the famous final scene. It was during that third time on the set that I met Adrienne King, Harry Crosby, Kevin Bacon and the other actors."

THE OFFER

While Cunningham and Miner controlled the production, in consultation with Philip Scuderi and his partners at Georgetown Productions, the crew of *Friday the 13th* answered directly to cinematographer Barry Abrams and camera operator Braden Lutz, primarily Abrams.

Barry Abrams not only commanded great respect from the crew, all of whom were his friends, but also from Cunningham. They had become close friends, and Abrams represented the

The crew of *Friday the 13th*. This picture was taken at the start of filming, during the filming of the scenes involving Annie. Cinematographer Barry Abrams (beard) stands at the front left of the picture while Sean Cunningham (moustache, white shirt) stands with his arm around one of the signs. Braden Lutz (cap, blonde/white hair, bulky frame) stands behind Cunningham in the picture. (Photo courtesy of Nalani Clark/Tad Page/Robert Shulman)

usually dormant creative side of Cunningham's brain. "The filming went very well and Barry and Sean were two very different people who nonetheless worked very well together and were very close friends," Virginia Field says. "Sean was a businessman, very simple, while Barry was full of passion and creativity. The filming went very well."

The amount of deference and respect that Cunningham had for Abrams was evident prior to the start of filming on *Friday the 13th* when he, along with Steve Miner, offered Abrams a profit participation deal for *Friday the 13th* in lieu of a salary, which ended up, as mentioned, being roughly $750 per week. Cunningham offered other crew members such a deal – and would make the same offer to actress Betsy Palmer later on during production when trying to secure her for the role of Pamela Voorhees – but Abrams was the first person Cunningham approached with such an offer.

Having worked with Cunningham and Miner previously on *Here Come the Tigers* and *Manny's Orphans* – neither of which yielded any measurable financial returns – and weary from several low budget productions throughout the 1970s, with little to show for it, Abrams – who supported himself, like many of his crew, through his work on commercials and industrial/technical films - summarily rejected the offer, which would've made him a millionaire over the subsequent decades. "Sean and Steve offered me a piece of the film and I said 'No' to them," Abrams recalled. "I liked Sean, and we were friends, but I didn't think *Friday the 13th* was going to be any more successful than the previous films, and a paycheck was really important to me at that time because I had a wife and a kid to support. If anything, I think the offer made me suspicious that Sean and Steve were out of money. It wasn't until we were midway through filming that I realized we had something here – in terms of something that would be successful – and I regretted not taking the deal, but at the time, it was the smart decision."

"Barry was offered points on the film but wanted a paycheck, not points," James Bekiaris recalls. "Most of us were getting five bucks an hour, seven-fifty if we were lucky. We were just happy to have jobs."

"Sean offered Barry points on the film and he refused," Daniel Mahon recalls. "It was something Barry laughed about."

"Barry was the leader of the pack," Richard Murphy says. "We were all offered profit deals on *Friday the 13th* and we all turned it down, especially Barry. Barry laughed at Sean and Steve when they asked him about taking a profit deal instead of a paycheck. Barry said, 'Give me my money.' He laughed right in their face."

"As we got deeper into the filming, I think we all realized that this was something that had a real chance to be successful, especially Barry," Robert Shulman says. "One night, midway through the filming, I got drunk with Barry and Barry said, 'This fucking movie's going to make ten million dollars.' Of course, it made a lot more than ten million dollars."

CHAPTER 6

WEEK ONE: BABES IN THE WOODS

"With Friday the 13th we were play-ing on childhood fears in terms of the things that scared us all when we were kids. What scared us the most as kids? Isolation."

- Sean Cunningham

Besides the main Camp No-Be-Bo-Sco filming location, much of the rest of *Friday the 13th* was filmed around Blairstown, especially in and around the township's downtown core. *Friday the 13th* was also partially filmed in the nearby town of Hope, New Jersey, with a few shots taken from neighboring Pennsylvania. The shooting schedule prepared prior to the start of filming called for a production schedule that allowed for filming between Monday and Saturday of every week – day and night shooting - with Sunday designated as a day off for the cast and crew.

Crazy Ralph warns Annie about going to Camp Crystal Lake (AKA Camp Blood). Both Walt Gorney and Rex Everhart, who played Enos, were distinguished New York stage actors prior to being cast in *Friday the 13th*. (Photo courtesy of Richard Feury)

The Monday through Saturday work schedule was certainly fluid, as evidenced by the fact that the date of September 3, 1979 – the day before the first day of principal filming – fell on a Labor Day Monday. The production script – or shooting script

A shot of the bridge that Annie walks past in the film. (Photo courtesy of Robert Armin www.robertarmin.com)

– used throughout filming was marked as a third draft script and was approximately 85 pages long. This script was dated August 21, 1979 and credited solely to writer Victor Miller, with no acknowledgement of writer Ron Kurz's contributions. From here, it was time for the cast and crew, having settled in Blairstown, to make a film, make *Friday the 13th*, and make history.

ANNIE AND ENOS

The first scenes filmed for *Friday the 13th*, in the first week of September, involved the character Annie, played by Robbi Morgan. In these scenes, Annie arrives in the downtown section of Crystal Lake, in search of a ride to Camp Crystal Lake. Annie receives a ride from a truck driver named Enos, played by Rex Everhart, a 1978 Tony Award nominee. He takes her roughly halfway to Camp Crystal Lake. Then, a hitchhiking Annie is given a ride, in a jeep, by an unseen Pamela Voorhees.

The scene when Annie first arrives in Crystal Lake is dated in the film as taking place on a 'present day' Friday the thirteenth -- June 13, 1980, the only Friday the thirteenth of either 1979 or 1980.

Robbi Morgan drove out to the Blairstown location after being cast by Julie Hughes in the New York casting office. Since her scenes were completely separate from the rest of the main cast, Morgan – who was in Blairstown less than 48 hours - never met Adrienne King or any of the other cast members. "I remember that I wasn't there long at all," Morgan recalls. "Maybe only one day. I think we shot the daytime scenes and then shot a nighttime scene at the campsite [referring to the scene where Annie's corpse is visible in the passenger seat of Pamela Voorhees' jeep]. I didn't meet the other actors. I was gone after my shoot."

Since Betsy Palmer hadn't even been cast as Pamela Voorhees yet, Morgan never crossed paths with the actress during the filming of *Friday the 13th*, but Morgan and Palmer did share a prior connection. "My brother had appeared in a stage version of *Peter Pan* with Sandy Duncan and Betsy Palmer," recalls Morgan who also had a background with genre filmmaking, sort of, having previously appeared, as a child actress, alongside Debbie Reynolds in the 1971 psychological-thriller film *What's the Matter with Helen?* "Sandy played Wendy and Betsy played Peter. I used to run into Betsy quite a bit over the years – in between her plays and my acting jobs – but never saw her around the time we both did *Friday the 13th*, either during the filming or after the film was completed."

A shot of Walnut St. in Blairstown. This is the exact spot where Enos' truck was parked in the beginning of the film. (Photo courtesy of Robert Armin www.robertarmin.com)

The scene where Annie arrives in Crystal Lake was filmed in the downtown section of Blairstown. The crew filmed around this area throughout filming, as well as around neighboring Hardwick Township, although much of the shot footage didn't make it into the finished film.

The scene where Jack, Marcie, and Ned drive along in Ned's truck, on their way to the campsite, was filmed on Millbrook Road in Hardwick Township. The crew also, as mentioned, shot some miscellaneous footage at some unspecified Pennsylvania locations. "I remember being at a gas station in Hope and shooting some stuff around there," Robert Shulman recalls. "Hope is right near Blairstown, so we were always around there. We also hit one town in Pennsylvania, which was an antiques town, and did some shooting there."

"That scene where the girl's walking through downtown was right near a local prep school called the Blairstown Academy," Richard Skow recalls. "I remember that the crew did quite a bit of shooting around the area, outside of the camp, but I don't think it ended up in the finished film."

The main street buildings that Annie moved past in the film remain virtually unchanged today. (Photo courtesy of Tony Urban www. tonyurbanphotography.com)

A shot of the old mill as it appears today. (Photo courtesy of Robert Armin www.robertarmin.com)

The scene where Annie asks for directions to Camp Crystal Lake represented an attempt by Cunningham, one of many, to add a sense of grim foreboding to the film. "The scene where Annie comes into the tiny diner and announces she's going to Crystal Lake, and the people just stare?" Cunningham said. "That was just trying to set mood, so the audience would think, 'Oh, there's something out of the ordinary going on here!'"

The tunnel Annie walks through in the film. (Photo courtesy of Tony Urban www.tonyurbanphotography.com)

Since Everhart and Morgan never appear inside the same frame while in Enos' truck, it's easy to assume that Everhart and Morgan might've shot their dialogue scenes separate from each other. There's also the question of whether Everhart actually drove the truck in the film or if the illusion was accomplished with sound effects, as is the case in most films.

Morgan, for her part, doesn't recall ever having been in the truck with Everhart. "Enos wasn't there in the truck when we did that scene," Morgan says. "I really had no one to act to. I was just sit-

ting in the passenger seat and delivering my lines to no one at all. Either that, or they had someone else in the driver's seat that I was reading my lines to, but I don't remember Enos ever having been there."

Some of the crew-members recall that Everhart – who died of lung cancer in 2000 – was driving the truck, at a slow speed, and was with Morgan. One fact that's not in dispute is that the truck was surrounded by crew members throughout the filming of the scene. "Rex Everhart was driving during that scene, unbelievably, because Braden [camera operator Braden Lutz] had to be on the outside of the truck, and had to shoot over Robbi in that scene," Richard Murphy recalls. "Braden Lutz was on the cab of the truck for that scene, and was hanging outside of the truck for that scene. I was on the tank of the truck, on the roof of the truck, in order to get the sound for the scene. We ended up taking a group picture – with Barry, Sean, the whole crew – in Hope, New Jersey when we were shooting the initial scene in the film with Annie in the oil truck."

CRAZY RALPH

The character of Crazy Ralph – or Ralphie The Rat Boy as he was known during the early scripting stages – was a construction on the part of Sean Cunningham and Victor Miller for the purpose of providing a voice of doom. A last minute addition to the film by Cunningham, Crazy Ralph wasn't even listed on the shooting schedule.

"The Crazy Ralph character was meant to be the soothsayer character that exists in every small town," Cunningham says. "He's the guy who drinks too much, and says all of these crazy things that have a kernel of truth in them. Everyone thinks he's crazy, but he turns out to be right in the end. I felt that kind of character would be a good fit for our story."

Walt Gorney, the actor who played Ralph, was a Broadway veteran like Rex Everhart. Gorney – who died in 2004 – was a serious actor, dedicated and professional, but he liked to keep to himself and the cast and crew – those few that spent any meaningful time with him during the filming of *Friday the 13th* – regarded him as being eccentric and odd.

The spot where Enos' truck was parked in the film isn't much to look at, but still holds appeal for *Friday the 13th* fans who flock to Blairstown every year. (Photo courtesy of Tony Urban www.tonyurbanphotography.com)

"Walt was actually a very well-trained New York actor," Steve Miner says. "I do remember, sometimes, in between scenes, you'd see him off in the corner, talking to himself, but when it came time to shoot a scene, he was money in the bank."

"Walt was someone Sean knew," says Virginia Field who later worked with Gorney on *Friday the 13th Part 2*. "Strange."

The signature arches that appear in the film are easy to spot today. (Photo courtesy of Tony Urban www.tonyurbanphotography.com)

"Walt would come to the set a day at a time," Richard Murphy recalls. "I remember they got him dressed, got him in town for that first scene, and they did his 'You're doomed' thing and then he was sent back to New York."

"Walt Gorney was an old thespian and was very eccentric," recalls David Platt who also worked with Gorney on *Friday the 13th Part 2*, as well as the 1986 New York-shot drama film *Seize the Day*, in which Gorney had a bit part. "He was an old-fashioned Broadway lifer who always stayed in character, and liked to stay in character. Walt wasn't as successful in his acting career as he would've liked, but couldn't, or wouldn't, give up acting."

"Walt Gorney was a real character," recalls Cecelia Verardi who also worked with Gorney again on *Friday the 13th Part 2* on which Verardi served as a makeup artist. "He was warm, eccentric and playful. He liked to talk to people; anyone he could find to talk to. The first day with Walt was the scene in town, in downtown Blairstown, where he's warning the girl to stay away from the camp. It was a very intense scene because Walt had a very startling presence, especially when he was on the bike. Walt had a real presence. Walt himself wasn't anything like the character he played in the film."

The exterior of the coffee shop/diner/store where Annie stopped for directions in the film. (Photo courtesy of Tony Urban www.tonyurbanphotography.com)

DON'T GO IN THE WOODS

During her brief stay in Blairstown, Robbi Morgan bonded with Tom Savini and his assistant and longtime friend, Taso Stavrakis. For Savini and Stavrakis, working with Morgan gave them the first chance to demonstrate their artistry with makeup effects, along with their dexterity and versatility.

Savini and Stavrakis were, aside from their effects prowess, more than capable stuntmen and stunt coordinators. "During my time there, I mostly hung around with Taso and Tom who were both so much fun to be around," Morgan says. "We got along great."

For the jeep scene, the vehicle was driven by the dashing Stavrakis with whom Morgan developed an immediate attraction to, and vice versa. Morgan herself proved to be a capable stunt performer herself during the scene where Annie jumps from the speeding jeep to escape. Morgan did the stunt herself. "That was Taso driving the jeep," Morgan recalls. "I remember we shot the scenes in the woods really quickly in order to save the light because they wanted to take me up to the camp to do the jeep scene at night [the scene where Alice

discovers Annie's throat-slashed corpse in the passenger seat of Pamela Voorhees' jeep]. I'm a trained acrobat and dancer so jumping out of the jeep was easy. The truck wasn't going as fast as it looked in the movie, but it was still moving along pretty fast."

"Robbi Morgan didn't spend much time on the set but we hit it off in a short period of time," Savini recalls. "She became 'acquainted' with my assistant."

This store in Hope, New Jersey was used for the interior of the coffee shop/diner that Annie visits in the film. (Photo courtesy of Robert Armin www.robertarmin.com)

"The three of us had such a good time that we bought matching t-shirts," recalls Stavrakis of his time with Morgan and Savini during the

Shot of Moravian Cemetery in Hope, New Jersey which is glimpsed in the film. (Photo courtesy of Robert Armin www.robertarmin.com)

filming of *Friday the 13th*. "I think Robbi bought them and they said 'Mini Maniac' (Robbi), 'Minor Maniac' (Me), and 'Major Maniac' for Tom."

For Morgan, the scene where Annie flees required her to run through the thick forest, while limping, and then to trip on a branch and fall to the ground. Stavrakis wielded the knife that cuts across her throat. "Taso killed me," Morgan recalls with a laugh. "It wasn't scary running through the bushes

because there were crew members standing around me and yelling out instructions like 'Run here, limp this way, turn that way.' When I stop and look up, I was looking at Taso. He was such a nice guy so I just acted as terrified as I could. I just pretended that there was a killer in front of me; not necessarily Mrs. Voorhees, because Betsy wasn't there. It was just Taso."

Annie's death scene required Savini, with Stavrakis' help, to create an appliance that fit comfortably around Morgan's neck and throat. It also had to be sturdy enough for Stavrakis to freely cut through without hurting Morgan. Savini's "other" makeup effects assistant, Cecelia Verardi, was also present for this. "The neck was a foam latex appliance that was applied to Robbi, over a bladder," Savini recalls. "The appliance was precut and when the knife passed by, Robbi lifted her head, opening the cut, and then we pumped blood out through the bladder."

"This was all new to most of us, and it was shocking to witness at first," Robert Shulman says. "The first murder happened on the first week, with the girl in the woods, and Tom Savini created a very good latex prosthetic. The blood just pumped out of her throat. It was eerie to watch."

The graveyard visible in the film remains virtually unchanged from when *Friday the 13th* was filmed. (Photo courtesy of Tony Urban www.tonyurbanphotography.com)

"Tom had a couple of machetes with cutouts that we'd used in *Dawn of the Dead*," Stavrakis recalls. "I think that's what he put on Robbi's throat for a gag shot."

"I remember that Robbi Morgan had an appliance glued around her neck for that scene," Cecelia Verardi recalls. "Behind the appliance, there was a blood bag, and they cut into the bag to create the effect."

The cemetery as it appeared in 1979. (Photo courtesy of Tony Marshall)

In addition to Savini's artistry, the sequence where Annie runs through the woods makes great use of sound, specifically the sounds of the forest and the wildlife that echo throughout the scene. This is a credit to the work of soundman Richard Murphy whose sound effects provide a great

compliment to the stinger provided by the throat-slashing effect. "The sound was so real in the scene where Robbi was killed," Richard Murphy says. "I think we used a wipe dissolve for that scene, and Braden wore the plaid shirt to play the killer in that scene. The scene was down for a couple of hours while Tom worked on the prosthetic for the girl. When the girl put her head back into the prosthetic, and Taso cut her, the blood just dripped out and it looked like the girl was getting her throat cut. It was shocking to see something that real."

"Braden" was of course camera operator Braden Lutz who played the killer here, along with Taso Stavrakis. Though Stavrakis supplied the cut across Morgan's throat, Lutz was present, knife in hand, in the frame just before. It was Lutz who wore the plaid attire seen fleetingly during the scene, and it was Lutz whose feet are seen stalking Annie through the forest.

As the camera operator, and in the closest proximity to what's happening in any given scene, the agile and physically-imposing Lutz was a good choice to play the killer or "prowler". But Braden Lutz wasn't the only member of the crew who performed this duty. "We all took turns playing 'Betsy Palmer' in the film before they cast an actress in the role and if you played the killer, you wore a yellow raincoat," Richard Murphy recalls. "We all took turns wear-

1979 shot of the cemetery reveals a spacious area. (Photo courtesy of Tony Marshall)

er] were trying to line-up past-their-prime actresses. They were turned down by several before landing Betsy Palmer. The point being that not having the killer cast probably dictated parts of the schedule."

"I remember that Tad Page and Braden Lutz donned the killer's boots and wore the yellow raincoat in the film," Cecelia Verardi recalls. "Until they cast someone to play the killer, they shot as much as they could without having to actually have an actress there, so different people on the crew would take turns being the killer, but it was mostly Braden and Tad."

With Annie, and her grim fate, Cunningham was trying to mirror the film *Psycho* (1960) by introducing a would-be heroine or protagonist who's subsequently murdered. In this regard, Annie was *Friday the 13th*'s Marion Crane, the character famously played by actress Janet Leigh in *Psycho*. "I was strongly aware of that setup for *Psycho*," Cunningham said. "That the first girl you are introduced to dies. I purposely set-up Annie as the lead, and she isn't the lead at all. That's why I think the audience is so surprised when she becomes the first victim, because they didn't expect her to die."

The cemetery in Hope, New Jersey was home to several war veterans. (Photo courtesy of Tony Marshall)

ing the yellow raincoat, which became the codename or insignia for playing the killer in the film. Braden played the killer because, as camera operator, he was the handheld killer in all of the scenes. Cindy Veazey played the killer. Cindy was a good friend of Sean's. The biggest surprise was that Peter Brouwer wore the raincoat and played the killer in one of the scenes."

"Sean and Steve Miner didn't come-up with a villain until pretty late in the shoot," Robert Shulman recalls. "Several of us were dressed up in slickers at one time or another when a glimpse of the killer was needed, so the size varied a bit, though always in the dark. The boys [Cunningham and Min-

A trained acrobat and dancer, Robbi Morgan had little trouble performing this stunt herself. (Photo courtesy of Henri Guibaud)

Besides cameraman Robert Brady, who was fired during filming, the other member of the *Friday the 13th* crew who departed Blairstown prior to the end of filming was Katherine (Katharine) Vickers. She was hired to be both the hairstylist and makeup girl. Unlike Brady, Vickers wasn't fired but rather suffered a ruptured appendix during filming that made it impossible for her to complete filming and forced her to leave the set.

Besides the scenes with Annie, the most significant scenes shot during the first week of filming involved the characters of Jack, Marcie and Ned.

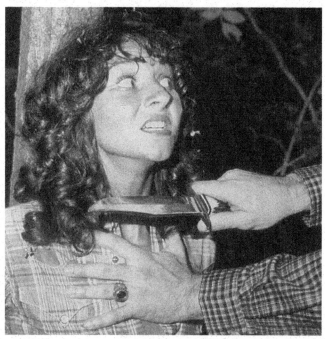

The plaid attire in this shot belonged to camera operator Braden Lutz while Taso Stavrakis actually slid the knife across the neck appliance through the use of a cutaway shot. (Photo courtesy of Henri Guibaud)

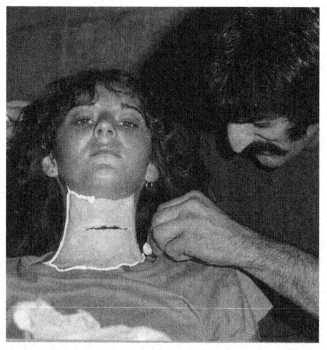

Tom Savini tweaks Robbi Morgan's neck appliance in preparation for the filming of Morgan's death scene. (Photo courtesy of Tom Savini)

As a result, the hair and makeup chores were taken over by Cecelia Verardi who was on a very steep learning curve, to say the least. "I was a liaison between the actors and the production on *Friday the 13th* and one of my main jobs was to make sure the actors arrived in the makeup cabin, or at the filming area, on time every day," Verardi recalls. "That's how I became such good friends with Laurie Bartram and Harry Crosby. I took over the makeup when the first makeup girl, Katherine Vickers, had a ruptured appendix and had to leave the film. She later sent me a rather mean postcard, blaming me for her being off the film. She was mad at me for taking her job."

These scenes encompassed a long monologue on the part of Marcie, a sex scene between Jack and Marcie, and the deaths of all three characters. The conceptualization and filming of Jack's death scene, in particular, proved to be the first major test for Sean Cunningham, Steve Miner and Tom Savini. If Savini had been a rising star in the effects world

Shot of Annie's corpse in Pamela Voorhees' jeep. (Photo courtesy of Tom Savini)

in the aftermath of *Dawn of the Dead*, the execution of Jack's death scene – or "the Kevin Bacon arrow-in-the-throat effect" – would raise Savini's profile to iconic status.

Like the rest of the cast members, Kevin Bacon, Mark Nelson and Jeannine Taylor weren't prepared, to say the least, for what they were going to go through. In the film, Jack, Marcie and Ned are clearly three college-aged kids who travel to Camp Crystal Lake for a summertime adventure before the dawn of an upcoming year at college.

Kevin Bacon's previous appearance in the film *National Lampoon's Animal House* gave him some degree of celebrity during filming, but not with co-star Jeannine Taylor who was unaware of Bacon's appearance in the film. (Photo courtesy of Richard Feury)

Nelson and Taylor had no screen experience prior to *Friday the 13th* and thus had to adapt to the filmmaking process and terminology. Bacon's sizable role in *Animal House* gave him some degree of fame amongst certain elements of the cast and crew.

"There was no kind of rehearsal process," Taylor recalls. "I don't know how the casting process worked because I auditioned alone for Barry Moss and Sean Cunningham, and then just with Sean for the callback, but it seems that they were looking for contrasting types for the three of us and I think they did achieve that mix. As for being intimidated by Kevin having done *Animal House*, I had no idea he'd been in it because I hadn't seen the movie and knew nothing about it. (I've seen it since and I think it's hilarious.) Kevin was very modest and never mentioned that he'd been in a big movie."

"I liked Jeannine and Kevin a lot, but no, we weren't close friends and we weren't enjoying a carefree adventure," Mark Nelson says. "We were trying to do the best job we could on our first movie, in a very short time. I don't remember if the three of us commuted from the set back to New York during the filming, but I doubt it because the shoot was too brief. I worked on the movie for about two weeks, and I think we were all together for that time."

"I honestly don't recall having any problems adapting to film terminology," Taylor says. "Sean knew I had no film experience aside from a few commercials, so I think he may have purposely kept things as simple as possible for me. I seem to remember that I was moving my head too much at first, and he mentioned that I needed to keep it more still for the camera. When I saw the movie much later, I thought that I appeared to be hiding from the camera in some spots. The acting training I'd had with William Esper in New York had stressed the kind of naturalistic style needed for a lot of film and TV work, so I wasn't completely unprepared."

PREMONITIONS

The scene where Jack and Marcie are outside Ned's cabin and she tells Jack about a nightmare she had, represents the longest monologue in *Friday the 13th*, alongside Pamela Voorhees' monologue later in the film. Marcie's premonition is preceded in the film by a scene at the lake, filmed later, where Marcie thinks she sees something or someone hiding in the trees.

The final part of Marcie's nightmare occurs in the latrine/shower stall, right before her death, where she opens a curtain, sees nothing and remarks, "Must be my imagination" before she turns and stares into the face of her off-screen killer. "Well, Marcie's premonition was already written into the script, and she shares her fear when she talks about her recurring nightmare, so there's that apprehension," Taylor says. "I tried to use that where it was needed, and to totally forget it where it wasn't. The character has a haunting fear, but she's not a 'fearful' person, if that makes any sense."

NED ON THE BED

In the earlier versions of the *Friday the 13th* script, the character of Ned was conceptualized as a muscle-bound guy who suffered from polio. "I remember reading a version of the script that said that Ned had polio, and I think they just decided to abandon that and just keep the character simple," Mark Nelson says. "I saw Ned as being a gentle soul who used humor to hide his insecurities."

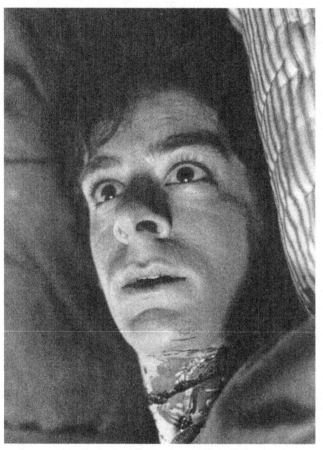

Shot of Ned's throat-slash effect. (Photo courtesy of Harvey Fenton)

The one constant element of the Ned character throughout the screenplay drafts was his practical joking trait. This persona would serve as a template for countless future horror films, most especially the *Friday the 13th* sequels. The slasher film *Terror Train*, filmed in the fall of 1979 and released after *Friday the 13th* in 1980, also featured a similar character, as did *Prom Night*. But Ned established the joker blueprint that countless future horror-slasher films – most notably *The Burning* (1981), and *Halloween II* (1981) - emulated: you're a practical joker, you make light of a potentially grave situation, you die.

Ironically, Steve Miner later tried to turn the tables on this formula in *Friday the 13th Part 2* (1981) by introducing a practical joker character who fatefully avoids death. This was a rare exception. Much like *Halloween* established that premarital sex was a death sentence, *Friday the 13th* established that being a practical joker, or class clown character, was as well.

Nelson recalls that it was fourteen-year-old Ari Lehman who was the shadowy figure standing on the front porch of Ned's cabin when Ned approaches. If true, this sequence would've had to have been shot in the last week of filming when Lehman returned to the campsite.

Since Lehman did end up meeting Nelson, Kevin Bacon, Harry Crosby, and the rest of the cast members during his final visit to Blairstown, this could simply be a faulty recollection, more than thirty years after the fact. "I do recall that it was Ari who was standing on the ledge of the cabin," Nelson says. "There was no one in the cabin when I walked inside the cabin and disappeared off-screen."

For the scene where Ned appears on the top bunk, eyes wide open, throat slashed from ear to ear, Nelson merely had to keep his eyes open and remain still. This was Savini's easiest effects chore, especially since Nelson's death takes place off-screen. The shooting script also kept the exact circumstances of Ned's death a mystery.

In author Simon Hawke's *Friday the 13th* novelization, published in 1987, Hawke described an inquisitive Ned walking into the cabin where he's jumped from behind and a knife is ripped across his throat. "When I was on the top bunk, I would try to remain still, play dead, but I kept blinking like crazy," Nelson recalls. "It took a few takes to get it right."

Betsy Palmer hadn't been cast in *Friday the 13th* when this scene was filmed, but Nelson did get to meet the actress when she arrived toward the second half of *Friday the 13th*'s production schedule. "I did meet Betsy Palmer in the makeup cabin, and she and Tom Savini played a trick on me," Nelson recalls. "Betsy was leaning her elbows on a table, with a prosthetic hand in the right sleeve of her coat, which Tom had given her. Tom introduced us. I went to shake her hand, and Betsy's real right hand came out of the middle of her coat and grabbed my hand. I practically screamed the roof off. Too bad they didn't record it for the movie."

FOUR ON THE FLOOR

As mentioned, the concept of the Jack character having an arrow rammed through his throat, from behind, was something that writer Victor Miller conceptualized in the early scripting stages. Of course, neither Miller nor Sean Cunningham had any real grasp of how this effect could be brought to life. The responsibility fell entirely onto the shoulders of Tom Savini who would thrive under the challenge, but not without a lot of help and perfect timing.

Although Cunningham had tremendous confidence in Savini's abilities, he was skeptical the effect could be fully realized, and was prepared to film an alternate version of the scene whereby Jack simply had his throat slashed from under the bed.

Savini, however, was supremely confident that he could make the effect work, especially since he'd executed a similar "throat piercing" effect on the film *Martin* (1978), directed by George A. Romero. "The arrow-through-the-neck effect in *Friday the 13th* was a variation on an effect I'd done in *Martin*,"

Kevin Bacon and Jeannine Taylor play around during the filming of their sex scene. (Photo courtesy of Richard Feury)

Savini says. "I'd done a mold of my friend, John Maldonado, on *Martin* and brought that with me to *Friday the 13th*. From there, the plan was to fill a cold bag with blood and then push the arrow through the bag and then the blood pours out. It was a magic trick."

The biggest challenge proved to be the basic logistics of getting Kevin Bacon in proper position under the bed and getting the blood to flow out of the neck-mold efficiently and smoothly. Virginia

Steve Miner and Tom Savini collaborated on this storyboard for the arrow-through-the-neck death scene. (Photo courtesy of Tom Savini)

Field and her design team had carefully scored the bed so that Bacon, who wore a bodysuit, could slide his head vertically through the opening in the bed that had been torn out so it appeared that he was laying flat on the bed. "We used Dick Smith's blood formula for most of the effects in *Friday the 13th*, and I'd just started using it when we did *Friday the 13th*," recalls Savini of the blood formula created by makeup and special effects legend Dick Smith. "We used it for all of the effects, but I wasn't as proficient with it as I would've liked to be, and sometimes the blood wouldn't flow the way I wanted it to."

The filming of the scene was excruciating for Bacon who had to remain in an arched position, never relaxed, for the entirety of the filming. "Kevin Bacon was in a full bodysuit for that scene and the poor guy had to be on his knees for hours," Richard Murphy recalls. "We couldn't get a good shot of Kevin laying down in the scene so the poor guy had to be on his knees for six hours while Tom and the rest of the crew figured out what to do. We tried to get an overhead shot of Kevin lying down on the bunk, but that wouldn't work either so Kevin had to be under the bed the whole time."

Prior to filming, Steve Miner and Tom Savini worked out a detailed storyboard that entailed Bacon, Savini, and Taso Stavrakis all being under the bed, with Savini working the arrow through the neck and Stavrakis pumping the blood through a tube which was attached to a blood pump. Complicating matters was the fact that the scene called for a hand to reach out from beneath the bed and clasp Bacon's face just before the arrow goes through Jack's throat.

Enter Richard Feury, *Friday the 13th*'s still photographer, who found himself unexpectedly called upon to assist by being the fourth person under the bed. Although the hiring of a still photographer might've seemed like a splurge for the frugal Cunningham, he had previously used a still photographer on *Here Come the Tigers*, and Feury, like much of the crew, was enthusiastic, talented, and cheap. "This was my first film job and my job was to basically take publicity stills that would be used to promote the film," Feury recalls. "I would stand outside during scenes and wait for the actors to rehearse the scene, and then I'd walk in and shoot pictures. That's what I was doing for the scene with Kevin Bacon when I was asked to play a part in the scene."

Needing a 'hand' for the scene, Cunningham and Miner looked around at the skeleton crew standing in the cabin when Feury's hands caught Cunningham and Miner's attention. "We were all standing around Kevin, trying to figure out how to tackle this scene, and Sean and Steve realized that they needed a hand for the scene, and a smooth-looking hand because the killer in the film was a woman," Feury recalls. "I remember that Steve turned and looked at me, at my hands, and said, 'You've got nice-looking hands. You go under the bed.' That was it."

With all of the planning in place, it was finally

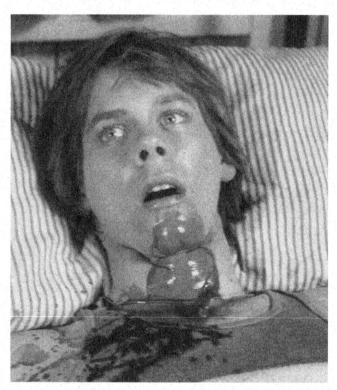

The successful realization of the arrow-through-the-neck sequence required the collaboration of several people. (Photo courtesy of Harvey Fenton)

time to film the scene. According to everyone who was present in the cabin, the filming commenced beautifully, entirely in sync with the storyboarding that Miner and Savini had done previously. There was just one problem. The blood that was supposed to spurt out of Bacon's throat failed to materialize.

For all intensive purposes, this scene was a single take proposition, so any problems had to be corrected during the actual filming, on the fly. "This was, basically, a one-shot deal, and what happened was that the hose on the blood pump became disconnected," Stavrakis recalls. "The whole thing was almost blown for good."

It was Taso Stavrakis who, from under the bed, grabbed the hose and blew as hard as he could until the blood, at last, flowed outward. "I had to think quick so I just grabbed the hose and blew like crazy which, thankfully, caused a serendipitous arterial blood spray," says Stavrakis who recalls Feury having especially 'delicate' hands. "The blood didn't taste that bad either."

The successful completion of the scene brought cheers of joy from the small crew gathered in the cabin, especially from Cunningham for this scene represented a harbinger of good fortune. "I've always said that Tom was, in many ways, the real star of the film," Cunningham says. "That scene just illustrated Tom's genius; doing something that all of us thought was logistically impossible. Tom was the magician, and we've lost that with films today. *Friday the 13th* was one of the last films where you could really see the magic being done by hand whereas you see films today that are all driven by CGI."

"When we shot that scene with Kevin, it was a closed set because there was also the love scene between Kevin and the girl that had to be filmed," Barry Abrams recalled. "Kevin and the girl had a ball doing their scene together, and then Sean let Tom take over the scene and work his magic. Sean had the ultimate trust in Tom."

"They built a fake neck and chest, and I was crouching under the bed for hours with my head sticking out through a hole," Kevin Bacon recalled. "It was absolutely awful, but I did have a classic horror movie death, which is you fuck the girl, you smoke the joint, you're dead, so that was good."

"The pump didn't work and Taso ripped the hose and blew the blood through," Richard Murphy recalls. "Taso could only do it once. Even someone like Taso could only do that once. It was one of the greatest examples I've ever seen of solving a problem on the spot."

"I did watch the filming of the arrow-through-the-throat scene, and saw Taso get under the bed and blow through the plastic tube when the mechanism failed," Mark Nelson recalls. "It was amazing to watch."

"For the Kevin Bacon scene, the generator was really breaking down so I had to tie into the electrical box to keep the generator working," Tad Page recalls. "It was magic. The generator did not discriminate. It broke down when it wanted to! Hot or cold, it was used to power lights which were used in all scenes and in all weather, including when we made rain. It seems to me that we 'tied-in' to a cabin's electric wiring for either Kevin's arrow-through-the-neck scene or his 'smooching' scene with Marcie. Sean commented at my delicacy while working with live wires as 'That man is working hot.'"

"That scene, in particular, really made me a star," Savini says. "It was a scene that was done on-screen with virtually no cutaways. We didn't cheat at all. Everyone loved the arrow scene. Kevin Bacon loved it. He thought it was cool."

"I put blood on him [Kevin Bacon] in that scene when it was needed," Cecelia Verardi recalls. "I remember that Kevin was very tired by the time the scene was finished, but also very excited about what Tom had done. Everyone was very happy. I think that scene made everyone believe that the movie might turn into something after all."

SEX EQUALS DEATH

Just as the Ned character popularized the practical joker archetype in the horror genre, the characters of Jack and Marcie established another motif: sex in a horror film equals death.

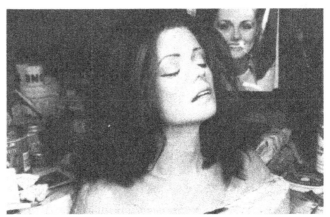

The realized mold of Jeannine Taylor's head with Taylor's reference picture in the background. (Photo courtesy of Tom Savini)

The sex scene in *Friday the 13th* was filmed prior to Kevin Bacon's death scene, the filming of which was witnessed by Victor Miller who'd travelled to Blairstown to consult with Cunningham and Miner. Like Bacon's death scene, the sex scene was in the shooting script. While the sex scene's filming didn't require nearly the effort and imagination that was put into Bacon's death scene, its influence would be just as substantial, for very different reasons.

The sex scene itself didn't feature any clear nudity, but was nonetheless quite graphic and intense. "I was extremely nervous because I was going to do this very private, naughty thing," said Jeannine Taylor of her sex scene in the film with co-star Bacon. "I was a modest person. I still am, really. So I did it very clumsily. I was just really bad on that first take, and I knew it. I was inwardly cringing. With that, just to show you what kind of person Sean was, he said 'Cut,' took me by the hand, privately walked me away from the rest of the crew and said very slowly and quietly in my ear: 'Now, we can all do better than that.' He was very gentle and compassionate about it, like talking to a skittish horse or something. It calmed me down immediately. I did a little better on the next take."

Jeannine Taylor poses alongside a fake version of her skull. (Photo courtesy of Tom Savini)

The most significant aspect of the sex scene between Jack and Marcie has to do with the inescapable fact that both characters are murdered following sexual intercourse. A message, deliberate or not, is sent to the audience. Although *Friday the 13th* wasn't the first horror film to equate sex with horrible death, *Friday the 13th* – and especially its many sequels – made this concept into an art form.

The progenitor of the sex-equals-death formula was *Halloween* (1978) where the unmarried teenage characters Bob and Lynda were both graphically murdered following sexual intercourse.

Halloween filmmakers John Carpenter and Debra Hill say that the deaths were a function of circumstance and didn't represent any kind of harsh moral judgment that the film, or the filmmakers, were trying to impose on the viewer.

For his part, Cunningham sees the formula as merely being a representation of classical literature in which sex and death are often synonymous. "I don't want to sound as though I'm over-intellectualizing, but orgasm and death are synonymous in Elizabethan literature," Cunningham said. "An orgasm is called a small death. The fact is, death and sex get linked a lot, just as water and security are often linked in a Freudian context. As the dead person in the scene is revealed, the orgasm happens. Cutting back

Jeannine Taylor's fake head wasn't used for the filming of Taylor's death scene. Tom Savini glued the axe onto Taylor's skull for the filming of the scene. (Photo courtesy of Tom Savini)

to them makes some kind of emotional sense that I don't really understand. I just know that it's true."

Actress Jeannine Taylor, one-half of the sex scene, feels the correlation between sex and death in horror films is a reflection of society itself and a reaction to the dark impulses that rest in the imaginations of viewers. "The subject has come under scrutiny by feminist and film scholars, as we all know, which I think is a good thing," Taylor says. "It sells tickets, but why? I think our society needs to look at why. Women and men both need to know why this sells tickets. I have a hunch that a completely lucid, truthful answer to that question will be scarier than any scary movie."

The sex scene with Jack and Marcie represents the second example of the sex-equals-death formula in *Friday the 13th*. The first example occurs at the beginning of the film where the characters of Barry and Claudette are both murdered after engaging in sexual activity. The difference being, Barry and Claudette had yet to complete the sexual act before their deaths whereas Jack and Marcie both clearly reach orgasm in the film.

CHANELLING KATHARINE HEPBURN

The scene where Marcie walks into the latrine cabin – built, virtually from scratch, by Virginia Field and her design team – and breaks into a Katharine Hepburn impersonation wasn't at all part of the *Friday the 13th* script, but was entirely an invention of actress Jeannine Taylor, with encouragement from Sean Cunningham and the rest of the crew.

This improvisation was a necessity because the script didn't contain enough description or dialogue to fill the time required where Marcie moves from the latrine area to the shower stalls.

The dialogue from Taylor's Katharine Hepburn impersonation was taken from the film *The Rainmaker* (1956), a performance for which Hepburn was nominated for an Academy Award. For the purpose of *Friday the 13th*, the scene serves to lighten the tension in anticipation of Marcie's violent death via an axe in the skull. "I just improvised it," Taylor recalls. "Nothing in my head beforehand. It 'came over the airwaves,' so to speak, and when

nobody yelled, 'Cut! What the hell are you doing?' I thought they might leave it in. My character is generally goofing around in the scene up till that point, so it came out of that, and the mirror. It's the silly camp counselor doing Hepburn, so it's a bad imitation, and she cracks herself up. Anyway, it was more fun than just washing my hands, which was what I was originally supposed to do."

THE SHOWER SCENE

Marcie in the shower stall area represents a second homage to the film *Psycho*, with a bit of a twist. Whereas the opening of the shower curtain in *Psycho* triggers immediate violence, Sean Cunningham's idea with the shower scene in *Friday the 13th* was to do things in reverse. Marcie opens the curtain and finds nothing. Then she turns around and sees the face of her killer, right before an axe crashes into her skull.

"I have to give Virginia Field credit for that set," Cunningham said. "I told her my idea and she built it. An outdoor bathroom is a place where you're most vulnerable. It's totally isolated from the rest of the camp. Anything can happen there and there's

Jeannine Taylor poses for the camera. (Photo courtesy of Tom Savini)

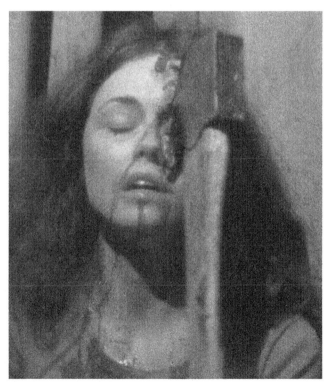

The completed version of Jeannine Taylor's death scene. (Photo courtesy of Henri Guibaud)

no one around to help you. I purposely had that set built for a dolly shot. I wanted to make that tracking and have the actress turn around and walk down this long row and go into yet another room in which there is another stall that shouldn't be opened. Then you open it and there's nothing there. Each time, you're exposing another layer, another dark place."

The ominous rainstorm that pounds during this scene was created by effects expert Steven Kirshoff with the help of a fire truck. "Well, I suppose that would be the first night shoot, when a fire truck came onto the set and a very realistic rainstorm was created," Taylor recalls of the filming. "As I recall, most of the shower scene was shot that night."

Jeannine Taylor doesn't recall looking at anyone on the *Friday the 13th* crew in particular, not Braden Lutz or Tom Savini. "For the scream, I was seeing the image I had in my mind's eye, not looking at anybody real," Taylor says. "I do vividly recall having the axe hot-glued directly to my face. Wouldn't you? Tom Savini was very reassuring when he did this, and I never doubted for a minute that it would not burn me, which it didn't, and he used a lot of hot glue, to make the gore and so forth. Got it all off too, quite painlessly, and I never even got a pimple!"

Savini did a mold of Taylor's head, and crafted a lifelike replica, with the intention of driving the axe into the fake head for the filming of the scene. When the axe failed to hold during the first attempt, Savini was forced to make other plans and settled on attaching the axe to Taylor's own skull. "We tried it and the axe slid down the skull every time," Savini recalls. "It wouldn't stick into the mold the right way, no matter how hard I swung the axe."

"I've read that the special effect with the axe going into the model of my head did not work because the mold didn't hold, and Tom Savini was disappointed about that," Taylor says. "What's amazing to me is that he immediately found another way, and I never even knew there was a problem because nobody transmitted it to me. Everyone stayed calm and focused and it all got done, and there was something really special about working through the night, breaking for 'lunch' at 3AM."

An inspired little touch to the axe-in-the-skull sequence was the insertion of a brief pause where the axe bangs into the overhead light, forcing the killer to briefly re-grip the axe and then swing again, all in one motion. This wasn't a cre-

A shot of what appears to be a makeshift workspace at the campsite used during filming. (Photo courtesy of Tony Marshall)

ative invention by Cunningham or Savini, clever and subtle as it is, but rather a result of what happened when Savini swung the axe and ended up clipping the overhead light in a cutaway shot that was done when Taylor wasn't even present.

Like Mark Nelson, Taylor also met actress Betsy Palmer when Palmer arrived on location. "I had to have a break from shooting because I came down with strep-throat, so I returned to the set later to finish some small stuff, and it was nearly fall, with

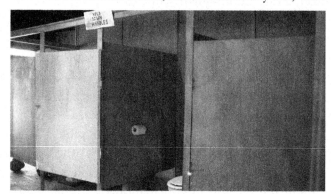

The toilet that Marcie used in the film, as it appeared in 1979. (Photo courtesy of Tony Marshall)

a nip in the air," Taylor recalls. "Another night shoot, and there was Betsy Palmer, standing on the shore of 'Crystal Lake,' getting into character while waiting for a shot to be set-up. She was so funny! Wearing her now famous Mrs. Voorhees baggy sweater, and literally growling, getting her voice down into a lower register and pacing along the lake, 'physicalizing' her character's maniacal energy, and at the same time carrying on a perfectly normal conversation with me, only saying whatever she said in a low, scary growl. It was hilarious, given her glamorous 'blonde Betsy Palmer' image, and she was really having fun with the whole thing. It was definitely surreal and I just loved her."

CHAPTER 7

WEEK TWO: FINDING MRS. VOORHEES

"When my agent urged me to make Friday the 13th, I asked him, 'Are you sure Bette Davis and Joan Crawford launched their comebacks in these kinds of films?' He assured me they did. I did such horrible things in that movie, killing all of those kids."

– Betsy Palmer

The first week of filming on *Friday the 13th* ran efficiently, raising the confidence level of the cast and crew that this project might have more worth than was first apparent. The spectacular execution of the arrow-through-the-throat effect was a revelation to everyone. It convinced Sean Cunningham that Tom Savini could deliver all of the effects that were listed in the shooting script. Not that Cunningham had any doubts about Savini, but the death scenes in the shooting script had never been realized in a film before.

Although the weather in Blairstown cooled off noticeably by the end of the second week, the frosty, inclement weather – which cast a pall over the entire production – didn't arrive in full force until well into the third week. Then it attacked the campsite with a vengeance.

The barn in which Barry and Claudette are killed at the beginning of the film. (Photo courtesy of Brett McBean www.brettmcbean.com)

The biggest event that occurred during the second week of filming, and which had the biggest impact on both the film and the recollections of the cast and crew, was the securing of an actress for the role of Pamela Voorhees. By this time, the cast and crew had shot as many scenes as they could without having an actress physically present. With the casting of Pamela Voorhees still unresolved, the morale of the crew began to sag. Sean Cunningham was under tremendous pressure to immediately find an actress and get her to the campsite before the production reached a standstill. So, Cunningham left the set of *Friday the 13th* for a brief period in order to settle the matter.

BARRY AND CLAUDETTE (AND MARIANNE)

For the most part, the filming of *Friday the 13th* stuck very close to the 85 page shooting script the cast and crew were given prior to the start of filming. One glaring exception was the filming of the opening pre-credit sequence where the characters of Barry and Claudette are murdered.

Originally, the sequence – set in 1958 – was supposed to develop and climax in the forest area of Camp No-Be-Bo-Sco, but the eventual filming of this sequence departed radically from the shooting script, and was shot in the upstairs landing of the campsite's barn area. The reasons and the circumstances surrounding this decision are a deep mystery within *Friday the 13th*'s production history.

Besides the switch in filming locations, there are a number of other little differences. First, the shooting script contains a header which identifies the location as "Camp Crystal Lake" as well as the date identified as July 4, 1958. In the film, the title reads "Camp Crystal Lake 1958" with no mention of the July 4th date.

In the film, the camp counselors (who are denoted in the shooting script as "Counselors in Training") are sitting around a campfire, singing the folk song *Tom Dooley* whereas the shooting script features lyrics ("The River is Wide, I cannot cross over...") from the folk song *The Water is Wide*. Both

Willie Adams and Debra S. Hayes became romantically-involved during their short time working together in Blairstown. (Photo courtesy of Barry Abrams)

songs had previously been made famous by the American folk and pop music group The Kingston Trio who'd enjoyed hits with *Tom Dooley* and *The Water is Wide* (recorded as *The River is Wide*) in 1958 and 1961, respectively.

Willie Adams, who played Barry, was a young New York actor excited about making his film debut. Like many young actors, Adam was energetic, and enthusiastic and willing to do anything for an opportunity. Adams' stay was scheduled to be for the day of filming that had been allotted for the filming of the opening sequence, two days at the most.

Debra S. Hayes, from New Jersey, who played Claudette, was also scheduled to only be on location for a day or two. The rest of the camp counselors in the opening campfire scene were extras culled from the Blairstown area.

Aside from the characters of Barry (named after cinematographer Barry Abrams) and Claudette, one other role was cast for the opening sequence: the part of Marianne. She's another camp counselor that Claudette references in the film ("Does Marianne kiss as good as I do?") but is never seen.

In the shooting script, Marianne appears after Barry and Claudette are murdered in the forest and her horrified expression is seen as she makes the gruesome discovery.

In an earlier draft of the script this character had been named "Chloe". She had been a virtual extra until a rewrite turned her into Marianne who ends up, in the shooting script, searching for Barry and Claudette in the forest. The earlier drafts of the script also featured a sequence where the unseen Pamela Voorhees gets into a struggle with Barry during which her ring finger is severed.

The Barry character was named after cinematographer Barry Abrams. Willie Adams was originally hired just to play the role of Barry in the opening, but Adams asked the crew if he could stay on in Blairstown as a production assistant. (Photo courtesy of Barry Abrams)

The shooting script deleted the severed finger but did include a sequence where a childlike voice cries "Help me, help me" over the track, a device later used when the character Brenda goes out into rain and, after hearing the childlike voice, is killed in front of the camp's archery range.

When Sean Cunningham and Steve Miner decided to move the opening sequence from the forest to the barn, the Marianne character was excised from the film, as Cunningham and Miner eventually decided to re-imagine the entire opening sequence.

Cunningham and Miner both claim that the changing of the opening sequence, and the switching in locations from the forest to the barn, had to do with inclement weather. Since the freezing conditions didn't, according to the memories of the cast and crew, really become a problem until later on, this probably had more to do with the unpredictable bouts of rainy weather that visited the campsite.

There was also the matter of the creaky, unreliable generator that acted up throughout filming. "Originally, we had planned to shoot that scene in quite a different way," Cunningham said. "It was written to occur by the lake, on the campgrounds. There was to be a chase through a boathouse and by the water, and a few other things. The first night we had planned to shoot it, it snowed. The second time, our

Claudette's death scene was filmed but omitted from the completed film largely due to the massive amount of blood present during the scene's filming which Sean Cunningham felt made the scene un-releasable. (Photo courtesy of Richard Feury)

generator failed. So, we had to choose a location that had its own current source, which turned out to be the interior of a barn. Working on a limited budget, there wasn't much choice other than doing it that way."

"We were forced to choose the barn out of necessity, because that was the one location we could think of that had its own power source," Miner says. "We really didn't have a choice because of the limited budget we had. It would've been a great scene. I liked the scene we did, but the original sequence would've been very exciting."

Since the cast and crew didn't have to deal with snow, or frost, until the third week of filming, this suggests that either Cunningham is mistaken, or that the sequence was filmed at the end of the filming schedule which isn't likely given the timeline of events that took place at the campsite.

"I recall that it rained that night and that's the reason the scene was moved into the barn, and not so much the cold," Cecelia Verardi says. "I think they could've filmed that scene around the cold, but it rained so much that they felt that they had to move the scene into the barn so the production wouldn't fall behind schedule."

Sean Cunningham originally intended the boatshed to serve as a backdrop for the pre-credit sequence with Barry and Claudette. The deaths of Barry and Claudette were originally supposed to take place in the forest. (Photo courtesy of Brett McBean www.brettmcbean.com)

Although Willie Adams was only supposed to act in *Friday the 13th*, he eventually stayed on location throughout the bulk of filming as a production assistant, a testament to his charming personality. Adams had auditioned for one of the main roles in the film – for the roles of Bill and Jack – before being given the role of Barry. "Willie Adams was very playful, very young, fanciful, an aspiring actor from New York," recalls Cecelia Verardi who served as a production assistant alongside Adams during the filming and who also assisted with the makeup effects for the scene in the barn. "He

had a small role in the film, but he was so in love with being on the set that he offered his services, offered to do anything, and the crew all knew him and liked him and decided to keep him on as a production assistant. He came in from New York."

Contrary to previous recollections stating Adams and Hayes had been a real-life boyfriend and girlfriend prior to filming, it now appears that the romance that sparked between them during their brief time at the campsite location was much more the kind of short-term spontaneous fling that's commonplace on film sets. "I do remember that Willie and Debra actually hooked-up, according to Willie," Tad Page recalls. "Willie bragged to the rest of us that he'd scored with her."

"I did meet Debra and I remember that she was brought in from New Jersey," Cecelia Verardi recalls. "I don't think she and Willie had known each other but they hit it off right away, and they both stayed at the motel with the rest of us, but Debra wasn't with us for very long."

The barn scene acts as an homage to the opening sequence in John Carpenter's *Halloween* which, in turn, was an homage to the opening sequence in the Orson Welles' film *Touch of Evil* (1958), as well as, to a lesser degree, the horror film *Black Christmas*.

The opening sequences in those films contained elaborate tracking shots where the camera served as the point-of-view of the killer. With *Halloween*, Carpenter had taken the technique one step further by employing the Panaglide, Panavision's newly-minted version of the Steadicam, and by executing the sequence in what appears to be one continuous shot, although, in fact, it does contain several cleverly-concealed cuts.

For *Friday the 13th*, copying *Halloween*'s opening scene was a practical impossibility. Although filmed in Panavision, *Friday the 13th* had no access to a Steadicam much less the hallowed Panaglide that *Halloween* utilized.

Cunningham's idea was to adopt *Halloween*'s point-of-view motif, positioning the camera to double as *Friday the 13th*'s killer throughout much of the film. Cunningham figured that a gritty, handheld style of shooting would make the technique in *Friday the 13th* seem somewhat fresh and not so much a direct replica of *Halloween*. "I don't recall us ever using a Steadicam on the film, and certainly not a Panaglide, given what a low budget film this was," Tad Page says. "The prowler shots were mostly hand-held shots that were carried out by Braden Lutz."

The scene where the camera tracks in on Barry and Claudette as they attempt to have sex was done with a handheld camera, aided by some clever use of lighting in the background. As was often the case during filming, camera operator Braden Lutz represented the killer that a terrified Barry and Claudette eventually cower from in the remainder of the scene. "Braden Lutz and Tad Page really made that scene work with the way they were able to move the camera and adjust the lighting simultaneously while we shot the scene, especially since the scene moves from darkness into the light of the barn," Barry Abrams recalled. "The Steadicam was still fairly new when we did *Friday the 13th*, and we didn't have any money for a big lighting package, and we generally used very small lights throughout the filming. It helped that Braden Lutz was a big, strong guy who could move so well with the camera."

In the film, the pre-credit sequence concludes with Barry stabbed and Claudette killed off-screen, as indicated by the white light that flashes over her face before the credits roll, an effect created in post-production.

The original plan was for Claudette's throat to be sliced with a machete and to spurt blood, not far removed from Annie's death scene. Although the effect for this version was created and staged, it proved unworkable. For his part, Tom Savini would later claim that he wasn't present for this effect, but merely applied the machete to Debra S. Hayes' throat. It now appears that Savini was present, especially since he was the only person on the set qualified to do the blood effect for the scene. "Tom was there and he did the blood effect for that scene," recalls Cecelia Verardi, Savini's makeup assistant. "It was very gory. The girl's neck was covered with blood and there was blood all over the floor of the barn when Tom did the effect. I don't know why the blood scene wasn't used in the film. It might've been because Tom wasn't able to control the blood as much as he wanted to. There was a pool of blood."

What now emerges is that Savini's blood effect simply wasn't filmed properly, and there was too much blood present for the scene to be restaged. The shooting script's description of Barry and Clau-

dette's deaths was, unlike some of the other deaths in the film, very non-specific in terms of gory detail, describing Barry as being killed with the blow of a hunting knife, and Claudette being killed by a hatchet. "My memory is vague but it seems to me there was a lot of blood in that scene that just wound up on the floor, or in their clothing, and just wasn't recorded," Savini recalls. "My most vivid memory is applying the machete to the girl's throat and watching her scream her head off, which she did very well."

COMIC RELIEF: OFFICER DORF

Aside from *Friday the 13th*'s lakeside setting, and certain other tonal elements, the character Officer Dorf, played by Ron Millkie, represents the clearest homage to the film *Last House on the Left*, which featured two bumbling cops in the form of a Deputy (Martin Kove) and a Sheriff (Marshall Anker).

Although Officer Dorf was played in the film by actor Ron Millkie, the person riding Dorf's motorcycle was Robert Tramontin, who ran a Harley Davidson dealership in Hope, New Jersey and provided the police motorcycle that was used in the scene. (Photo courtesy of Harvey Fenton)

In *Last House on the Left*, the two characters serve as a comedic intercut; a lighthearted counterpoint to the savage violence that occupies every inch of the rest of that film. In *Friday the 13th*, the Officer Dorf character is introduced before most of the film's carnage takes place.

Many critics felt the scenes in *Last House on the Left* served to undermine the rest of the film's chilling impact, a belief also held by Wes Craven and Sean Cunningham who, today, both disown this use of comedic relief in that film.

In *Friday the 13th*, however, the introduction of Officer Dorf – a character who was created, on the urging of Philip Scuderi, by writer Ron Kurz - has a much different effect. The character represents the last authority figure that the would-be camp counselors see before they're murdered. Dorf, bumbling and silly as he is, is the last vestige of safety and security in *Friday the 13th* before the film is overwhelmed by complete isolation.

The path that Officer Dorf rode down in the film. (Photo courtesy of Brett McBean www.brettmcbean.com)

When Ron Millkie arrived at the Camp No-Be-Bo-Sco filming location, he was immediately introduced to Kevin Bacon, Laurie Bartram, Harry Crosby, Mark Nelson and Jeannine Taylor, all of the cast members who appeared with Millkie in his first scene. Adrienne King was absent, the Alice character not present in this scene. "I arrived in Blairstown and I read with the kids – Harry, Jeannine, all of them," Millkie recalls. "I rehearsed my scene with Harry and the kids and then we shot the scene. One time, I remember that Harry walked up to me and said that he was 'unduly impressed' with my performance and we shook hands."

In the scene, Dorf arrives at the campsite and is confronted by Bill, Brenda, Jack, Marcie and Ned who gawk at his motorbike and Dorf's ultra-seriousness. "Kevin grabbed the bike in the scene, improvising, and I told him to get his hands off the bike, and to get away, something like that, also improvising," Millkie recalls. "I think Sean had told Kevin to improvise something in that scene, which Kevin was very good at, and so he hovered around my bike and grabbed the bike. When Kevin was hovering around the bike, I could tell that he was a very strong actor because he had a powerful presence."

Millkie, a SAG member, ended up spending two days on the film under this agreement. "I shared a room with Harry at the truck-stop motel," Millkie recalls. "I also had dinner with Harry and

The *Friday the 13th* cast members were rarely all together at the same time during filming due to varying work schedules. (Photo courtesy of Harvey Fenton)

the kids at a local diner, although I don't remember Adrienne King being there. I picked-up that there was a bit of distance between Adrienne and the rest of the kids who were all great kids. I remember that Kevin had a girlfriend with him."

The motorbike that Dorf rides in the scene wasn't the property of the Blairstown Police Department, but belonged to a man named Robert Tramontin who operated a Harley Davidson dealership in nearby Hope, New Jersey. "I was contacted by the director, Sean Cunningham, and special effects artist Tom Savini at my Harley Davidson dealership in Hope, New Jersey," Tramontin recalls. "They needed a police motorcycle for a scene in the picture that they were working on in the local area. I have supplied motorcycles for movie companies in the past so I agreed. After delivering the motorcycle on set, I guess the director discovered that the actor who played Officer Dorf did not know how to ride a motorcycle. As I was, and still am, a holder of a SAG card from previous work, they asked if I would drive the bike as a double. I again agreed. The scene was where Officer Dorf rides down a washed-out road to question the campers. I was supposed to ride the bike down the road, stop and then they cut to the actor getting off the bike."

It was Robert Tramontin and not Millkie who rode the motorbike in the scene, especially in the sequence where Dorf awkwardly pulls away from the campsite and almost wipes out completely. "I weighed about 195 pounds at the time and Ron Millkie probably weighed 160 pounds at the time, so the continuity is off a bit," says Tramontin who didn't receive screen credit for his work on the film. "Then, after his dialogue, he got on the bike and was

This shot of Officer Dorf and Sgt. Tierney standing on the shore was taken without Adrienne King being present. (Photo courtesy of Richard Feury)

warned by one of the campers to be careful because the road was in such bad shape. Officer Dorf disregards that and then I get back on the bike and do a slight doughnut on the bike and go up the road and drop the bike as if to have an accident, then look back at the campers, kick the bike, like it was the bike's fault that I crashed, then pick up the bike and ride away. The crash part was later edited out of the movie so all you see is me driving after I do the doughnut."

"One thing I remember is that we shot the Dorf cop scene differently than the final cut where he just rides off after inquiring about them smoking pot," Tad Page says. "We shot it with him falling off the motorcycle as he departed and either Mark or Kevin said something like: 'Big chief, bust'em ass.'"

According to Tramontin, the bike used in the film was a brand new 1980 Harley. "When my father first saw the movie, he gave me hell for using a brand new Harley to do a crash scene," Tramontin recalls. "I don't think anybody has noticed what he immediately saw. In 1980, all new Harley Davidson motorcycles came with a small red and white decal on the speedometer (instructions on brake in speed). He picked it out! Although no damage was done to the bike, I still caught hell. All in all, it was a great experience, and for a low budget horror movie that was probably not going to do much, it really set the mark. I still see Ron Millkie now and then. We are good friends. He and I are very proud to be part of this cinema experience."

During his short stay, Milkie also filmed the scene where Dorf and Sgt. Tierney (played by Ronn Carroll) wave from shore at Alice as she drifts in a canoe. "I spent one day in front of the camp for the scene on the bike, and then I spent one day shooting at the lake for the final lake scene," Millkie recalls, echoing the memory of Carroll who also recalls standing on the shore and staring out at the lake, pretending to see actress Adrienne King who was, in fact, nowhere in sight when Carroll and Millkie shot this scene. "I just looked out at the water and pretended that there was someone out there. I don't think I'd even seen the entire script, so I had no idea what was going to happen in the film. After that I said goodbye to Harry and the rest of the kids, shook hands, and then a bus driver took me away from the camp and dropped me off at a bus station, and that was it."

EASY TARGET

During their time at Carnegie-Mellon, Savini and Stavrakis liked to don capes and engage in mock swordfights in between their studies. Savini's skill with a bow-and-arrow came in handy during the filming of *Friday the 13th* for the scene where the character of Laurie is standing in front of the archery range, putting a dummy target in place, and an arrow whizzes by, just missing her.

In the film, the arrow was fired by Ned, but it was actually Savini. "I fired the arrow that just misses her in the scene, and it wasn't difficult because I was good with a bow," Savini says. "I was very careful, and there was no danger of Laurie [Laurie Bartram] getting hurt, but she was pretty spooked when the arrow went right by her."

Although actress Laurie Bartram developed a bond with Savini, the stunned reaction on her face wasn't acting. While it might appear in the film that the arrow was fired from a comfortable distance, the reality is that Savini was right near Bartram and the dummy target when the ar-

Tom Savini was in close proximity, just out of the camera frame, when he fired the arrow that whizzes by Laurie Bartram in the film. (Photo courtesy of Henri Guibaud)

row was fired. "Tom just moved forward and fired the arrow when he was about six inches away from Laurie," Robert Shulman recalls. "He was close enough so that he was just out of sight of the camera. It wasn't the way stunts are usually done."

Kevin Bacon, Harry Crosby, Adrienne King and Mark Nelson were also present for this. "The actors would come and go throughout filming, but they were all there for the scene at the ar-

The archery range where Ned pulled a prank on Brenda, and where Brenda was later killed in the film, still stands today. (Photo courtesy of Tony Urban www.tonyurbanphotography.com)

The archery range scene between Brenda and Ned served to establish Ned's practical joker persona. (Photo courtesy of Henri Guibaud)

chery range with Laurie," Cecelia Verardi recalls. "Tom just fired the arrow, and even though it wasn't supposed to be done like that, he just did it."

Savini's technical competence and precision earned the admiration and respect of the cast and crew alike, no more so than Bartram, with whom Savini enjoyed a trusting, warm relationship throughout filming. "I had a crush on Laurie and she spent time with me in the little cabin at the camp, though she stayed at the hotel with the other actors," Savini says of his time with Bartram who died of pancreatic cancer in 2007 at the age of 49. "We watched movies on the Beta machine I had there, and she spoke a lot about being a born again Christian. I thought she was gorgeous."

THE MANY FACES OF PAMELA VOORHEES

As filming on *Friday the 13th* approached the midway point in the filming schedule, some members of the cast and crew were told that actress Louise Lasser was going to play the role of Pamela Voorhees. Lasser had been one of the candidates back in New York. Now she seemed to be the favorite. Not for long. "Louise Lasser was the actress that we thought was coming to play the part," Robert Topol recalls. "Sean had three or four names and he just went down the list, and he either got rejected, or they wanted too much money, and he just went down the list and checked every name that he could think of."

When the casting of Louise Lasser failed to materialize, Cunningham still didn't turn his immediate focus to Betsy Palmer. Instead, Cunningham, in consultation with Barry Moss in New York, turned his focus back

to Academy Award winner Dorothy Malone.

To this end, Cunningham, very much aware that the crew's morale was starting to ebb, left Blairstown for a day and drove upstate to meet with Malone in person. "Morale was very low before Betsy arrived," Richard Berger recalls. "Sean left the location and went upstate – either to New York or to Montreal in Canada – to meet with actress Dorothy Malone about playing Pamela Voorhees."

Whatever happened during Cunningham's meeting with Malone, it was obvious to the *Friday the 13th* crew, upon Cunningham's return, that Cunningham's meeting with Malone hadn't gone well. "When Sean came back, he looked discouraged," Berger recalls. "Sean said that Dorothy Malone 'didn't look

Before securing Betsy Palmer for the Pamela Voorhees role, Sean Cunningham left Blairstown to meet with Dorothy Malone. (Photo courtesy of Jason Pepin)

very good' and was 'too old to play the part.' Not that Sean needed a beautiful woman to play the part, but Sean said there was no way she could do it, based on whatever he saw. Then Sean called Betsy Palmer."

Betsy Palmer wasn't aware of any of this as she was driving back to her Connecticut home. She had recently wrapped an eighteen month stint on Broadway in a production of *Same Time, Next Year*. It was during this drive home that Palmer's

Mercedes broke down, a twist of fate that served as a major catalyst for Palmer's involvement with *Friday the 13th*. "I'd had that car for many years, and could never get it fixed properly, but it had always served me well, gotten me where I needed to go, until that night," Palmer recalls. "I got home at five in the morning, and was in a situation where I desperately needed to buy another car. If I hadn't needed a car, I don't think I would've done *Friday the 13th*."

Curiously, Victor Miller recalls that he and Cunningham met with Palmer in Connecticut right near the start of *Friday the 13th*'s filming, and that she had effectively been cast and hired by Cunningham prior to Miller's lone visit to Blairstown (for the filming of Kevin Bacon's death scene). "Filming had started when we visited Betsy Palmer," Miller recalls. "She lived twenty minutes away and so we had a chat with her and as far as I knew that was it. I never heard Louise Lasser's name at the time or Dorothy Malone's but I do remember quite well that Sean said he had Estelle Parsons but when the filming [*Friday the 13th*'s filming] got thrown back, she had to drop out because of a previous commitment. That is what Sean told me at the time and hence the trip to grab Betsy. She [Palmer] was not on location when I visited. She had been hired before that when Sean and I visited her at her home in Connecticut."

Since Palmer had been a candidate in New York, and lived in Connecticut, it would've been entirely practical for Cunningham to have met with Palmer at any time during pre-production and even during breaks in filming, without committing to giving Palmer the part. Miller insists that Palmer was virtually hired by Cunningham very early in *Friday the 13th*'s production schedule. "I would be guessing, but I do know that it [Palmer's hiring] was before they took off for New Jersey," Miller recalls. "Before any shooting in New Jersey at all."

Although Palmer had a very sparse recent filmography, the then 52 year old actress had enjoyed an illustrious career and life that had seen her cross paths with such show business luminaries as Joan Crawford, James Dean ("We [Dean and Palmer] had an eight month fling," Palmer says), Henry Fonda, Jack Lemmon, and on. She was, like Dorothy Malone and the other candidates, an older actress with a pedigree, the 1960s and 1970s, as mentioned, being the era where older actresses on the down-

side of opportunity were appearing in exploitation and horror films, most notably Joan Crawford who'd made a second career out of this. "Betsy was kind of like the Katie Couric or Jane Pauley of her time, so it was very unconventional casting," Cunningham says. "It was a gamble, especially since she hadn't done a movie in a long time, but it paid off and she clicked in the role almost immediately."

The baggy sweater that Betsy Palmer wears in the film was given to Palmer by costume designer Caron Coplan for the sole purpose of keeping Palmer warm. (Photo courtesy of Richard Feury)

Palmer was a light actress and nothing she'd done before had remotely prepared her – or audiences - for her introduction to the horror genre and to *Friday the 13th*. "My agent called and asked me if I wanted to do a horror movie," Palmer recalls. "A horror movie? I couldn't believe it. I was a light actress, a nice old lady. No one had heard the term 'slasher' before *Friday the 13th* so I had no idea what kind of movie this was until my agent sent me the script to read. I read the script and thought it was a real piece of shit. My agent told me that the producers were offering $1000 a day for ten days, and so I figured I could do the job quickly, get in and get out, and then be able to pay for my new car. I also figured that no one would see the movie. It was a job. Eventually it became more than just a job, but not much more."

Ever the professional, Palmer studied the *Friday the 13th* script her agent sent her and went about creating a character profile for Pamela Voorhees that centered on the birth of Jason Voorhees and his eventual drowning in 1957. "Being an actress who uses the Stanislavsky method, I always try to find details about my character," says Palmer who used the proceeds from her role in *Friday the 13th* to buy a Volkswagen Scirocco. "With Pamela, oddly enough, I began with a class ring that I remember reading in the script that she'd worn. Starting with that, I traced Pamela back to my own high school days back in the early 1940s. So it's 1944, a very conservative time, and Pamela has a steady boyfriend. They have sex – which is very bad of course – and Pamela soon gets pregnant with Jason. The father takes off and when Pamela tells her parents, they disown her because having pre-marital sex, and having babies out of wedlock, isn't something that good girls do."

From a psychological standpoint, and in the context of the horror genre, Palmer envisioned Pamela Voorhees as being the single mother from hell. "I think that she took Jason and raised him the best she could, but he turned out to be a very strange boy," Palmer says. "Anyway, I imagined her taking lots of odd jobs and one of those jobs was as a cook at a summer camp. Then Jason drowns and her whole world collapses. What were the counselors doing instead of watching Jason? They were having sex, which is the way that she got into

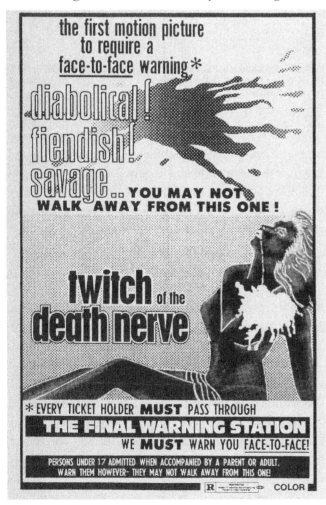

Script supervisor Martin Kitrosser, a Mario Bava fan, felt that parts of *Friday the 13th* were derivative of the Bava film *Twitch of the Death Nerve*. (Photo courtesy of Troy Howarth)

trouble. From that point on, Pamela became very psychotic and puritanical in her attitudes as she was determined to kill all of the immoral camp counselors. The two camp counselors who get killed at the start of *Friday the 13th* were having sex."

Like Barry Abrams, and some of the other *Friday the 13th* crew members, Palmer was offered a profit sharing deal in lieu of her salary, but she wasn't interested in that, and so the $10,000 salary that Palmer received for *Friday the 13th* effectively bought out this profit sharing deal.

With this deal in place, Palmer, who recalls staying at a motel with Adrienne King and some of the other cast members during her work on *Friday the 13th*, approached this most unsavory job with all of the enthusiasm she could muster. "Summer was gone and it was very frosty and there was snow," Palmer recalls of her trip to Camp No-Be-Bo-Sco. "I drove to the campsite and the first thing I saw was the 'Welcome to Camp Crystal Lake' sign which put me in a good frame of mind."

Whatever Palmer's feelings were about the *Friday the 13th* script, the actress brought energy and enthusiasm to the campsite. She immediately embraced the cast and crew, all of whom were won over by her personality and sense of humor that belied the deranged villainess she'd been recruited to play in the film.

"Betsy brought history, professionalism, a name to the film," James Bekiaris says. "The rest of us were just a bunch of kids. Betsy had been convinced that this role would help her career. I remember this steely look she was able to project in her performance which was quite a contrast to her own sweet personality. We all knew that Louise Lasser had been the first choice, but I don't think Betsy ever heard about Louise Lasser."

"Betsy saved the film with her energy and her performance," Richard Berger says. "When she arrived, she was bright and bubbly, like she was on her game show appearances. Betsy baked brownies for the cast and crew during filming. She saved the production from collapsing with her spark. The first day she arrived, she took some of us out for Chinese food. I remember that because that was when Steve Miner asked Barry Abrams if 'There were any good restaurants around here?' and Barry just laughed and shook his head and said, 'There's nothing decent between here and New York City.'"

"The Pamela Voorhees character was, to me, all about insanity and madness, and I wasn't sure, at first, whether Betsy could do that, because she'd never played a role like that in her career," Cunningham says. "I wasn't sure if Betsy could handle it, but she proved to be uncanny at showing the madness of the character. Once I knew we had the acting down for that part, it was just a question of whether Betsy could handle all of the stunts that we were going to put her through."

"Betsy was down to earth, had a sense of humor, and wasn't demanding, unlike others," Virginia Field recalls. "She was easy to work with. There's a scene in the film where Adrienne and Betsy are fighting in the main cabin and I'd built a table to put in the living room and was worried that Adrienne and Betsy would break it. I said to Betsy, 'You break the table, it's yours,' jokingly, and I probably shouldn't have said that, but Betsy wasn't bothered about that or anything. She was a real pro and could laugh at anything."

"Before Betsy Palmer showed up, we'd been passing around the yellow raincoat, having different people play the killer in the film, so it was a relief to finally have an actress play the part," Richard Murphy says. "Betsy was a nice person and Sean and Steve were smart with the casting of Betsy and with all of the elements in the film but especially Betsy."

"We didn't know who Betsy was," Tad Page says. "I think we knew her from a game show that she'd been on but that was it. She was a lot of fun and a very sweet lady."

"The only person I ever acted in the film with was Adrienne King, and I don't recall meeting any of the other actors," Palmer says. "I stayed at the motel where the actors stayed, and I was right next door to Adrienne King. There was no hairdresser, nothing like that. I met with Tom Savini who was a wonderful guy and then Tom showed me a picture of Jason, who was a mongoloid. I couldn't believe it. I asked Tom who that was and Tom smiled and said, 'That's your son, Jason. He's a mongoloid.' It was very scary. I also spent time with Taso [Stavrakis], another great guy, and I was aware, prior to filming my scenes, that Taso had played the killer in a lot of the previous scenes."

Hallmark Releasing distributed *Twitch of the Death* (AKA *A Bay of Blood, Bay of Blood*) in 1972 under the title *Carnage*. (Photo courtesy of David A. Szulkin)

"*Friday the 13th* was my first movie and Betsy Palmer was like a mother figure to me on that film," Denise Pinckley says. "She was a very sweet, funny woman and she was very kind and supportive to me as I was trying to do my job."

"Betsy Palmer was the only name that anyone recognized," David Platt says. "Betsy had a deal with the producers where they had her for one week, a certain period of time. She had a history, she was experienced, and she had a body of work. She was very sweet."

"They were looking for Betsy a long time," Robert Shulman recalls. "By that time, we'd shot all of the scenes with different people playing the prowler, different-sized prowlers. They'd looked at ten similar actresses before they cast Betsy. This was the era of Joan Crawford and Bette Davis in terms of old stars with name value doing B movies and horror movies."

"In our shop at the camp, Betsy would often come and hang-out to chat, telling us stories of her illustrious career," Taso Stavrakis recalls.

"Betsy, myself, and Tom spent a lot of time together and I don't think Betsy was prepared for all of the makeup work she was going to go through, but she had fun with it, and never complained."

"There was subtle fanfare on the set when Betsy arrived," Cecelia Verardi recalls. "Some of the younger people didn't really know who she was. We welcomed her and she welcomed us, and she was very pleasant. She also did her own hair in the film. I didn't do her hair."

"They gave me nothing; no hair, wardrobe, just that baggy sweater," Palmer says. "It was a lousy acting job, but then I've always loved the stage and hated film. Film is too rushed. Hurry up, do this, go here. I hate that. The one thing that made *Friday the 13th* a happy experience was how nice everyone was to me. I also thought Sean was a very good director. One of the first things Sean said to me was that he didn't want there to be any overacting in the film. I think *The Shining* came out the following year, with Jack Nicholson who was really over the top with his performance, and Sean wouldn't allow any of that. He wanted madness and intensity."

"Jack Nicholson was born over-the-top, but it's very risky for unknown actors, and Betsy wasn't very well known as a movie actress, to go over-the-top," Cunningham says. "I thought her performance would be great if Betsy just acted pretty much like herself, nice and sweet, and that the madness would come out through the dialogue."

Betsy Palmer's arrival in Blairstown meant that Braden Lutz and other crew members no longer had to don the role of the film's killer, although since *Friday the 13th* featured the killer's point-of-view in many scenes, Lutz continued to don the killer's identity in this capacity. Having Palmer on location made the rest of filming go much smoother. The killer finally had a face.

Palmer's voice was especially useful for the filming of Brenda's death scene. In the scene, Brenda is drawn out of her cabin by a childlike voice that cries "Help me" through the rain. Brenda eventually follows the voice to the archery range where she's killed off-screen.

Cunningham thought about having his son, Noel, provide the childlike voice for the scene, or using Barry Abrams' son, Jesse, who was also on location. It was a surprise when Palmer volunteered to supply the voice and proceeded to mimic a childlike cry right in front of Cunningham and the crew, as a rough audition for what was Palmer's first scene in the film, even though she's never visible during the sequence. "I'd done *Peter Pan* on the stage, and I was pretty good at doing different voices, especially children," Palmer says. "That was my voice."

Palmer's voice was recorded "live" and wasn't augmented in post-production. Palmer also interacted with Laurie Bartram, who was doused with a fire-hose throughout the scene's filming. "I worked with that girl, Laurie, in that scene, and I watched her walk around because they wanted my voice to match," Palmer recalls. "She was a very pretty girl, very nice."

One can only speculate as to how Louise Lasser or Dorothy Malone or the other candidates would've reacted to the trying and unusual circumstances that Palmer encountered during her time in Blairstown, or how the film's direction would've been forever altered.

That was history. What might've been.

The real Pamela Voorhees had arrived.

THE GHOST OF MARIO BAVA

As is often mentioned, *Friday the 13th* was born out of the successful model that *Halloween* established, while Sean Cunningham and Steve Miner also adopted the lakeside milieu, as well as the shock filmmaking techniques, culled from their experience of filming *Last House on the Left*. Since *Friday the 13th*'s commercial release in 1980, many critics and fans have also suggested that *Friday the 13th* borrows heavily from another film, the 1971 Italian horror film *Twitch of the Death Nerve* (AKA *A Bay of Blood*, *Bay of Blood*, *Carnage*).

Directed by Mario Bava, who died on April 25, 1980, just weeks before *Friday the 13th*'s theatrical release, *Twitch of the Death Nerve* is set at a bayside location. It follows several duplicitous, greedy characters who will stop at nothing, including gruesome murder, to get their hands on priceless bayside property left behind by a murdered countess.

Although the specter of bizarre, gruesome murders – of which *Twitch of the Death Nerve*, a pro-

Sean Cunningham claims he'd never seen the 1971 Mario Bava horror film *Twitch of the Death Nerve* (AKA *A Bay of Blood, Bay of Blood*) prior to the filming of *Friday the 13th*. (Photo courtesy of Troy Howarth)

genitor of the slasher film genre, is full of — taking place at a bayside setting suggests some inspiration on the part of the makers of *Friday the 13th*, this is disputed. Most Bava experts feel the comparisons between the films are overblown, and that there are few stylistic similarities between the films.

In fact, most Bava experts cite *Friday the 13th Part 2* (1981) as being a much more direct rip-off of *Twitch of the Death Nerve*, citing two murder scenes in *Friday the 13th Part 2* in particular – the double-impalement of a couple making love and a wheelchair bound character having a machete slammed into his skull – as being direct copies of scenes from Bava's film.

"In all honesty, I think the similarities have been overblown," says Troy Howarth, author of the book *The Haunted World of Mario Bava*. "Yes, there are similarities, but to suggest *Friday* is a carbon copy of Bava's film is ludicrous. Bava's film is dark comedy. *Friday the 13th* is a dead serious slasher film. If anything, I think it [*Friday the 13th*] borrows more, in terms of inspiration, from Carpenter's *Halloween*, which really brought the slasher film into its own. Also, it's worth nothing that Sean Cunningham has

denied seeing the film prior to making *Friday*, and while he may be skirting the truth in that, I simply don't see enough concrete similarities to suggest that he was trying to rip-off Bava's picture."

"The murders in *Friday the 13th* were not patterned on those in *Twitch*, but were designed by [Tom] Savini with the stage trickery approach to makeup effects he had mastered," says Tim Lucas, a Bava scholar and the author of the eponymous book *Mario Bava: All the Colors of the Dark*. "What the two films have specifically in common is setting their horrific murder scenes in contrast with a beautiful lakeside view. In *Twitch*, the cast kill each other off in order to clear the path to its ownership. Human greed was one of Bava's main themes. *Friday the 13th* replaces this with a more common revenge story, mixed with campfire story tropes, which I believe was the real reason behind its success."

"The lakeside setting and the sweater Betsy Palmer wears [which is similar to the outfit that Claudio Volonte wears in *Twitch*] are similar, and the basic setup of a killer dispatching a group of horny teens...but there again, Carpenter's film was a more direct model," Troy Howarth says. "Also, Bob Clark's *Black Christmas*, to a degree. If anything, I see more obvious cribbing in *Friday the 13th Part 2*, with the skewering of the two teens making love."

"I don't see *Friday the 13th* as a failure to reproduce Bava's stylistic effects, but as a failure to do anything original," Tim Lucas says. "When I look back over my own lifetime as a critic, I see *Jaws* as the movie that changed Hollywood and *Friday the 13th* as the movie that changed horror – both for the worse. *Friday the 13th* had the good fortune of savvy timing; it came out just as a new generation of young people started exploring horror. I saw *Friday the 13th* as pretty common stuff, built around a thin story consisting of every cliché in the book, but these clichés were new to people and they ate it up like popcorn. I don't see any style in *Friday the 13th*."

"To my mind, Cunningham is a blunt, functional filmmaker," Troy Howarth says. "I don't see a lot of stylistic flair in *Friday the 13th*, to be honest, and I truthfully prefer some of the sequels. Bava's film is darkly-funny and filtered through his ironic sensibility. Bava was also not what I would term to be a moralist as a storyteller. His point-of-view was more wry and detached. It is easier to read *Friday the 13th* as a conservative piece than it would be to see Bava's film that way, though, truthfully, I think Carpenter unwittingly set that game in motion with *Halloween*, and I don't believe he and Debra Hill intended for *Halloween* to be seen that way."

Most Bava scholars believe that *Friday the 13th Part 2* contains more similarities to *Twitch of the Death Nerve* than does *Friday the 13th*. (Photo courtesy of Peter Stein)

"The first *Friday* doesn't overtly copy any one film, but it's certainly part of an evolving sequence of horror hits," explains Stephen Thrower, author of the book *Nightmare USA: The Untold Story of the Exploitation Independents*. "The mystery killer/body count aspect was already established thanks to *Halloween*, although *The Toolbox Murders* and *Black Christmas* deserve mention as precursors too. You could say that all *Friday the 13th* did was to take the idea of a rural murder spree from *The Texas Chainsaw Massacre*, relocate it to the leafy Northern States, and replace Tobe Hooper's bickering hippies with *Halloween*'s high school pot-smokers!"

Were the members of the *Friday the 13th* production team aware of Bava's work when they started work on *Friday the 13th*? Were they, even subconsciously, influenced by Bava's film? The most direct connection has to do with Hallmark Releasing who distributed *Twitch of the Death Nerve* in 1972 under the title *Carnage*. In addition, Stephen Minasian claims to have met Mario Bava "sometime in the late 1960s or early 1970s," during Minasian's many European travels during that time period.

"Remember, these guys [Robert Barsamian, Stephen Minasian, Philip Scuderi] were theater owners and distributors of films, and they had experience handling some European movies that had strong violent content back in the 1970s," says author and film historian David A. Szulkin. "Hence the borrowing from *Twitch of the Death Nerve*. It's not that Sean Cun-

ningham was 'influenced' by Mario Bava. I doubt Sean even knew who that was at that time he made those movies. Nobody gave a shit about those Euro films back then, really, and Sean just isn't the type of guy to be sitting around stroking his chin and admiring Mario Bava's mise-en-scene. The guys from Boston probably suggested certain scenes because they remembered seeing those setups in the films they released. I think Phil Scuderi was ahead of his time in exploiting movies that revolved around graphic violence. He saw that market before the studios did. It took the success of *Halloween* and *Friday the 13th* to make that sort of thing bankable in Hollywood."

Sean Cunningham claims that he first discovered Mario Bava's work while at a film festival in the mid 1980s, after which he became an ardent fan. Steve Miner pleads ignorance, as do writers Victor Miller and Ron Kurz who don't recall having had any discussions about Bava's film, or work, much less even knowing who Bava was in 1979. Tom Savini says he hadn't seen *Twitch of the Death Nerve* prior to working on *Friday the 13th*, although Savini has, like Cunningham, become a big fan of Bava's films in the years that have followed the making of *Friday the 13th*.

At this point, the matter would end were it not for Martin Kitrosser, a longtime associate of Philip Scuderi's who was the script supervisor on *Friday the 13th*. Kitrosser was already a big fan of Bava's work, and it was Kitrosser – a later genre filmmaker who's best known for being filmmaker Quentin Tarantino's longtime script supervisor – who noticed striking similarities between *Friday the 13th* and *Twitch of the Death Nerve* during the filming in Blairstown. He sensed that *Friday the 13th* was directly-inspired by – and directly-imitating – the teens-in-the-woods section of *Twitch of the Death Nerve*.

Kitrosser was so sure that *Friday the 13th* was a copy of *Twitch of the Death Nerve* that he suggested to Sean Cunningham and Philip Scuderi that they dedicate *Friday the 13th* to Bava. This request, obviously, was rejected by Scuderi who felt that the dedication would underline *Friday the 13th*'s debt to Bava's film. The depth of Kitrosser's love for Bava is evidenced by the fact that Kitrosser - who later co-wrote the script for *Friday the 13th Part 3* (1982) – named his own son Mario Bava Kitrosser.

CHAPTER 8

WEEK THREE: CAMP BLOOD CHRONICLES

"*There were anti-Semitic beavers at Camp Crystal Lake.*"

– Barry Abrams

The third week of filming on *Friday the 13th* was marked by freezing conditions that swept over the campsite filming location. Toward the end of the third week, temperatures ranged from between twenty-five and 35 degrees, a far cry from the comfortable 70-75 degree conditions that existed at the start of filming.

As mentioned, Betsy Palmer's arrival at the campsite revitalized *Friday the 13th's* cast and crew and bolstered everyone's confidence in the project.

In contrast to this was the arrival of Robert Barsamian, Stephen Minasian, Philip Scuderi, the three partners of Georgetown Productions who came to monitor the filming and their investment. This was greeted with much less enthusiasm.

Up to this point, Alvin Geiler (b. August 29, 1917 – d. November 25, 1996), a long-time associate of Scuderi and his partners, had been keeping tabs on Sean Cunningham and the progress of filming. Geiler watched the purse-strings, watched Cunningham and signed the checks that were distributed to the cast and crew.

When his partners left the campsite, Scuderi stayed on through to the end of principal filming. In particular, he wanted to witness the filming of the climactic lake scene which he felt was the key element to *Friday the 13th's* success.

The main cabin. (Photo courtesy of Brett McBean www.brettmcbean.com)

THE MEN IN BLACK

Philip Scuderi's arrival in Blairstown, along with Georgetown Productions partners Robert Barsamian and Stephen Minasian, was disarming and uncomfortable for the cast and crew, especially Sean Cunningham and Steve Miner whose relationship with the Boston trio was always strained.

"They were the men in black from Boston," Betsy Palmer recalls with a laugh. "There were three of them and they wore black hats and they looked like they were mafia hit-men. They would just stand around and watch everything, and we didn't know who they were, and we were told not to speak to them. Eventually, we found out that they were the money men who financed the film."

"They were the hats and suits from Boston," Robert Topol recalls. "We'd see them around; making sure that their money was being well-spent. We all knew to stay away from them and not to try and talk to them."

Cunningham's deal with Georgetown Productions called for him to receive twenty-five percent of the profits from *Friday the 13th*, along with any related properties. Obviously this turned out to be several sequels, a remake, books, games, even the syndicated television series *Friday the 13th: The Series* which aired from 1987 to 1990.

Steve Miner also has an ownership stake in the film, something that writers Ron Kurz and Victor Miller – both, technically, co-creators of *Friday the 13th* – do not.

Cunningham and Miner had a surprising amount of control and leverage over *Friday the 13th*, including financial matters. In fact, it was Scuderi and his partners who were more worried about the profit-sharing deal on *Friday the 13th* than Cunningham and Miner, who felt they couldn't trust the Boston investors. Creatively, Cunningham and Miner triumphed, for the most part, with the lake scene being one of the few elements that Cunningham would acquiesce to Philip Scuderi's suggestions.

The business acumen that Cunningham and Miner displayed on *Friday the 13th* far surpasses anything they would achieve on a filmmaking lev-

Barry Abrams in Blairstown. (Photo courtesy of Tony Marshall)

el. Miner, in particular, was so adept with the cold, mechanical business aspects, and had such a calm, laid-back personality, that no one on the crew, not even Cunningham, envisioned he was destined for a successful directing career, both in feature films and episodic television. "Steve Miner was very minor," Virginia Field says with a laugh. "He was a businessman and he wasn't that involved with the making of the film itself. I had no idea at all that he was a hidden director, and a very good director, as it turned out. I didn't get to know Steve very well on the films we worked on together."

Although Scuderi and his partners supplied the bulk of the money to make *Friday the 13th*, Cunningham's deal gave him final say on all business and creative decisions, including how, and to whom, the film would eventually be sold. As such, Scuderi and his partners had to reckon with Cunningham at every level of the process; they could stonewall Cunningham, in terms of withdrawing money, but they couldn't ignore him.

"I was well-paid for my work on *Friday the 13th*, and when I wrote *Friday the 13th Part 2*, I actually had a percent profit contract with Georgetown which was estimated to be worth three million dollars!" Ron Kurz recalls. "I never got a penny of it (I was well-paid though while working on it). Georgetown said Paramount should pay. Para-mount said it was Georgetown's responsibility. Lawyers I had got nowhere. Ah, the movie business."

"They [the Boston investors] were only preoccupied with financial matters and were always around the set during the filming of *Here Come the Tigers* and *Friday the 13th*," Richard Murphy recalls. "Sean had total creative control of the film and there was no way the Boston guys had any say over Sean and the way he made the film. Sean had all of the leverage. He was the producer and director and had his own money in the film, and didn't really need them. He had lots of leverage over the Boston guys. The story we heard was that the Boston investors were really nervous that Sean would sell the movie to someone else, like what George A. Romero had done with *Night of the Living Dead*, and they wanted as big of a piece of the film as they could get because they felt that this was something that was going to be a big hit. They were very deferential to Sean on the set, but they were always around."

"I think they [the Boston investors] had a big creative influence," David A. Szulkin says. "They were putting up the money so they had a say in the movies Sean made. It's my opinion that they suggested a lot of the gags (the gore scenes) in the *Friday the 13th* movies. I got the impression, from talking to various people involved in the movies, that Phil [Scuderi] was the creative force. Steve [Stephen Mi-

The Van Dusen cabin served as the main cabin in *Friday the 13th* and the home for the film's strip monopoly scene. (Photo courtesy of Tony Urban www.tonyurbanphotography.com)

nasian] also contributed creatively to the movies he produced but my impression is that Phil was the main man, an outgoing, bigger-than-life sort of guy. Steve prefers to 'remain behind the scenes.'(his words)"

As when they operated under the Hallmark Releasing banner, Georgetown Productions were notorious for bouncing checks and missing payments, a result of the volatile nature of their weakening theater chain. One story that gained traction over the years, regarding the filming of *Friday the 13th*, is that Georgetown was delinquent with their payments to Cunningham during production. Allegedly, Cunningham ran out of money at some point, and the cast and crew went without paychecks during the production schedule, and threatened to quit from the film as a result.

There's also been the suggestion that the profit sharing deal that Cunningham and Miner had approached Barry Abrams, Betsy Palmer, and some of the other crew members with, in lieu of salary, was a direct result of the wobbly, unreliable cash flow that Cunningham received via Boston.

The fact is, there were no missed paychecks during filming. The cast and crew were paid on a weekly basis and none of the crew members, save for still photographer Richard Feury, recall any disruption in the payment process. There was, however, a great deal of nervousness amongst the cast and crew as to whether said checks and paystubs would be valid once they left the wilderness of Camp No-Be-Bo-Sco. "I was in a car with Barry Abrams and Richard Murphy after we'd just gotten paid," David Platt recalls. "We all looked at each other nervously and figured we'd better race to the bank and cash the checks given what a cheap shoestring production this was."

A close-up shot of the fireplace. (Photo courtesy of Brett McBean www. brettmcbean.com)

As mentioned, Cunningham was, is, very personable and unflappable, and had a tremendous ability to not let pressures affect him or to sour the people around him. "It sounds so low-rent, but it wasn't like they'd [Philip Scuderi and his partners] write a check and the money would be in the bank," Cunningham said. "They would say they would write a check and then they wouldn't, and then it wouldn't arrive, and then you can't make payrolls and you're trying to pay the laboratories and stuff like that. They were theater owners, and cash would come in on the weekends, and they would have a limited number of places where they could spend the money. It was the squeaky wheel thing. There was a lot going on. Every week it was always a battle. You had to fight so hard just to pay the bills, which is a fight that was completely separate from how hard it is to make any movie, even when you have the money."

Steve Miner was very much like Cunningham in terms of having an outwardly positive approach and maintaining an ability to compartmentalize the onset of difficult circumstances. In their dealings with Philip Scuderi, and associates, Cunningham and Miner took any disputes they had indoors, away from the cast and crew. "There were a lot of discussions that went on behind closed doors, when the Boston guys showed up, and that's the way Sean and Steve were when there were any problems," David Platt says. "Sean and Steve had a very close and supportive relationship. When something bad or serious needed to be discussed, they went behind closed doors."

"Whenever morale was low, like when we were waiting around for Betsy Palmer to arrive, Sean would sense that and would create an upbeat mood," Richard Berger recalls. "One day at lunch, Sean looked at me and said that I reminded him of Warren Beatty, because Warren Beatty wore glasses in those days and I guess Sean thought I looked like him. I don't know how much I looked like Warren Beatty, but hearing that from Sean did a lot for my confidence."

"It was such a cheap, skimpy production in every regard but Sean and Steve had a great love of film and I think that carried them through," Caron Coplan says. "Steve Miner was a neighbor of mine in Connecticut and I remember that, before we started on *Friday the 13th*, he was all excited about doing this movie. He'd point at a piece of wood outside his house and say, 'Let's paint some wood. Let's build a set.' In the end, they sold their rights to Paramount and became millionaires off the film. The rest of us got nothing."

"There was a production office at the camp and Sean and Steve had a friend from Connecticut who handled the payroll," Richard Murphy recalls. "It wasn't a great deal of money. I think I made 600 bucks a week, and I'm sure the rest of the guys on the crew got the same, except for Barry and Braden."

"Sean and Steve were like partners in crime in terms of how they ran things and worked in tandem," Tad Page says. "When Sean wouldn't give us bologna for sandwiches, that was probably a sign that the movie was in trouble, but we never knew how much pressure Sean was under because Sean never let on that there were any problems. I was paid 700 dollars a week and never went unpaid, although I wish I'd taken a piece of the movie instead."

"It was a very hardworking, no-nonsense cast and crew," Jeannine Taylor recalls. "There were no squabbles, power struggles or ridiculous egos. Not that I ever witnessed. Just a lot of genuine enthusiasm and a sort of fly-by-the-seat-of-your-pants, can-do spirit that emanated from Sean, to Barry and Steve, and to everyone on the set. People really had a good time on that shoot. Everybody did their job, no one took themselves too seriously, and there were a lot of laughs."

"We got weekly checks," Robert Topol says. "Not much money. I recall a flat weekly salary which ranged, on the crew, from 150 to 750 dollars a week. Sean always kept a positive attitude. Barry, Sean, Steve, Virginia were a tight-knit group and they had the type of relationship where they could say anything to each other. The most surprising thing about Sean, given the kinds of films he made in his career, was how much he would talk about character and story, which he did over and over again."

"We were paid every week," Cecelia Verardi says. "I don't recall any problems or threats or work stoppages."

The Mechanic's Lodge doubled as Alice's cabin in the film. (Photo courtesy of Tony Urban www.tonyurbanphotography.com)

Harry Crosby and Adrienne King mostly worked with each other during their time in Blairstown. (Photo courtesy of Harvey Fenton)

To the degree that Sean Cunningham was preoccupied with financial pressures on the set of *Friday the 13th*, or pondered the production collapsing completely due to lack of funds, it was something that Cunningham only shared with those close around him, namely his wife, Susan, Steve Miner, and Adrienne King.

"Talented, tenacious, endearing and very protective of his actors," King said of Cunningham. "We worked very well together and he directed with love and creativity, not fear and loathing like some others. He kept a calm set, even though the world was caving-in around him...running out of money! The actors didn't know and he kept it that way. He wanted everyone focused on their roles and characters and Sean was able to offer the right words at the appropriate times."

LET THERE BE LIGHT

Although, *Friday the 13th* was filmed entirely in Panavision, the campsite location presented many photographic and lighting challenges for cinematographer Barry Abrams and his crew who used a very modest lighting package for the film.

Since most of the film takes place at night, amidst a failing generator, lighting scenes became increasingly difficult throughout filming and required a great deal of creativity. "Sean and I spent a lot of time, maybe three days, just talking about the cinematography and the overall look of the film before we started shooting," Abrams recalled. "One of the first things we decided was that we weren't going to use fluorescent lighting. Not having the budget for a big lighting unit, we wanted to establish a narrow contrast range so as to not lose any contrast in the lighting. We wanted the film to have a dark, grainy look and for the camera to see what the characters in the film see."

Abrams and his crew basically used only what was required, and what their miniscule budget would allow. "Panavision was the only way to go on a movie like this, in terms of the range and scope it gave you, and the Panaflex cameras had greatly evolved by the time we did *Friday the 13th*," Abrams said. "In terms of the lighting, we used what we needed. HMIs {Hydrargyrum medium arc iodide} had just come in so we used Tungsten Lighting for the film and we especially made great use of little Mole-Richardson lights. I think most of the lights we used in the film were between 650 and 2000 watts. The biggest light we ever used in the film was maybe 5000 watts."

"We had a small amount of equipment," James Bekiaris recalls. "There were no HMIs, all Tungsten lighting. Heavy units. Small generator at the camp. We'd always be carrying cables all over the camp. There was no rigging of the lights, nothing like that, and no pre-lighting so we just had to get it all done. We would hide lights behind columns, on open rafters, and the lights we used in the

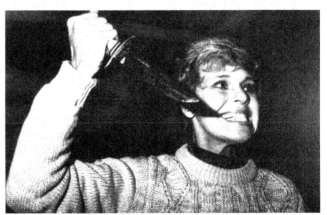

Betsy Palmer's arrival in Blairstown revitalized the production. (Photo courtesy of Harvey Fenton)

cabins were very small units. One thing we tried to do in the film was to create a bluish 'bounce' level of ambience for certain scenes in the film. Barry and Sean really had their act together on the film. There was no indecision. They had vision."

"Barry's creative vision was instrumental to the film's success, especially since he didn't have much to work with," Sean Cunningham says. "Barry had a lot of creative finesse and he used that to solve problems. I remember that he would often improvise many of the lighting sequences in the film, often using very basic, simple techniques."

"Our package was primarily made up of the Mole-Richardson lights," Tad Page recalls. "We didn't have any HMI lights on board. They were available at the time but were outside of our budgetary constraints. Our biggest lights were MR (again, Mole-Richardson) 'Ten-ers' or 'Ten Ks' which is slang for 10000 watt Fresnel lights (with Tungsten bulbs) and 'Seniors' AKA 'Five Ks' (5000 watts). For daylight requirements I remember using MR 'Mighties' gelled with full blue and bounced into four by eight foam core. We also carried four by four silver reflectors known as 'Shiny Boards.' Rain (effect) was the complicating factor on *Friday the 13th*, and there was much melting plastic and hazardous electrical conditions. Don't remember any scene being too difficult to light but keeping everyone safe from electrocution proved the most challenging. I'm talking about night shots here, primarily."

The lighting and photography in *Friday the 13th* is so cleverly-concealed that there doesn't appear to be any technique at all. The most impressive example of this is in the scenes that take place in the main cabin, especially in the nighttime scenes where

Nighttime shot of "Steve Christy's diner" as it appears today. (Photo courtesy of Dean A. Orewiler/Dean A. Orewiler Portrait Art)

the generator is "down" and the cabin is illuminated only by a lantern or fire from a fireplace. "When we shot the strip monopoly scene, I was in the clubhouse, watching from the other room and we lit that with tiny units," Abrams recalled. "We did a wide shot for that scene so what we did was that we put lights all along the bottom of the walls which allowed the actors to move through the cabin, right past the lights. The main challenge with the filming of every scene was to make sure the shots were in focus. When the lens is wide open for a scene, the depth of field falls so the focus has to be good. When I saw the movie for the first time, the first thing I was looking for was to see that it was in focus and I was very relieved that the film was 99 percent in focus throughout."

"Our exteriors on the job were quite simple, relatively speaking," Tad Page recalls. "Where supplemental lighting was required, we used full blue-gelled Tungsten lights to balance to daylight and dichroic nine light fays. Of course, twelve by twelve silks, 'blacks' and 'nets' and four by four shiny boards to manipulate everyday light. Four by eight white foam core (for bounce) was a staple as well. Barry Abrams was not a big fan of hard light for interiors when shooting close in on people. Hard lights were used to bring effects (sun, street lights, moon) in through the windows or through an interior doorway to suggest lights being on in another room. Face and foreground area lighting was generally accomplished with soft lights like egg-crated 2k zip lights, 1K baby softs and bounce light setups like a twenty-four by 36 white show card or four by four white foam core with a Mickey or Mighty into it. We hung a lot of lights on this job. The cabins at the camp lent themselves to that with open rafters and a rustic construction that allowed the liberal use of nails, tape and clamps. We used under-light on the walls and put lights behind the couch which saved the cost of and use of rigging lights."

"Probably the most inventive camera trick we used on *Friday the 13th* was in the scene where Steve Christy's in the diner," Abrams said. "We painted the windows with green gel for that scene and that was one scene in the film where you do see the use of fluorescent light."

"Barry's work on *Friday the 13th*, his style, was gritty and scary," Max Kalmanowicz says. "Not

The interior of the diner that Steve Christy visits in the film. Barry Abrams covered the windows with green gel for the filming of the scene between Steve Christy and Sandy. (Photo courtesy of Dean A. Orewiler/ Dean A. Orewiler Portrait Art)

pretty. There's nothing pretty about the film, not even the grass, or the trees. Barry's photography generates a feeling of malaise in the film that was very effective and very suited to the material."

"That (the lighting in the diner} would have been to color-balance the Tungsten light that we punched through the windows from outside the diner to the fluorescent light inside the diner," Tad Page says. "Barry was the DP so he designed the lighting for every scene in the film. Barry was a big fan of the super soft shadowless lighting that came into vogue back then. Lots of bounce light and a LoCon one or two on the lens was the formula. Beyond that, the locations dictated the look."

The filming of Steve Christy's death scene was a unique challenge in that the scene required a deft mixture of handheld photography and lighting. As mentioned, one of *Friday the 13th*'s visual signatures was the film's use of the handheld "prowler" shots and this motif was especially necessary in this scene since the shooting script called for Steve Christy to be killed off-screen.

In the scene, Steve Christy approaches the camera while simultaneously being blinded by light that flashes in front of his eyes. The off-screen killer in this scene was played by – who else? – Braden Lutz. Abrams, Cunningham and Lutz decided that the off-screen death would be an effective counterpoint to the rest of the gory sequences in the film. As such, the scene was filmed with Peter Brouwer approaching Lutz and then shrieking backwards from the camera as he simulates the effect of being stabbed.

One of the most inventive camera tricks in the film involved the later reveal of Steve Christy's

upside-down corpse, hanging from a tree. This shot was taken by Brouwer himself while he hung from a bar in a gazebo. "I actually was hung from a bar in a gazebo," recalls Brouwer. "I let go of a handheld camera and just swung right into frame."

THE SOUND OF VIOLENCE

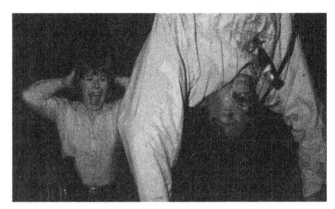

Alice screams at the sight of Steve Christy's corpse. This particular sequence was filmed in and around a gazebo with actor Peter Brouwer hanging upside down into the camera frame. (Photo courtesy of Richard Feury)

The bountiful wilderness backdrop surrounding Camp No-Be-Bo-Sco provided for many interesting opportunities for sound recording -- as highlighted by Annie's death scene which was set against an orchestra of bird sounds and snapping twigs. It was also the setting for some peculiar misadventures.

Steve Miner developed a nightly ritual where he would go down to the lake and go fishing around the dock area. Miner was particularly obsessed about tracking down a bass that constantly eluded him. "Steve Miner would go fishing down at the lake every night," Daniel Mahon recalls. "One night, I went down there and saw him hunting this bass that was around the dock and he just couldn't get it, and it was driving him crazy. So I took a rod and threw it out and got it on the first try. Steve just went crazy about that. We let the bass go."

Barry Abrams had a traumatic experience at the lake when he went down to urinate. While there, Abrams was attacked by an aggressive beaver who tried to grab for his genitals. "I was taking a leak down at the lake and the beaver appeared out of nowhere and snapped at my privates," Abrams recalled. "I tried to move away from him, but he wouldn't go away and he just kept snapping at me. I got out of there right away and told the guys up at the camp that there was this 'fucking anti-Semitic beaver' down at the lake."

The rest of the cast and crew preferred to stay inside during off-hours, especially when the nights grew increasingly chilly and rainy. One other exception was soundman Richard Murphy, who would often go out into the woods at night in search of distinct noises that could be used in the film.

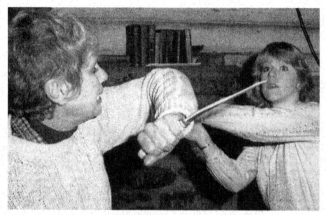

The fight scenes between Adrienne King and Betsy Palmer were choreographed by Tom Savini. (Photo courtesy of Harvey Fenton)

As with the cinematography and lighting, the sound on *Friday the 13th* was accomplished with a very inexpensive and modest sound equipment package. "We didn't have enough knowledge and we didn't have enough equipment when we did the film," recalls Murphy. "We mainly used a shotgun ['shotgun' microphones which are attached to the camera] for the film's sound, and we also used KM-81 microphones and I believe we also used Tram Lavaliers [Tram Lavalier microphones]. We used Nagra tapes [audio tapes] for the sound, which were quarter inch tapes, and that was our basic package. We had three mikes for the whole shoot, and there were no radio mikes. Basically, I spent most of the film running shotgun and pointing at people throughout filming."

Like the rest of the New York-based crew, Murphy was a city slicker, uncomfortable in the wilderness. "I went into the woods in the dark, with a mike and tape deck, to record some animals," Murphy recalls. "I was in the woods, smoking a joint, a city rat from Brooklyn who didn't know anything about the woods. I had a chair and I sat there for five, six minutes and it was very quiet, and you could hear every little noise, every branch, every

movement, and because we were doing this slasher movie about kids getting killed, I really started freaking out and scared myself with the headset I was wearing. I started hearing branches. Steve Miner laughed at how out of place I was and wanted to get a picture of me out in the woods, which he did."

As mentioned, Sean Cunningham's wife, Susan, was present throughout filming. She had an editing bay at the campsite where she edited the film. Murphy worked in tandem with her to match the sound effects. "Susan was there to edit the film while Steve Miner, who was supposed to edit the film, produced the film," Murphy recalls. "Susan would tell me what they needed in terms of sound effects for any given scene and I would do my best to get what she wanted."

HOLD THE BOLOGNA

Sean Cunningham entered the filming of *Friday the 13th* with the burden of life and financial pressures. Although outwardly calm and relaxed towards the cast and crew, the pressures he faced manifested in various ways, most notably in the cheap, frugal way the *Friday the 13th* production operated.

A prime example of this was how the cast and crew were, or sometimes weren't, fed on location. Jean Zipser, a nearby resident, now deceased, was hired to provide craft service at the campsite, but quickly grew frustrated and embarrassed at the lack of resources she was given. "Sean was very cheap," Tad Page recalls. "He was a terror on the set, in that regard, and we had to fight to get dinner and we had to fight to even get bologna for our sandwiches. Sean had a schedule and he cracked the whip to get the job done. Of course, we didn't know, at the time, just how much pressure Sean was under."

"Were we eating filet mignon or drinking champagne? Obviously, no," Richard Murphy says. "At the same time, we were all just happy to be learning how to make a movie."

"Sean was very cheap on the set in Blairstown," Robert Shulman recalls. "Jean Zipser ran the craft table, and Sean gave her ten cents a day

Betsy Palmer's slapping of Adrienne King during filming caused some animosity between the two actresses. (Photo courtesy of Harvey Fenton)

for food, and she couldn't do anything with it. It got to the point where she didn't want to face us after awhile, and she was near tears, because she was so embarrassed that she couldn't feed us."

"We mostly had cold-cuts," Robert Topol recalls with a laugh. "It wasn't much but the cast and crew would eat together, for the most part, and the rough conditions brought us closer together."

ADRIENNE AND BETSY

Betsy Palmer's first week at the campsite was spent with Sean Cunningham and Adrienne King, filming her character's scenes with Alice. But she also spent a good amount of time in Tom Savini's makeup chair to prepare for the film's decapitation sequence in which Alice chops off Pamela Voorhees' head with a knife.

Palmer's wardrobe consisted of a baggy sweater given to her by wardrobe designer Caron Coplan. "They gave me the baggy sweater to wear in the film to make me look bulkier and more physically-imposing, even though I'm only five-foot-seven," says Palmer. "I also wore long underwear for the scenes to make me look stronger, but I kept thinking, 'Who the hell am I going to scare?' When we started filming my scenes, I think I was still getting over the shock that I'd been cast in a horror movie."

According to Caron Coplan, the now infamous baggy sweater wasn't a stylistic touch but rather a matter of necessity given the freezing conditions that greeted Palmer's presence at the campsite. "I provided the clothes for all of the actors in the film, including Betsy, and I got all of the wardrobe from Canal Jeans on Broadway, and Cheap Jack's, or from my closet," says Coplan. "I brought a Mexican peasant blouse which one of the girls wears early in the film as a sweatshirt. The baggy sweater came from one of those places and I gave it to Betsy because it was so cold and we had to keep her warm. There was no other reason. It had nothing to do with Betsy being a small woman, or looking skinny, because I remember that she was fairly tall and strong-looking. At that point in the filming, there was a lot of night shooting, and it was bitterly-cold,

A shot of Alice as she discovers Annie's corpse in Pamela Voorhees' jeep. The actual reveal of Annie's corpse was shot separately. (Photo courtesy of Richard Feury)

and the rainy nights were brutal and unpredictable for the filming. The season was changing."

Palmer's relationship with King during filming contained rough edges right from their first meeting and was compounded by the bruising, physical scenes they filmed together. Except for the scene where Pamela Voorhees tells Alice about Jason and the camp's history, all of the scenes between King and Palmer placed the two women in close quarters combat, with King mostly on the receiving end.

One of the first of their scenes filmed was where Pamela Voorhees discovers Alice hiding in a storage closet, after which Alice strikes Pamela in the head with a frying pan. When the scene was filmed, the rubber frying pan lost stiffness and flopped over. This was a bad omen.

The scene where Pamela slaps Alice around in a storage cabin (also known as the "rifle range shack" or as Steve Christy's office in previous script versions) was especially contentious with Palmer hitting King a bit too hard for King's liking. "I think it was in the shack when she has the rifle pointed at me and then I slap her around," Palmer recalls.

"Well, from the stage, you're taught to really punch except that you pull the punches and hit an imaginary mark. I said to Adrienne, 'Come on, Adrienne, let's do it. Let's go all out for this.' So I really started smacking her and then I smacked her really hard and she fell to the ground. Then she yelled, 'Sean, Sean' and Sean had to run over and console her. After that, we did it the fake way. Sean told me he was going to add the sound effect of me hitting her, but I don't think he ever did. I think he just told me that so I wouldn't hit her for real anymore."

Savini, with input from Taso Stavrakis, planned and staged the scene on the beach where Alice and Pamela grapple and Pamela slams Alice's head into the sand. Once again, King found Palmer too rough in this regard and let her feelings be known to Cunningham. "I was like, 'Okay, the gloves are coming off,'" King recalled. "It was a serious physical challenge. I wound up battered and bruised, but I felt a new level of acting was achieved."

"You don't hit in movies," Cunningham says with a laugh. "That was a concern. Betsy hadn't done a film in a long time and I was worried whether or not she could still act effectively on screen. She did great, but you don't hit the actors."

The decapitation sequence was in the shooting script, but described in a way that gave Cunningham the option of filming the sequence as a cutaway effect in the event that Tom Savini wasn't able to deliver the real thing. Savini, anxious to duplicate the excitement generated after the skillful execution of Kevin Bacon's death scene, was determined to engineer a memorable decapitation.

Savini and Stavrakis created a mold of Betsy Palmer's head, her facial features posed in a screaming, terrified maw. Palmer's mold, like all of the other molds Savini created for the film, was baked to readiness in the cafeteria oven.

Once Savini had a suitable mold of Palmer's head, it was off to the beach which was so cold the sand felt like cement. "When we were filming on the beach, it was so cold that I put ice in my mouth to prevent the cold air from appearing on camera," Palmer recalls. "I would've died of pneumonia if it hadn't been for the baggy sweater I had on. We were standing on the beach, and then Taso and Tom walked over to me and said,

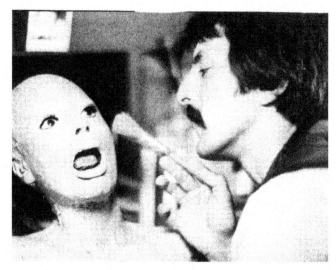

Tom Savini works on Pamela Voorhees' "head" in preparation for the film's decapitation sequence. (Photo courtesy of Tom Savini)

'Hey, Betsy, do you want to watch yourself get decapitated?' or something like that. I was shocked."

Unlike her strained, though short-lived, relationship with King, Palmer developed great affection for both Savini and Stavrakis, and vice versa. Palmer represented the old guard of show business and Savini the cutting edge extreme of low budget horror filmmaking. "I'm very flattered when people tell me how much they love my performance in the film, and when they refer to me as the star of *Friday the 13th*, but I think the real star of the film is Tom Savini," Palmer says. "Tom was so sweet and funny and very talented. He kept talking about how Dick Smith was his favorite makeup artist and how much he wanted to be like him. One time, Tom had to leave the set to go have a meeting with Dick Smith. When he came back, he was so happy because Dick Smith had liked his work. Tom was so happy."

"Tom's such a genius that my temptation was to go over-the-top with the gore effects," Cunningham says. "We could've easily had lots more effects in the film, but I thought that would've been overkill because once you've shocked the audience, they can get numb. I was able to balance this during the editing process when I could be more objective. I also knew that the film couldn't end with the decapitation. It had to have that big shock, the jump-out-of-your seat shock, like Magic Mountain."

"We really got away with that decapitation scene," King said. "The way it was done with slow-motion was almost like a ballet. I know it's bizarre to look at a decapitation scene that way, but I think everybody involved in that first *Friday* probably looks back on it a little differently. There had not been too many slasher films made at that time, so there was a real sense of innocence involved in making that one."

"The scene [the decapitation] was in the script, but, again, Tom just amazed us with his imagination," Miner says. "The decapitation appeared on-screen in the most powerful and visceral way possible."

The filming of the decapitation sequence was somewhat of a social event on the set of *Friday the 13th*. Everyone gathered down on the beach to watch, including casting director Barry Moss, who had just arrived in Blairstown. Like with Kevin Bacon's death scene, the execution was basic in theory but required a lot of dexterity and timing on the part of Savini and Stavrakis.

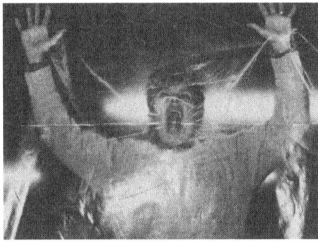

This shot was taken in Camp No-Be-Bo-Sco's cafeteria and shows Betsy Palmer playing for the camera, pressed against a plastic sheet. This shot was taken by still photographer Richard Feury and was later published in *Time* magazine. (Photo courtesy of Richard Feury)

For the effect's filming, the mold of Palmer's head was attached to a mounted body cast. Palmer's hands – the hands that reflex after the head falls off the body – belonged to Stavrakis. The blade that sweeps through the frame was swung by Savini. "After she gets decapitated, she raises her hands in the air, in a death reflex, and you can see the hairy knuckles," Savini says. "That's because Taso was wearing a head and shoulder piece of Betsy Palmer which was placed on his back. The head was already severed and it was held in place by toothpicks. All that was left was for me to swing the blade hard enough so that it separated the head from its position. We had to over-crank the camera so the whole thing would play in slow-motion. We were lucky that the head ended up spinning in the air like it did."

STRIP MONOPOLY

Although cast members Laurie Bartram, Harry Crosby and Adrienne King improvised much of the Strip Monopoly scene, it was created by Victor Miller, who continued making script contributions beyond the start of filming. "I was working on the script after the start of filming and you'd better believe I wrote that scene," says Miller. "Sean felt he needed a humorous scene like that in order to lighten the mood in between the kills and that's what I came up with."

"The strip Monopoly pages were added and given to Laurie, Harry and me the day before the night we were shooting it," King recalled. "A lot of the stuff we did was improvisation and if it happened, and it worked, it was left in. The scene where Brenda's body [actually Tom Savini's] comes flying through the kitchen window and I react...when my raincoat gets caught in the stove...well...it's not like that was planned. Sean said, 'It's real, it works...that's a take!'"

ADRIENNE AND SEAN

As director and leading lady, Sean Cunningham and Adrienne King were bound together by their respective roles, and the Spartan filming conditions that placed them in close proximity to each other throughout the principal filming schedule, and beyond.

For Cunningham, Friday the 13th was the last stop on the road, while the film marked King's first – and last - starring role in a feature film.

By the time the principal filming schedule of Friday the 13th neared the homestretch, many of the crew members had developed a tepid view of King, related to the perceived favoritism and preferential treatment that they felt Cunningham gave to King.

The crux of the crew's unhappiness was related to how King – who was an artist and photographer but had no known filmmaking experience – would express her ideas and suggestions to Cunningham about how scenes should be photographed and staged.

A paystub from *Friday the 13th*, addressed to key grip Robert Shulman. The check was signed by Alvin Geiler, the only credited executive producer on *Friday the 13th* and a longtime business associate of the Georgetown Productions partners. Alvin Geiler died in 1996 at the age of 79. (Photo courtesy of Robert Shulman)

"There was resentment towards Adrienne, who was very spoiled on the film," Robert Shulman says. "What would happen was that Sean would be choreographing a scene with us, and the two of them would be discussing the scene, and this went on and on."

As filming progressed, Cunningham adopted more and more of King's creative suggestions, much to the chagrin of the grizzled crew, who stood around idly while these discussions took place. "There was one time where we were doing a scene and we were all standing around while Adrienne and Sean talked for ten minutes about how the scene should be filmed," Shulman recalls. "Adrienne would explain the way she thought the scene should be done and would always get her way."

Cunningham and King both vigorously deny that their relationship in Blairstown crossed into personal territory, as many of the crew members suspected during filming, other than the friendship that developed out of their collaboration. Just as Cunningham helped to guide the in-experienced King through the film, King became a sounding board for Cunningham, in terms of the various problems he faced throughout filming.

Cunningham and King remain friends today, both serving the sentence that is Friday the 13th, which has followed them for the rest of their lives, and from which there is no escape.

The making of a movie is a lot like summer camp, in terms of the short-term antics, conflicts and relationships that spark on film sets, and which are usually extinguished once filming has ended and everyone returns to civilization. With the exception of the film itself, what happened in Blairstown definitely stayed in Blairstown..

The Strip Monopoly scene pages were added during production. (Photo courtesy of Henri Guibaud)

Laurie Bartram gets drenched at the archery range during the filming of her character's death scene. Although rain was created for the film, through the use of fire-hoses, it also rained heavily during filming. (Photo courtesy of Barry Abrams)

CHAPTER 9

WEEK FOUR: THE LAKE SCENE

"The lake scene was the last scene we shot in the film and we thought it was going be very easy and straightforward. We thought we'd go down to the lake, get the girl in the canoe and the boy in the water, get the sun just right, and just shoot it. Boy, were we wrong!"

– Barry Abrams

Cast and crew gather for the filming of the dock scene. (Photo courtesy of Cecelia Verardi)

The fourth and final week of principal filming on *Friday the 13th* was a very busy week, dominated by the planning and attempted filming of the climactic lake scene. Expected to be simple and straightforward to film, the scene proved unattainable during *Friday the 13th*'s main filming schedule, at least to Sean Cunningham's liking. It would require several more attempts, over the span of another month, before the scene was successfully completed.

This last week of filming on the production schedule wasn't the end of filming on *Friday the 13th*. Cunningham, along with a skeleton crew, would shoot more insert scenes near his Westport, Connecticut home base that would appear, in bits and pieces, in the finished film.

The end of *Friday the 13th*'s filming in Blairstown was greeted by the arrival of October 1979. It represented the end of a chaotic, fun, wild journey for the cast and crew, who've spent the rest of their lives looking back at their time spent in Blairstown, the film, with a combination of bemusement, nostalgia, and weariness.

A PLACE IN THE SUN

The scene where the camp counselors swim and suntan around the lake was shot during the time when the campsite had turned bitterly cold. The crew members had to brush frost off the dock built by Virginia Field and her design team for the film.

Other than that, the scene represents the last moment in the film where the camp counselors are happy and together in daylight before the film turns increasingly dark and bloody.

The dock scene was filmed towards the end of the production schedule. (Photo courtesy of Cecelia Verardi)

By this time in *Friday the 13th*'s filming, the cast members had formed somewhat of a clique, and cliques in between, even though the filming schedule often had the cast members working separately, and at different times. Like their college-aged characters, the cast members represented a carefree group of young performers who were just happy to be alive, to be making a film, and were full of optimism about the future. The only action that occurs in this otherwise playful scene is when the character Ned fakes a drowning, is pulled out of the water and then given mouth-to mouth resuscitation by Brenda.

Laurie Bartram had used the filming of *Friday the 13th* to make decisions about the future. While Bartram enjoyed her time with the cast and crew at the campsite, she was closest with Harry Crosby and their friendship would continue past the end of filming, back in New York. "We became friends during filming," Crosby says. "It was nothing romantic, and we weren't dating or anything like that. She was a very likable and talented actress and a wonderful person. She was a Christian and when we got back to New York, she took me to a Church in Harlem, which was a very interesting experience. I lost touch with her later on but was very fond of her."

"I remember hearing, or being told, that Laurie was a college athlete," Richard Murphy recalls. "I think that had to do with the scene where she jumped

The daytime scene at the dock was filmed amidst frosty conditions. (Photo courtesy of Harvey Fenton)

into the water and pulled out the guy who was drowning. When she goes out to swim, and you see the killer watching from the bushes, we had to film that at higher and higher angles because there were less and less leaves as the filming went on. We had to blow the frost and snow off the dock for that scene."

"I remember Laurie as being a lovely, smart, generous person," Mark Nelson says. "For the swimming scene, I almost passed out because I had to doggy paddle, tread water, over and over again until they finished filming the scene. When I got out of the water, I felt really sick. The good part was that I got to kiss Laurie."

"She had a tremendous sense of humor, a wry wit as they say, and I'm sorry our paths never crossed again and we lost touch" Tom Savini says. "She was one of the most beautiful women I'd ever seen, certainly on a movie set."

"I didn't know Laurie was religious until I saw her say Grace one day before she ate, which was certainly unusual in our group," Robert Shulman says. "Other than that, it seemed like she had a lot of fun doing the movie."

"She [Laurie Bartram] was grappling with her commitment to her Christian faith, and how to fit this into her life as an actor," Jeannine Taylor recalls. "By the end of the shoot, I felt certain that she'd made up her mind to leave acting and devote herself to living a faith-based life, far away from the entertainment industry. One could see her working

to remake her life into something more spiritual. For instance, she thought that the bathing suit she wore in the scene at the lake was unflattering. (Funny, I thought she looked great). Instead of asking wardrobe to find her something else, she told me, 'Never mind. This is my lesson in humility.' She said this with her usual dry wit, but she also actually meant it. I knew there was something extraordinary about her and I also knew she would choose to leave performing. For that moment in time, we were on the set of a horror movie that was going to be 'picked up' and put into wider release, and be condemned by the Catholic Church and virtually everyone else in authority at the time, or so it would seem. I've often wondered over the years what Laurie must have thought of it all. I was terribly saddened to hear she had passed away. The world lost a very beautiful spirit."

Mark Nelson got sick during the filming of the scene involving Ned's fake drowning. (Photo courtesy of Harvey Fenton)

"One of my many jobs on the film was to stay with the actors and make sure they got from Point A to Point B, and I spent a lot of time with Harry and Laurie, and we became very good friends," Cecelia Verardi says. "I stayed with Harry and Laurie, especially, during the day and made sure they got to where they needed to be. We were working day and night, so there wasn't much free time. Laurie wasn't thrilled about being in the movie, but she was very playful. Seeing her bloody body later on made her have a sense of humor about the whole thing and Laurie had a great sense of humor. Harry was amazing. He was charismatic, spiritual, quiet, but he also made you laugh. Harry doted on Laurie, was very fond of her, but in a very subtle way."

Obviously, Harry Crosby – who recalls being paid $750 dollars, total, for his work in *Friday the 13th* - carried the most prestige amongst the cast members because of his famous last name, while Kevin Bacon had some degree of notoriety from his featured role in the film *Animal House*.

That left Mark Nelson and Jeannine Taylor, who were complete unknowns, along with star Adrienne King.

A romantic subplot involving the characters of Alice and Bill was discarded during the scripting process. (Photo courtesy of Harvey Fenton)

"Harry Crosby got the most attention because of lineage," James Bekiaris recalls. "He was the big name and was regarded as being special on the set. Adrienne was willing to do whatever she had to do. She was attractive, and had a girl next door look that made you care about her. Kevin Bacon was just a young actor."

"Adrienne King was a horrible actress," Richard Berger says. "Harry was a really nice guy. Years later, I met Harry's mother, Kathryn, at a screening of the film *High Society* and I told her that I'd worked with her son on *Friday the 13th*."

"They were a bunch of kids happy to be doing a movie," Virginia Field recalls. "Kevin was fine. Perhaps Harry was a bit spoiled, more than the other actors who were just happy to be alive. Harry was very nice. The kids were friendly. Adrienne was nice but not very interesting."

"Kevin Bacon and Harry Crosby used to pump iron and do push-ups before their shirtless and swimming scenes," Adrienne King recalled. "My fondest memory would probably be when we first started the film and it was still warm and sunny and all of us were together for the first time. We had a great time together; we were all in our twenties and we were all so excited about working together."

"Kevin Bacon had some fame because of *Animal House* and was a lot of fun to be around," Tad Page says. "Adrienne was standoffish, a real straight arrow type. Harry Crosby was a good guy. Laurie Bartram was really straight."

"Kevin was a shy, sweet kid who I thought was seventeen or eighteen years old when we did the film because he looked so young," David Platt says. "Adrienne was a nice, sweet girl who I think overacted a lot and wasn't particularly interesting or talented. Harry was very nice, very unpretentious, very hardworking."

"Adrienne King was usually busy on other parts of the set, and since we really didn't have many scenes together, I unfortunately didn't have much opportunity to get to know her, which was too bad," Jeannine Taylor says. "I remember her as a total pro, with fantastic concentration. I did spend a bit of time talking with Harry Crosby, who had lost his famous Dad not long before. He sometimes shared anecdotes about growing up as the son of Bing Crosby, which was a real treat. I also enjoyed listening to Harry play the guitar, which he played very well. I was curious about everyone and everything at that point, and much more a listener than a talker."

"Kevin was a really good-looking guy and was more confident than the other actors," Robert Topol recalls. "I thought Kevin was very effective in the film. Harry Crosby had a prestigious family name. Mostly, I think the actors were just happy to have jobs in a movie."

"One night, I invited Tom Savini and Harry Crosby over to sample some of New Jersey's sweet corn, which was in season at the time" Robert Tramontin recalls. "We gorged ourselves on so much sweet corn. That became our dinner."

"Adrienne was uncomfortable to be around and a little annoying," Cecelia Verardi says. "You didn't get too close to her, and she didn't get close to the others. She came across as a Connecticut, upper crust type, kind of pampered. Kevin Bacon was somewhat aloof, and was a real boy's boy. Not that he was gay or anything like that, but rather to say that he much preferred to hang-out with the guys instead of the girls. Jeannine was a Connecticut socialite type, upper class girl."

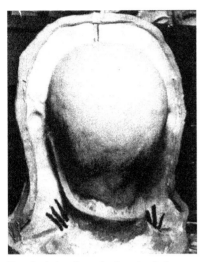

Tom Savini undertook a lengthy design and molding process to create the right look for young Jason. (Photo courtesy of Tom Savini)

MAKING JASON

Although Ari Lehman only recalls spending four days on the set, near the end of the filming schedule, he managed to meet most of the cast members and put in more hard work than any of them, with the possible exception of Adrienne King.

This was a result of the grueling effects work needed to turn Lehman into the monstrous Jason that rises from the lake. Lehman had begun working with Tom Savini and Taso Stavrakis in August of 1979, at Steve Miner's Westport home, and continued through September and then into October. "Yes, that [the filming of the lake scene and Lehman's witnessing of the filming of other scenes] all happened in the few days that I was on the set the last time in the fall to shoot the final scene with Adrienne," Lehman recalls. "In fact, Adrienne even confirmed that she remembered hearing the radio announcer on the Blairstown station saying it was fourteen degrees outside that morning [the morning in which the filming of the lake scene was first attempted]! I was on

the set for a few days that time, and they shot several of the death scenes at that time, including Kevin's and Harry's. I believe that Kevin's was shot first."

Lehman's recollection of witnessing Kevin Bacon's death scene belies the memories of several other crew members who all recall that the scene had been filmed much earlier. This would suggest that Lehman's either mistaken about this, all of these years later, or that certain elements of this scene were reshot towards the end of the filming schedule, a time when Kevin Bacon was definitely still present at the campsite.

In August, Savini and Stavrakis had fashioned a mold of Lehman's head from the makeshift effects cabin in Miner's backyard. With Lehman at the campsite, it was time to finish the job. "I worked with Tom Savini and his assistant, Taso Stavrakis, on and off for four weeks to create the original mold for the face," Lehman recalled. "After that, script additions called for the character to appear water-damaged. I went back to the studio for a few days before we tried it out on the set. Each time, it took around four hours to apply the

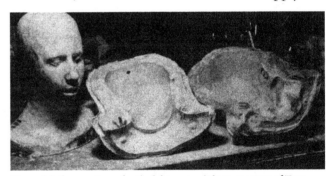

The mold of young Jason for the lake scene. (Photo courtesy of Tom Savini)

makeup, so if there was a 7:30 AM call for cast and crew, we would start applying the mask at 3:30."

Lehman stayed on the campgrounds with Savini, Stavrakis and the rest of the junior crew members, and, as mentioned, spent a lot of time around the twenty-something cast members. Lehman, Savini and Stavrakis were like the Three Musketeers at the campsite as they worked together to bring Jason to life. "Working with Tom Savini and his assistant, Taso Stavrakis, was a blast," Lehman recalled. "We were all living on the campgrounds, which lent a festive air to the production, especially after we were done shooting for the day. Tom and Taso liked to practice stage-fighting with fencing sabers all over

Mongoloid Jason. (Photo courtesy of Tom Savini)

the camp, jumping off tables and swinging on ropes. I had to learn how to defend myself from surprise attacks. We would go canoeing on the lake as well. One time we were out there late at night, dredging up muck from the bottom for the Jason makeup, when we heard a loud sound coming from the wooded shore. 'It's Jason' we joked. We were relieved to see that it was only a big bear, coming to the lake to get a drink."

Lehman's final stay at the campsite was preceded by the filming of Pamela Voorhees' dream sequence in which she envisions a drowning Jason. "We worked for weeks on the first mask, casting the teeth, eye, and head itself," Lehman recalled. "One time, when my entire head was completely covered in plaster, Tom put on Jim Morrison and the Doors' *Strange Days*. It was the first time I heard music like that, and I was impressed...Strange Days,

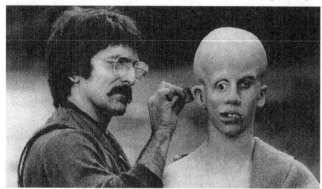

Tom Savini touches-up Ari Lehman's makeup for the filming of the climactic lake scene. (Photo courtesy of Tom Savini)

indeed! After we did the first prosthetic and filmed the drowning scene, a second one was required for the final scene, so I went back to the studio for that one, which was created to look more scary. They wanted Jason to be both repelling and pitiable at the same time, so Tom fashioned a new version which I wore in the final scene. Of course, we also covered the mask and myself in muck and vegetation that Tom asked us to scrape from the bottom

Ari Lehman and Tom Savini had worked together on the Jason design back in Westport, Connecticut, before Lehman travelled to Blairstown to film the lake scene. (Photo courtesy of Tom Savini)

of the Sand Pond the night before. Tom also applied additional latex, which he allowed to dry. When peeled back, it looked like decaying flesh. When everybody was happy with the look, Tom made some deformed false teeth, put a gruesome glass eye over my right eye, and Jason was born!"

While Tom Savini deserves all praise and glory for bringing Jason to visual life, Savini's contention that he created the "monstrous Jason" is undercut by the shooting script which describes Jason - the Jason that rises out of the lake – as a "grotesque form" with a face that's "horribly-bloated, purple, agonized." This description clearly denotes writer Ron Kurz's contribution in regards to the conceptualization of the Jason character, and bolsters Kurz's contention that he scripted Jason as being a monster, working off of Victor Miller's version of Jason who was simply an abnormal, disturbed - but entirely human - kid.

Of course, nowhere in the *Friday the 13th* script was there a reference of Jason being a mongoloid, and the "mongoloid Jason" is a concept that was entirely Savini's. Still, the look of Jason changed and evolved right through the filming schedule. "Doing the makeup itself was very problematic as Jason only became a mongoloid after the original look didn't work very well," Savini says. "In our original design, Jason had lots of hair and then we changed the look to make him have a weird-shaped head and chin. It was my idea. There was no script that had that kind of description, and how could there have been with the tight schedule we were on?"

THE SNAKE MUST DIE

The scene where Alice finds a snake in her cabin wasn't in the shooting script but was suggested by Tom Savini. "I found the snake in my cabin, and I spoke to Sean Cunningham and we decided to create a scene where one of the characters finds the snake," Savini recalls. "The script, what it was, left a lot of room for interpretation, both in terms of the effects and for adding little bits like that."

Savini mentioned the incident to Cunningham who, conscious of how slight the 85 page shooting script was, decided to manufacture a scene involving said snake, for the purpose of adding both foreshadowing and levity to the story. The mood dimmed when Savini's snake was killed at the campsite, the circumstances of which no one seems to recall.

The snake's real-life death (the snake in the film was chopped to pieces with a machete by Harry Crosby's character although Crosby denies he actually killed the snake) brought a rare outpouring of emotion from Cunningham. "The only disturbing moment on the set was when we killed the snake for real," Cunningham said. "Everything else was make-believe except for the snake, which was chopped with a machete. It's an important element in the film, it's a tone setting, but it was very upsetting to everyone, including myself, that we actually killed that snake. The reality of it was disturbing."

The emotion that Cunningham displayed over the snake's death was an anomaly for a production he marched through with the clinical, cold,

The "snake" scene was born after Tom Savini discovered a snake in his cabin during filming. The snake seen in the film was actually killed on location. (Photo courtesy of Jason Parker www.fridaythe13thfranchise.com)

weary professionalism that defined his pre-*Friday the 13th* career. "The movie had no emotional impact on me at all," Cunningham said. "It's all plumbing. The characters were, at best, thin. In fact, much later on, when I made a movie called *Deepstar Six* (1989) with a big ensemble cast...after three or four weeks came the time when there's an explosion and some of the characters die, and I was just depressed because there was more substance to them."

BILL FULL OF ARROWS

The biggest calamity that occurred during the filming of *Friday the 13th* was the scene where the character of Bill is pinned to the door of the generator cabin with arrows. During filming, Harry Crosby's

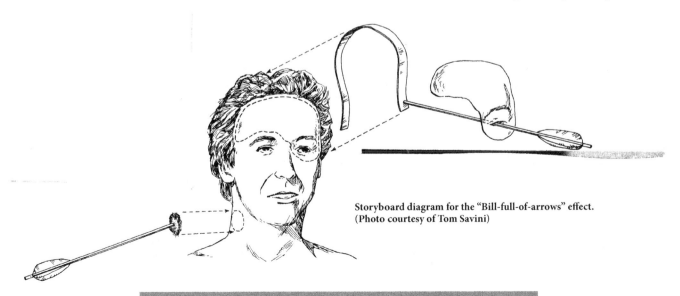

Storyboard diagram for the "Bill-full-of-arrows" effect. (Photo courtesy of Tom Savini)

Harry Crosby displays a sense of humor in preparation for the filming of the fateful scene where Bill is mounted to the door of the generator cabin. (Photo courtesy of Tom Savini)

kis recalls. "He probably spent more time with us than he did with the rest of the actors in the film. The three of us were inseparable during filming."

Crosby – who says he never met Betsy Palmer during the filming of *Friday the 13th* - was in awe of the effects magic that Savini and Stavrakis were capable of, and was more than willing to put his trust in them for his own death scene. "Harry stood on a ledge and Harry's belt was clipped to the door," Savini recalls. "We took the arrows and pushed them up through Harry's jeans and we built an appliance for the arrow that was stuck in Harry's eye, to give the impression that it was really in there. After that, we applied the blood to his face."

Savini had been experimenting with Dick Smith's blood formula on *Friday the 13th*, and used it for Crosby's death scene. He mixed up a blood formula that included a wetting agent called Photoflo. Unfortunately, the blood formula created a tremendous burning sensation in Crosby's eyes, so much so that he was temporarily blinded, and in great agony. "The blood formula was like a mask over my face and the blood welled up in my eyes," Crosby recalls. "When the *Mission: Impossible*-like mask was taken off, the air hit my eyes and face and caused my eyes to burn."

Although Savini recalls mixing said blood formula, he denies being present for the accident, which would've left Taso Stavrakis and Cecelia Verardi to oversee the effect. Regardless, the accident was a great embarrassment for Savini, in what had otherwise been a triumphant shoot up to that point.

eyes were burned, and he was subsequently hospitalized for a short period of time. The pain Crosby suffered is visible in the finished film. Bill can be seen twitching when Alice makes the gruesome discovery.

This was one of the few scenes in the shooting script that went into graphic detail. "The script said that the guy was killed in the tradition of the martyrdom of St. Sebastian, who was full of arrows," Savini says. "That's what we did to Harry, although the scene also became a spoof of Steve Martin's arrow-through-the-head routine from *Saturday Night Live*."

Besides co-star Laurie Bartram, with whom Crosby grew very close to during filming, Crosby spent most of his time hanging out with Tom Savini, Taso Stavrakis, Cecelia Verardi and her husband John. The scene in the film when Harry plays the guitar ("the song I played in the film was by Edvard Grieg, a Norwegian composer," Crosby recalls) was inspired by Crosby's own guitar-playing proficiency. "Harry would spend many a lovely night sitting in Tom's old barber chair, playing classical guitar while we painted props," Stavra-

"I mixed up the formula and I wasn't on location when that effect happened," Savini recalls. "Woman problems back home. There are a few safe formulas for blood used in the mouth and the eyes...I found out later. PhotoFlo is not one of the ingredients used in safe blood. It is a wet-

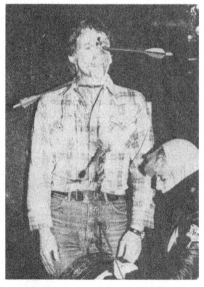

Harry Crosby with makeup effects assistant Cecelia Verardi (below). (Photo courtesy of Tom Savini)

ting agent used in the developing of film negatives and helps the blood saturate garments instead of just beading. So our unsafe blood had an opportunity to fill up Harry's eyes under the appliance used to keep the arrow looking like it was in his eye and it surface-burned poor Harry. Not a proud moment."

Crosby writhed in agony following the accident, and was then taken to a local hospital for treatment. Ultimately, Crosby was fine, and continued working without interruption, but the mishap caused a short-term panic on the set. Cunningham and Miner, in particular, were terrified that Crosby would either quit the film or sue the production or both.

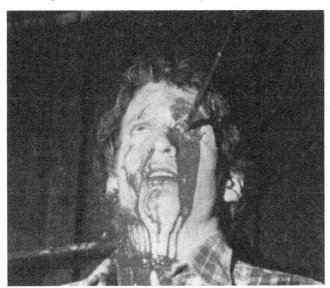

The finished version of the Bill-full-of-arrows effect. (Photo courtesy of Tom Savini)

This nervousness heightened when Crosby, following an examination at the hospital, went missing for a period of time, gone from his motel, only to be eventually discovered being "nursed back to health" by a female crew member in her room. Ultimately, the person most affected by the accident was Savini who was very humbled and shaken by the whole episode.

"The fake blood, the PhotoFlo, blinded him and he was taken to the hospital and then he disappeared and no one could find him," Daniel Mahon recalls. "He wasn't at the motel with the other actors. We found out that one of the female crew members had taken him back to her cabin and was taking care of him. Tom was really scared and his whole demeanor changed after that and I think 'the production' was a bit scared after that about Tom. During the filming, Tom would come to me for blades, knives, and I would show him what I had. After the

The blood formula that was applied to Harry Crosby's face damaged Crosby's eyes and almost brought filming to a halt. (Photo courtesy of Tom Savini)

accident, I was told not to sharpen the knives too much because the producers were afraid that Tom might kill somebody! Tom was also a bit scared too. One time I asked Tom if he wanted me to sharpen a knife for him to use and he said 'No' because I think he was afraid something else bad would happen."

"I was on the set during the filming of Harry's death scene on the door," recalls Ari Lehman. "Harry mentioned that his eye was stinging, causing it to twitch, so Sean immediately called for someone to bring Harry to the hospital. Harry said that he would rather finish the scene and then go. Sean reluctantly agreed. Harry's eye twitches in the scene because the makeup was seeping. Kudos to Harry Crosby, a real actor!"

"I remember that there were two types of blood for that scene, one with a Karo base, and that the PhotoFlo was used because it had the right viscosity and flowed better," Richard Murphy recalls. "Someone put that PhotoFlo on Harry's face and

In order to illuminate the main cabin for filming, Barry Abrams and his crew placed lights along the walls and in various other hidden locations throughout the cabin. (Photo courtesy of Barry Abrams)

then Harry started writhing on the floor. They only used the spill on Harry's face for the shot, as well as a stop-frame for the scene because Harry started writhing in agony as soon as the air hit the PhotoFlo."

"Harry Crosby was blinded and we all thought, 'Great. This is going to go down as the movie where Bing Crosby's kid got blinded,'" David Platt says. "We were all terrified until Harry came back. It was really bad. Very amateurish."

"Harry Crosby was a very nice guy but there was a big issue with the eye effect and the fact that he ended up going to the hospital," Robert Shulman recalls. "It was more than a minor irritation."

"Harry had the injury to his eye, but didn't make a fuss," Cecelia Verardi recalls. "Tom was very nervous about hurting Harry's eye because he could've been sued. Tom really toned down his act after the eye incident."

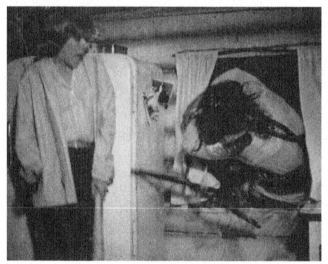

Tom Savini donned a wig to double as Brenda for the filming of the scene where Brenda's corpse is tossed through the window. (Photo courtesy of Tom Savini)

STUNTMAN TOM

The last major act of filming before the climactic lake scene was the sequence where Brenda's corpse is thrown through the window of the main cabin. With the previous effects, necessity had been the mother of invention for Tom Savini, but this particular sequence was born out of exhaustion and a shortage of time. "The whole crew was on the way out of the camp when we

had to shoot that scene," Savini recalls. "Everyone was so tired, and just wanted to get the shoot over with, so we planned the scene very quickly."

The sequence wasn't accomplished through any effect on Savini's part, but rather a feat of stuntwork. Laurie Bartram was present in the cabin, for the filming of the reveal of Brenda's corpse. "I put on a wig that sort of matched Laurie's hair color, and then I just told Sean and the crew that I would

Most of the other principal cast members were still on location when Adrienne King filmed her scenes as *Friday the 13th*'s last survivor. (Photo courtesy of Richard Feury)

jump through the window myself, instead of using a dummy," Savini recalls. "Even though I'd done stunts before, I'm not crazy and I wasn't thrilled about doing it, but it had to be done because we were really under time pressure to get it done."

THE BOY...JASON

Tom Savini, Taso Stavrakis, and young Ari Lehman put in several weeks of intense planning and work to get the technical elements just right for the climactic lake scene. But for Sean Cunningham and the film crew, the lake scene represented just one last chore they didn't think would be any more difficult or time-consuming than the previous scenes. There was a shocking lack of planning.

The story of the lake scene's filming began the night before and focuses on Cecelia Verardi, the jack of all trades on *Friday the 13th*. Her job was to watch the sky and wait for the moment when the sun was in the perfect position for filming. She wasn't alone. The rest of the crew, who had worked a gruel-

Despite her moral and religious beliefs, the cast and crew of *Friday the 13th* recall Laurie Bartram as having a great sense of humor. (Photo courtesy of Tom Savini)

ing day and night, all gathered on the beach and fell asleep. The idea was to have everyone on the beach so they could be ready to go at the precise moment the sun arrived, at dawn. Then they'd film the scene.

It was supposed to be that simple. The cast and crew would show-up at the lake, at dawn, and shoot the scene, and then make plans for leaving Blairstown. "I'd been up for twenty-five hours, all day and all night, the previous day and so had Adrienne [King]," Cecelia Verardi recalls. "My job was to watch the sky until the sun arrived at dawn, to make sure the sun was just right for filming, and then wake everyone up so we could do the scene. The plan was that we'd get the kid Ari into the water, get the crew to the water, check the sun, have Ari jump out, and then Adrienne screams and gets pulled under. Then we wrap the film. Real simple and smooth. This was the last day of filming and the last scene we had to do."

Laurie Bartram smiles for the camera in between takes. (Photo courtesy of Tom Savini)

The lake scene was filmed, in what turned out to be the first of several fateful attempts, at dawn, about six in the morning. King, exhausted from a marathon filming the night before, actually went down to the lake about

an hour or two before dawn, and proceeded to get into a designated canoe, drift into the water and fall asleep. "The other actors, Harry and Laurie, weren't around when we did that scene and were gone from the location," Cecelia Verardi recalls. "Adrienne was in the water, in the canoe, which was the idea, and she slept in the boat for an hour before we were ready to film. She was waiting for the shot and she fell asleep."

As it turns out, King, Ari Lehman, and Tom Savini were the only people who ever actually got into the water. When the scene was filmed, the canoe itself was only five to ten feet away from the shore where Cunningham and a skeleton production crew – primarily Barry Abrams and his unit from New York – worked. "Yes, I think I was the only one who got into the water with Adrienne and Ari when we did that scene, because I had to constantly adjust Ari's makeup," Savini says. "Sean and the rest of the crew were on land."

"The rest of the crew weren't in canoes when the scene was filmed, but were on the beach," Cecelia Verardi recalls. "The water was shallow enough for Tom and the others to wade into the water and talk to Adrienne and Ari, and to work with Ari on the makeup. It was a very small crew that was there for that scene."

Philip Scuderi was also present for the filming of the lake scene, Scuderi believing that the lake scene – and the concept of Jason rising from the bowels of the lake – was

Laurie Bartram and Tom Savini enjoy a playful moment in the main cabin. (Photo courtesy of Tom Savini)

crucial to *Friday the 13th*'s success. "The scene with Jason jumping out of the lake became Phil's obsession," recalls un-credited screenwriter Ron Kurz who spent several days on the *Friday the 13th* set. "I wasn't there when they filmed the scene, but I know that Phil was all over Sean to do it exactly right."

Kurz emphatically claims creative ownership of the lake scene, the chair-jumping moment when Jason jumps out of the lake, something that Victor Miller and Tom Savini, each of whom claim to have

Tom Savini and Ari Lehman pose together in front of the Sand Pond. (Photo courtesy of Tom Savini)

invented the scene themselves, dispute. "I came up with the idea of Jason the monster," Kurz says. "In Victor Miller's script, Jason was merely a normal kid who had drowned the year before, nothing more. As I was rewriting, I came up with the idea of making Jason 'different.' I made him into a mongoloid creature and I came up with the idea of having Jason jump out of the lake at the end of the film. I knew that once the audience was lulled into thinking that the closing credits were about to roll, that it was the perfect time for Jason to jump out of the water."

As disastrous as the first – and only – attempt to film the lake scene turned out to be for everyone, the person who suffered the most was Ari Lehman who had to survive in the freezing waters of the Sand Pond, covered in makeup and ungodly muck. "I was naked out there in the water except for a jock I had on," Lehman recalls. "Talk about humiliating. For the filming of the lake scene, I'd reach down into the dirt and rub mud over my body to make myself look really slimy."

Lehman denies, as stated by other sources, that he was given any kind of breathing tube for the filming of the lake scene. He recalls that he and Cunningham used a very primitive signal "cue" for the scene that resembled a silent snap count that a quarterback would use in a football game to offset a hostile, noisy environment. "There were absolutely no tubes used in this sequence," Lehman says. "Sean simply said, 'You are directing this scene, Ari! When you go down into the water, that's 'Action.' Then look up at the surface and wait for the bubbles to clear. When the bubbles are gone, jump out of the water!'"

Sean Cunningham concedes that the filming and planning of the lake scene was - aside from Savini's contribution – ill-conceived, to say the least. "The toughest part of the movie was the scene with Jason in the lake," Cunningham says. "First, it was freezing. Second, we had this fourteen year old kid who was under the freezing water, and we had

Sean Cunningham and Steve Miner pose with Ari Lehman at the Sand Pond. (Photo courtesy of Barry Abrams)

to get him to jump out of the water right on cue, with all of the makeup intact. The scene just took on a life of its own, and became much more difficult than we ever imagined. It was a nightmare."

In the shooting script, Jason's hand grabs Alice from beneath the water, and the canoe upturns. Then Jason pops up from below the surface of the water and yells "Mommy!" after which Jason drags a screaming Alice underwater. This brief dialogue was quickly excised from the scene. "My greatest challenge with the Jason scene was trying to understand the vision of Sean and Steve Miner," Barry Abrams recalled. "They understood absolutely how important this scene was to the film and, in my opinion, it is probably the one scene that accounts for the great success of the film. My memory is that we shot it more than twice because they knew it had to be right and they also knew exactly what 'right' meant."

"I actually thought it worked pretty well," Tad Page says. "I think if the timing hadn't been off, it would've been just right."

"It was an all or nothing scene," Robert Shulman says. "The lake scene was all about getting the time of morning scaled and all set up for that one shot we had to do. The lighting had to be just right in the morning so we had a short time period to get the scene done."

Once King and Lehman were finally in the water and the light was ideal, the scene was filmed. In an added wrinkle, Cunningham decided that King wouldn't be told when the scene was going to be filmed, specifically when Lehman was going to jump out of the water. The purpose of this was to provide shock and spontaneity for the scene, and for King. "After everyone had woken up, the plan was to put the kid in the water and don't tell Adrienne when we're going to do the scene, or when the kid's going to jump out of the water," Cecelia Verardi re-

Adrienne King drifts in the canoe. King actually fell asleep in the canoe before the filming of the lake scene was attempted and had to be awoken. (Photo courtesy of Harvey Fenton)

calls. "Adrienne came from her motel in the morning, after a long day and night of filming for all of us, and we were all dead-tired. Then Adrienne fell asleep in the canoe and had to be woken up for the scene, and it really caught her by surprise. It was supposed to be an easy scene, just show up and do it."

"All of our inexperience and all of the unforeseen problems came out in that scene," Richard Murphy says. "The young kid was given air inside his headpiece and what happened was that he couldn't hold his head underwater and keep the headpiece intact. We ended-up trying that scene three or four times and it was a real disaster and very upsetting to Sean. It was October when we finished it."

In retrospect, keeping King in the dark about the scene's execution might've been a bad idea, especially given how badly the timing was off between King and Lehman. When the scene was finally shot, Lehman jumped out of the water before King was ready, effectively spoiling the scene, and not just for that moment, but for the filming schedule as a whole. "Sean fucked up," Robert Shulman recalls. "He blew the cue to the kid in the water.

He said 'Action' too early and the kid jumped out too early and that blew the scene. Sean screwed up, and after that, he just said, 'Get Ari up here.'"

"The kid jumped out of the water before Adrienne was ready and she just freaks out and yells, 'Not now, you stupid fuck!' to the kid," Cecelia Verardi recalls. "Adrienne's hair and wardrobe had to be redone, the sun was lost, the kid was in the freezing water, and the effect had to be redone. The shot was lost. I wasn't there for the reshoots they did."

"The first time we tried it was all good except for one minor detail: I went out of camera range," Adrienne King recalled. "I think the hardest thing for me, as an actress, was to be able to lay there in [a] canoe for the second attempt and not anticipate the action. It took three different days of shooting but probably more like ten times over those three days."

"As I remember, the first attempt at the cli-  mactic lake scene, we had shot all night (as usual) and were forced to hang around for a few hours (it seemed) after sunrise until the light was right, or until the stunt was prepped or something," Robert Shulman recalls. "Even with our meager overtime rate, it was getting expensive.

Tom Savini readies for the filming of the lake scene. Aside from Savini's effects work, very little planning and preparation went into the lake scene's filming. (Photo courtesy of Tom Savini)

Adrienne was sort of lolling in the boat, drifting, and there was a countdown of some kind, and Sean cued Ari too soon, or with the wrong cue. Ari attacked over the side of the boat and Adrienne resisted because she knew the cue was wrong, and it was all useless. I think it would have taken too long to set-up again; the sun would have been too far advanced, or something, so the can was kicked down the road. I seem to feel like the second time didn't work either."

The filming of the lake scene was finally completed by the end of October, an arduous journey that included several more failed attempts. There's even been a suggestion over the years that the scene was eventually completed at Turkey Swamp Park in Freehold, New Jersey, but there's no clear evidence of this.

Tom Savini is out of frame as Ari Lehman rises from the depths of the lake to attack Adrienne King. (Photo courtesy of Tom Savini)

By the time the scene was filmed to Cunningham's satisfaction, the biggest challenge was concealing the increasing specter of winter that had taken firm hold of the surroundings. "I was lecturing a class of cinematographers at L'ecole Nationale Superieur Louis Lumiere and it was fun to ask them if they noticed anything about the background of the scene," Abrams said. "Answer: By the time we got it right, it was late in the fall and the foliage in the back-

Tom Savini was the only crewmember in the water with Adrienne King and Ari Lehman when the filming of the lake scene was attempted. The canoe itself was no more than ten feet away from the shore during the filming of the lake scene. (Photo courtesy of Tom Savini)

ground had begun to change color. In fact, I think it snowed the day we finally put it in the can. (Poor Ari and what a game kid – submersed in freezing water for the sake of art!). By the way, every one of these young cameramen and women, most of whom were not born when *Friday* was shot, jumped or screamed when they saw the scene for the first time. It works!"

Not wanting to take any chances, and knowing the scene's importance, Cunningham employed multiple cameras, mounted on the shore, to try and account for any possible mistakes. "Sean hadn't gotten the exact shot he had in his mind so on this third, and last, attempt he had multiple cameras, including a slow-motion camera, to catch it," Adrienne King recalled. "Don't forget, low budget. We only had two tries. They could only afford one

The filming of the lake scene was successfully-completed in October of 1979 after several failed attempts. (Photo courtesy of Barry Abrams)

change of clothes for me. The leaves were turning color and falling and the water was freezing, and neither Ari or I had a wetsuit of any proportion."

The fact that Adrienne King was, besides Ari Lehman, the only cast member still around at the campsite, a fact that mirrored Alice's "sole survivor" status, gave the filming of the lake scene a certain poignancy amidst the horrible filming conditions. "It took us three months to shoot that scene," King recalled. "The first two times something went wrong. Even though it was supposed to be in the spring, it was twenty-eight degrees. Snow was falling by the time we were getting ready to shoot it the third time."

The experience also further bonded King with Cunningham who was joined, at the end of the ordeal, by a very small cadre, primarily Barry Abrams and his band of followers. "Sean Cunningham was very apologetic about the screw-ups," King said. "He promised, 'This is the last time I'm going to ask you to do this.' We finally got the scene, but the water was so cold and I was wearing so little that I came down with a bad cold and was out of commission for two weeks."

CRYSTAL LAKE HOSPITAL

Although the climactic lake scene was always designated to be the "money shot", Sean Cunningham never thought of ending the film with Jason pulling Alice underwater. "We couldn't end the movie with that scene, as well as it worked, because that was a dream sequence, and we had to find out what happened to Alice," Cunningham says. "The entire film was grounded in reality, so in my mind, Jason was dead. I never intended for Jason to come back to life, much less doing any sequels. When we shot the ending, Jason was just a dream."

The lake scene was the film's unquestioned climax, but the hospital scene was the last scene in the shooting script. The hospital scene was sup-

Shot of Ari Lehman in the Sand Pond. (Photo courtesy of Tom Savini)

posed to have been shot during the second week of filming, but was pushed back to the end of the filming schedule. Contrary to the popular belief that the hospital scene was created spontaneously, the scene was, in fact, filmed virtually identical to the script, with hardly any noticeable changes.

In this scene, Sgt. Tierney explains to Alice that her fellow camp counselors are dead, while Alice goes on about how Jason attacked her in the lake.

Although Cunningham says he never intended for the ending of *Friday the 13th* to leave the door open for a sequel, actor Ronn Carroll, a friend of Cunningham's, felt that a sequel was inevitable. "When we shot the scene in the hospital room, I remember thinking that they were definitely leaving the door open for more films," Carroll says. "It was when Adri-

enne said 'Then he's still out there.' That really made me sure that Sean had a plan to continue the series."

The filming of the hospital scene took place at a hospital in Connecticut. The room itself was modified slightly by Virginia Field who pushed out the wall that Adrienne King leans against in the hospital bed. However, neither Sean Cunningham nor cinematographer Barry Abrams were present for the scene's filming, although both consulted on the way the scene was designed and shot.

The hospital scene was directed by Steve Miner and shot by cinematographer Peter Stein who was in Blairstown to do some pickup and second unit shots, having previously worked on *Here Come the Tigers*. "I believe that Barry and Sean were off doing other things, some other pickup shots, and that Steve Miner was the director with me for that scene," Stein recalls. "I think I was only there for two days,

The flashback scene showing young Jason's drowning was filmed in August of 1979, prior to the start of principal filming. (Photo courtesy of Tom Savini)

but it might've been only one day. I shot the hospital scene, but I also did some street scenes with them as a second camera. I believe it was car pass-bys. I did know this [the hospital scene] was at the end of the production schedule. I don't think I was ever at the camp, and I don't think I met any of the other actors, although, a few years earlier, I'd done a commercial with Betsy Palmer, and she was a very nice lady."

Although Cunningham says he never envisioned a sequel to *Friday the 13th*, a statement bolstered by Victor Miller, the planning and filming of the ending scenes certainly, maybe subconsciously, moved the film in that direction, especially turning Jason into a pop culture icon. "Maybe, given the success of the film, the idea that Jason might've been still out there forced the issue," Cunningham says. "If Pamela's dead, who's left to continue the killing? There's just Jason. Maybe it was inevitable."

BACK TO WESTPORT

In October, Sean Cunningham filmed some insert sequences in and around Bridgeport and Westport, Connecticut. These shots featured Adrienne King and Betsy Palmer, and focused primarily on close-ups related to the scenes where Alice and Pamela are on the beach or in the forest.

Although it's unclear whether any other cast members were involved in this additional filming in Connecticut, Laurie Bartram and Harry Crosby did make an appearance in Connecticut for a makeshift cast and crew party Cunningham held at his Westport home. "We had a party at Sean's house in Westport when we shot some inserts," Cecelia Verardi recalls. "Betsy, Harry and Laurie were there with the rest of us. Jeannine [Taylor] wasn't there and I don't think the other cast members were there either."

Of the filler sequences shot in Connecticut the most notable was a sequence where Palmer, in a childlike voice, mutters her "Kill her, mommy" line. "Sean called me up and said he needed me to come to his house in Connecticut and do the voice of Jason," recalls Palmer who, as mentioned, lived in Connecticut. "I remember we filmed near a local university, and there were a lot of close-ups but it

was so cold that there was steam coming out of my mouth, so I had to put ice cubes in my mouth, like I'd done when we'd filmed on the beach, back at the campsite."

GOODBYE BLAIRSTOWN

By early November, Sean Cunningham and Steve Miner had completed all of the filming on *Friday the 13th* and prepared to go into the editing room to bring form and shape to the footage.

The rest of the cast and crew, most of whom lived in New York, settled back home, in recovery from the roughly month-long odyssey of *Friday the 13th*'s filming, especially the group that had stayed at the truck-stop motel. "I was in the editing room, cutting *The Children* with Barry's wife, Nikki, when the guys came back into New York,"

This shot was taken between the last week of August and the first week of September of 1979 and illustrates the vast wilderness area that surrounds Camp No-Be-Bo-Sco. (Photo courtesy of Tony Marshall)

recalls Max Kalmanowicz. "They were really exhausted. I asked them about the movie and they talked about mosquitoes, the cold weather, and how things had been fucked-up, but not in a bad way."

Barry Abrams and his team had been close friends prior to *Friday the 13th*, and would stay close for years afterwards, but everyone else went their separate ways. None of the cast and crew would ever see Blairstown again, except in their memories and in their viewings of the finished film.

"As soon as we were finished at the campsite, the whole set was torn down," Tad Page recalls. "Gels, lights, everything. We all took everything we could. I took the bloody axe from the film."

Upon their return to New York, the cast and crew were invited, by Sean Cunningham, to a makeshift wrap party which was held at a country-western bar in New York called City Limits. Much like had been the case at the campsite, this was a very modest affair. "The wrap party was in typical Sean Cunningham style," Tad Page jokes. "We went to City Limits, a country-western bar, and we were given free admission, free draft beers, and a small buffet."

Everyone involved with the filming of *Friday the 13th* was filled with morbid curiosity as to whether *Friday the 13th* would ever live on past the Blairstown adventure and enjoy any kind of commercial success. Most thought the film would never see the light of day while others were worried that the finished product would resemble something pornographic and unclean.

For most of them, *Friday the 13th* had been a job, nothing more and nothing less. "One of the reasons I did the film was because I didn't think anybody would ever hear about it," Betsy Palmer says. "I don't think anybody, except for Sean, thought it would ever get released."

CHAPTER 10

BEYOND BLAIRSTOWN:
THE RELEASE OF *FRIDAY THE 13TH*

"It [**Friday the 13th**] was a curse for my directing career because, obviously, I have interests and tastes of my own but I found it very difficult to move beyond **Friday the 13th**."

– Sean Cunningham

"My children are proud, my neighbors are aghast, my parents are shocked, my friends are mystified and my agent is euphoric."

– Victor Miller in 1980 following **Friday the 13th's** theatrical release

The North American theatrical poster for *Friday the 13th,* which was conceptualized by designer Spiros Angelikas and painted by fantasy illustrator Alex Ebel. (Photo courtesy of Matt Hankinson)

In 1979, *Friday the 13th* transformed from a title to a logo, then developed into a concept and, finally, became a real story with flesh and blood characters. By Christmas 1979, Sean Cunningham and Steve Miner were well into the process of turning *Friday the 13th* into a finished product.

The rest is history.

In the spring of 1980 Cunningham, armed with a completed version of *Friday the 13th*, screened the film for potential distributors. A bidding war ensued, resulting in Paramount Pictures paying a whopping $1.5 Million for the North American distribution rights.

Released in May 1980, *Friday the 13th* was the surprise box office hit of the year. Cunningham found himself the architect of one of the most commercially-successful, independent films in history. "It was *The Blair Witch Project* before there was a *Blair Witch Project*," Cunningham says, comparing *Friday the 13th*'s commercial impact to the 1999 independent-

ly-produced horror film. "The reaction was similar."

Cunningham also found himself at the center of controversy. *Friday the 13th* became a lightning rod for film critics as well as church and political activists who decried it as being misogynistic and pornographic. In the film centers of Hollywood and New York, no one cared. After a decade of defeat, Cunningham found himself, almost overnight, a wealthy man and a very hot commodity; the latter being for a very short time.

The North American pressbook. (Photo courtesy of Jason Parker www.fridaythe13thfranchise.com)

For the rest of the cast and crew, the film's success triggered a series of repercussions-- both minor and long-lasting. While many of the crew members were able to anonymously slip back into regular film and television work, the actors found it difficult to shake the stigma associated with *Friday the 13th*. Their career prospects mirrored the grim fates of their characters.

Friday the 13th sent a tremor through both the film business and the overlaying society, the aftershocks of which still linger today. "I think *Friday the 13th* ultimately had a bad effect on the in-

The wide release Paramount Pictures gave *Friday the 13th* was unprecedented for an independently-produced film prior to 1980. (Photo courtesy of Jason Parker www.fridaythe13thfranchise.com)

dependent horror market, although we can't blame the film, or the filmmakers, themselves," says historian and journalist Stephen Thrower. "It was just another independent production until it was bought as a 'negative pickup' by Paramount. Unfortunately, I think you can trace the 1980s backlash against graphic horror to that moment."

In October 1980, roughly a year after the wrap of filming on *Friday the 13th*, and just several months after its theatrical release, production began on the sequel, *Friday the 13th Part 2*, released in May 1981. In the span of a year, *Friday the 13th* transformed from a low budget film production, shot in remote isolation, to a bankable brand.

Friday the 13th Part 2 was just the beginning in a seemingly endless series of sequels - ranging from *Friday the 13th Part 3* (1982) to *Jason X* (2002) - that have encompassed hundreds of millions of dollars in revenues. Beginning with *Friday the 13th Part 2*, these sequels gradually moved farther and farther away from the 1980 film, primarily with the growing prominence of the Jason character, so much so that *Friday the 13th* now seems like a completely separate entity from the rest of the franchise.

THE CUTTING ROOM

The ruthless efficiency in which *Friday the 13th* was planned and filmed served Sean Cunningham well when he undertook the editing of *Friday the 13th* throughout the Christmas season of 1979.

There weren't, as speculated, any additional or unused scenes filmed outside of the shooting script, and as a result, Cunningham didn't have many creative decisions. The editing of *Friday the 13th* was a matter of picking the best version of the scenes that were on film, with a few trims, nips and tucks. Susan Cunningham's editing at the campsite sped up the process even more. "We had so little money, and so little time, that it would've been stupid to have done any extra filming," Cunningham says. "Every scene that we filmed was kept in the finished film."

One scene Cunningham and Victor Miller planned and scripted but never filmed was where Alice makes the gruesome discovery of the 'missing' bodies: those of Jack, Ned, Marcie, whose remains are never found in the film. "We always thought that when the sun came up, all would be revealed, in terms of what happened," Cunningham says. "We didn't film any extra scenes like that."

For film editing, Cunningham was joined by Bill Freda, a New York based editor who had performed editing chores on *Here Come the Tigers*. Cunningham and Freda were joined also by Jay Keuper, while Susan Cunningham and Steve Miner, the original, intended editor, were also kept in the loop. "There was no magic with the editing of *Friday the 13th*," Sean Cunningham says. "The film had a beginning, middle and an end. The editing was nothing more complicated than that."

Paramount eschewed the original block logo design in their advertising and promotion of *Friday the 13th*. (Photo courtesy of Jason Parker www.fridaythe13thfranchise.com)

The biggest cuts imposed on *Friday the 13th* were in the death scenes. Once Cunningham and Freda assembled a rough cut, Cunningham was shocked to discover that the "dead bodies" twitched and moved, primarily in the scene where actor Harry Crosby was injured. "I was shocked when I saw it on a big screen," Cunningham said. "It can be very difficult for actors in these situations. I spent a lot of time on the moviola rearranging shots, because all of my corpses seemed to move! It's hard to notice on an editing console."

The "white light" effect that surrounds some of the victims in the film was added in post-production, along with the block letter "glass-breaking" sequence Cunningham had used for the advertisement in *Variety*. After going through the post-production process, the total bill on *Friday the 13th*, which had a filming budget (or filming cost) of roughly $550,000, ended up at the $700,000 mark, according to Barry Abrams.

Cunningham didn't trim much of the gore from the film during the editing process, nor would he have many difficulties with the Motion Picture Association of America (MPAA). They gave *Friday the 13th* an "R" rating without much of a fight. "I knew, when I saw the film, that it worked exactly the way we'd hoped," Cunningham says. "It was the magic mountain ride that I'd wanted to make. A year later, when I had to cut the film for the television debut, I only had to cut about twenty seconds because the gory scenes were all really concentrated in specific parts of the film. I think the biggest cut we had was the Kevin Bacon scene that went on a few seconds longer in the unedited form, but which I think is more effective and shocking in a shorter version. Other than that, I didn't have any big problems with the ratings board."

Future *Friday the 13th* films, especially *Friday the 13th Part 2*, would suffer greatly for the MPAA's perceived laxness in letting *Friday the 13th* skate by with an "R" rating. Surprisingly, given his filmmaking background, Cunningham has a very sunny view of the MPAA and the purpose they serve. "We have in the MPAA one of the greatest political gifts to artists in the world," Cunningham said. "Because of the MPAA, any person can make a movie about anything he wants. He can make it any way he wants. The MPAA stays sensitive to the mood swings of

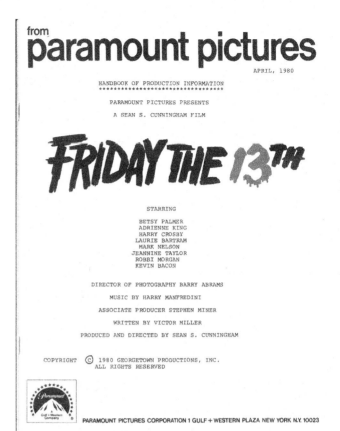

The North American press-kit. (Photo courtesy of Jason Parker www.fridaythe13thfranchise.com)

the country so they can adjust their ratings. I think it's wonderful we live in a culture where you can do anything in a movie, whatever it is. Nobody tells you that you can't do something, except the marketplace."

KILL, MOMMY, KILL

One of the key elements added in post-production was composer Harry Manfredini's musical score.

It wasn't until one of the first ever screenings in January 1980 that Manfredini had any clear idea of what *Friday the 13th* was going to be. "The film was complete when I first saw it," Manfredini recalls. "I was at a screening with just a few people and I was in total shock. I had never seen anything like it. One of the producers came up to me and asked me, 'Do you think you can make this scary?' I answered, 'Hmmm. It seems pretty scary already, but I think I can.'"

Manfredini also met cast member Harry Crosby at this screening. "I did get to meet Harry after the show was over, and I can tell you he was a really smart and talented guy," Manfredini says. "We talked about music, and shared ideas. I did not know the piece he played was [Edvard] Grieg. I thought it was something that he had written."

When planning the score for *Friday the 13th*, Manfredini took his cues from Sean Cunningham, and not the "producers" from Boston. "I had almost no contact with any investors, or Phil Scuderi, although maybe that was Phil who came up to me and asked if I could make it scary," Manfredini says. "I didn't know his name. As far as creativity and influence goes, I got all mine from Sean directly, and from myself. The score is a result of the two of us talking. If there was any other, I did not know it. We talked mostly on the phone, and he [Cunningham] was very happy with my suggestions and ideas, so we worked very smoothly together."

The European poster. Much of the overseas promotion of *Friday the 13th* featured the axe-on-the-pillow image. (Photo courtesy of Harvey Fenton)

Although Manfredini had a vibe for Cunningham's sensibilities, having worked with him on *Here Come the Tigers* and *Manny's Orphans*, Manfredini was a virtual neophyte to the horror genre, despite scoring the film *The Children*. "As far as impressions that I had, I was so green at the time, I just said, 'Great. Let's go,'" Manfredini recalls. "I am not really a big horror movie fan. At that time, I had not seen *Halloween*, and had never even heard of Mario Bava, although I had heard of Brian DePalma, and Dario Argento. As far as his [Cunningham's] influences, he never really mentioned *Halloween*, and never Mario Bava."

The staple of the musical score is the "stinger" that punctuates the film's gruesome events, and especially the "ki-ki-ki, ma-ma-ma" riff that announces the killer's presence, an iconic landmark in horror film history. "*Friday the 13th* is like *Jaws* in the sense that the killer, Mrs. Voorhees, doesn't really appear until the end of the film, so the challenge was to create music that provided an identity for the killer we don't really see throughout most of the film," Manfredini says. "Sean asked me if we could have a chorus, but that was too expensive for us. I love classical music, and one day, I was listening to a piece by polish composer Krzysztof Penderecki and the piece had a large chorus that contained striking pronunciations. All of the consonant sounds were extremely sharp, like a 'ki, ki, ki' type of thing. Not being able to afford 100 people, I had to find a way to mirror this sound."

The "ki-ki-ki, ma-ma-ma" riff relates to the scene in the film where Betsy Palmer, mimicking the voice of Jason, performs her "Kill her, mommy" sequence. "The idea was to take the 'ki' from 'kill' and the 'ma' from mommy and put them into a microphone, but in a very harsh, rhythmic tone," Manfredini says. "We gave the words a 1970s echo by running the words through a machine called an echoplex. From that point on, every time the stalker appeared in the film, I put that into the score."

Certainly, the ki-ki-ki, ma-ma-ma riff is one of *Friday the 13th*'s signatures, and also an imprimatur of the horror genre itself in the early 1980s, but perhaps the most curious aspect of *Friday the 13th*'s score has to do with the inclusion of a country song called *Sail Away, Tiny Sparrow*.

The song is featured in the film's two diner scenes: the first diner scene with Annie and the later diner scene with Steve Christy. "When I first got the film, the temp score for the film featured a Dolly Parton song called *My Blue Tears* which played over the diner scenes," Manfredini recalls. "In that song there is a line, 'Fly away, little bluebird.' I needed to write a country song that was something like that, so I thought, 'Hmmm...sail away, tiny sparrow.' It was a song about a girl who married her high school sweetheart, and now finds that life is not quite as she expected, the things of which country songs thrive."

The appearance of *Sail Away, Tiny Sparrow* has a disarming effect, completely incongruous with the rest of the film. This is especially true when the song plays during the climactic scene where Alice is drifting in the canoe, right before Jason jumps out of the water. The song also plays over the end credits. "I wrote it solely for the two diner scenes, but then when it came to the end of the film...the dramatic object was to convince the audience that the film was over," Manfredini says. "As Adrienne King is in the boat on the lake, that scene just goes on and on... excellent editing and cutting to extend it as far as possible, to convince the audience that this was the end, and any second, the credit roll was about to come up. So I wanted to create something musically that did just that. So I thought, and thought, and then it occurred to me that, 'Hey, she is in a boat.' She is

The European pressbook. Unlike Paramount, overseas distributor Warner Bros. did feature the original block logo design in much of their advertising and promotion of *Friday the 13th*. (Photo courtesy of Henri Guibaud)

sailing away, and so there I really had it, so I took the melody of the country song and elongated it and processed it to sound like a final scene, and it worked."

Many viewers feel the overall musical score in *Friday the 13th* owes a lot to *The Children*. This view is shared by Carlton J. Albright, *The Children's* producer and writer who believes that Manfredini's score for *Friday the 13th* was a knockoff. "If you watch the two films, and listen closely, it's virtually the same music," Albright says. "I went to a screening of *Friday the 13th*, and I think *The Children* had either just been released or was just about to be released. After the screening, Harry walked over to me and asked me what I thought of the film, and the music, and I just smiled and said, 'Harry, you're a very good thief.' Harry was a great guy, and a great musician, but he worked on *The Children* before he did *Friday the 13th*. We were first!"

Like John Carpenter's musical score in *Halloween*, which brought the scares in that film to glorious life, the musical score in *Friday the 13th* played a pivotal role in establishing *Friday the 13th's* visceral impact. "When I first saw it completed, Sean and I sat in the front row, and we would turn around to watch the test audiences react to it," Manfredini recalls. "They would fly out of their seats, and popcorn would go flying, so we knew we had accomplished what we set out to do. I don't think we knew that it was lightning in a bottle though."

SCREENING FRIDAY THE 13TH

Throughout February 1980, Sean Cunningham held various screenings of *Friday the 13th* that were attended by members of the cast and crew, and especially potential theatrical distributors, whom Cunningham was anxious to court. The most prominent of these screenings took place at the massive, storied Paramount Theatre, located in the Midtown section of New York, in February 1980.

The Paramount screening was especially notable because it represented the moment when Cunningham had begun to interject Harry Manfredini's powerful musical score, assembled in two weeks, into the edited film. "I went to the screening and all of the actors were there, most of whom I'd never met, besides Adrienne, and it was strange because nobody talked to me at all," recalls Betsy Palmer. "Sean Cunningham was a half an hour late for the screening, and we were all wondering where he was and when

European pressbook advertisement. (Photo courtesy of Henri Guibaud)

the movie was going to start. It turned out that Sean was busy putting the 'ki-ki-ki, ma-ma-ma' music into the film, which was a stroke of genius on his part."

"The cast and crew screening of *Friday the 13th* was held in a big theater, not some little screening room," Virginia Field recalls. "The Paramount was a huge movie theater in Midtown and it was really exciting to see the movie we'd worked on, a movie we didn't think would ever get released, play in a big theater like that. It was the first and only time I ever saw *Friday the 13th*, up until a few years ago when I screened it again."

Ron Millkie recalls attending an early cast screening that was held at New York's Huntington-Hartford building. "There may have been two screenings, but the screening I attended was held at a movie theater inside the Huntington-Hartford building," Millkie recalls. "I was at the screening with the kids, the rest of the actors from the film, and this was before the distributor bought the film. I remember being shocked that no one laughed at me during my scene. After the movie was over, Betsy came over to me and asked me what I thought of her performance in the film, how I thought she was, and I told her she was great. I think every actor at the screening was just there to see their own work in the film."

"I went to the initial screening in midtown Manhattan, in which all of the cast had been invited," Jeannine Taylor recalls. "I remember seeing Sean Cun-

ningham and his wife and saying 'hi' to them. When the lights dimmed, for some reason, I ducked out and didn't return, so I don't know what I would have thought because I didn't see it! I don't know why, but I just couldn't stay and watch it with everyone else. Call it an attack of shyness. I had them back then."

The screenings Cunningham held for potential distributors were promoted with the unused *Friday the 13th* advertisement – the one with the tagline "THE PERFECT DAY FOR TERROR" and the February 1980 release date – that Richard Illy had photographed in tandem with the photograph for the *Variety* advertisement. "I attended a premiere of the film with some of the investors and would-be distributors, and there were lots of people there," Illy recalls. "A lady from Paramount Pictures was sitting behind me and she said, 'I think I'm going to be sick' and then she said, 'I think this is going to be a big hit' because the violence in the film was very shocking for that time."

Original British quad poster design. (Photo courtesy of Harvey Fenton)

The February screenings of *Friday the 13th* quickly generated buzz and momentum throughout the film industry, on both coasts. After a decade of struggle, Cunningham sensed, at this point, that, for once, his instincts had served him well and that *Friday the 13th* was destined for commercial success. "I'm shocked," Cunningham said in 1980, following several screenings for distributors. "It's never happened to me. All of a sudden I'm getting offers. Hopefully I'm going to be very busy."

Of the potential distributors, Paramount, Warner Bros. and United Artists (UA) jumped out of the pack in terms of expressing serious interest in acquiring *Friday the 13th*. Metro-Goldwyn-Mayer (MGM), who merged with UA into MGM/UA in 1981, also showed interest but bowed out early in the bidding process. "I took it to Warner Bros., who'd had *Kick* [AKA *Manny's Orphans*] for eight weeks before turning it down," Cunningham recalled. "They wanted it. So did Paramount and United Artists. It was great to see them bidding against one another."

In the end, Paramount Pictures secured the North American distribution rights to *Friday the 13th* for $1.5 Million. Warner Bros. secured the overseas distribution rights.

Paramount's acquisition of *Friday the 13th* was spearheaded by distribution chief Frank Mancuso Sr. who was on a crusade to acquire projects financed and made outside of the rigid studio system and which would appeal to the teenage market that Mancuso saw as key to Paramount's continued growth in the 1980s. *Friday the 13th*'s eventual commercial success was a major factor – although not the only factor – that launched Mancuso into the position as chairman of Paramount Pictures; a role he assumed in 1984.

Two color British double-bill quad poster promoting *Friday the 13th* and *Friday the 13th Part 2*. (Photo courtesy of Harvey Fenton)

Paramount's acquisition of *Friday the 13th* also meant dealing with Philip Scuderi and Scuderi's partners, Robert Barsamian and Stephen Minasian, from Georgetown Productions. While Cunningham and Mancuso formed an instant camaraderie, dealing with Scuderi required a great deal of finesse, mostly on the part of Mancuso, a former Paramount booking agent, who'd had many dealings with Scuderi over the years, when the Esquire Theaters chain had been one of Paramount's more prominent "customers" on the East Coast throughout the 1970s.

Paramount's acquisition of *Friday the 13th* for North American distribution also gave Paramount the right to distribute any future *Friday the 13th* sequels. This was an agreement refined between Mancuso and Scuderi following *Friday the 13th*'s box office success.

This meant Paramount controlled distribution while Georgetown Productions controlled the copyright. Cunningham controlled the rights to *Friday the 13th* which gave him a say in every decision that was to be made, from 1980 on, regarding the *Friday the 13th* franchise.

Friday the 13th was acquired as a "negative pickup" by Paramount Pictures, a term that refers to a contract entered into by an independent producer and a motion picture studio wherein the studio agrees to purchase the movie from the producer at a given date and for a fixed sum.

Although the negative pickup deal wasn't exclusive to low budget independent films like *Friday the 13th*, with titles like *Superman* (1978) and *The Empire Strikes Back* (1980) being just two examples of big-budget blockbuster films that were also negative pickups, the deal was certainly idyllic for a film like *Friday the 13th*, and especially the numerous se-

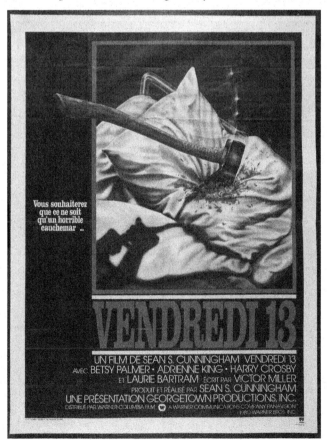

French poster artwork. (Photo courtesy of Matt Hankinson)

quels. This arrangement allowed Philip Scuderi and his partners to produce *Friday the 13th Part 2,* as an example, as a non-union production, having no direct relationship with Paramount. Paramount could never otherwise be involved with a non-union film.

This was, of course, pure semantics, but the negative pickup deal also gave Paramount something else: a degree of deniability. Since Paramount didn't finance or produce *Friday the 13th,* the staid, venerable studio could distance themselves from the foul odor that the theatrical release of *Friday the 13th* ultimately generated.

THE RELEASE

While the *Friday the 13th* cast members were almost universally oblivious to Paramount's attachment to *Friday the 13th,* and the implications of such a deal, the more savvy crew members immediately recognized Paramount's involvement as a clear sign that *Friday the 13th* was poised to receive some major national exposure.

French promotional advertisement. (Photo courtesy of Jason Pepin)

This was especially true when Frank Mancuso decided to give *Friday the 13th* a release on between 500 and 600 screens, an almost unheard of scale for such a low budget production. *Friday the 13th'*s actual theatrical release, in May 1980, debuted on over 1100 screens.

Mancuso's decision to open *Friday the 13th* on such a wide scale was a bold gamble. The strategy went against conventional thinking that dictated low budget films were best given a modest initial release, in parcels of regional theaters, thus allowing the film to build an audience through the network of drive-ins and neighborhood houses that was still fairly robust in 1980.

This slow-build, regional strategy had certainly worked for low-budget blockbusters like *Billy Jack* (1971) and *American Graffiti* (1973). *Halloween* had used the regional release strategy and benefitted greatly. There was no doubt that Mancuso believed in *Friday the 13th.*

The Children followed said regional strategy, opening in June 1980 on roughly 100 screens, to scant notice. "Sean was a favorite of Frank's, and Frank had a real passion and vision for *Friday the 13th* and decided to put *Friday the 13th* into 600 theaters at once," Max Kalmanowicz, the director of *The Children,* recalls. "That was almost unheard of, at that time, for a film like *Friday the 13th.* That was a serious investment and that told everyone – Sean, Barry, the whole crew – that *Friday the 13th* was going to do some serious business. Frank believed in it so much. I think *The Children* played on about 130 screens. Still, the movie [*The Children*] exceeded my expectations, both in terms of the quality of the film and the film's success. *The Children* and *Friday the 13th* both came out in the summer of 1980 and, the way I look at it, *Friday the 13th* took the top of the box office and we took the bottom, although *The Children* did fairly well and made money."

Friday the 13th was an anomaly that defied all of the conventional rules of filmmaking. This was true in the planning stages, the filming, and was especially true in terms of the film's release and eventual commercial success. Although Paramount would end-up spending over $4 Million promoting *Friday the 13th* during the summer months of 1980, Mancuso knew that the film itself was its greatest sales tool.

Cunningham thought *Friday the 13th* should

be marketed along the lines of the *Variety* advertisement, especially the block logo. He deferred to Mancuso and Paramount who had different ideas. "I got a letter from Paramount Pictures asking me to send the negatives of the shot I took for the *Variety* ad to them, but there was no mention of renting it or giving me any credit," Richard Illy recalls. "All I wanted was credit, but they offered me nothing. For 100 dollars, they could've had these

Italian poster artwork. (Photo courtesy of Matt Hankinson)

great shots of the logo which would've been much better than the poster they used, but they were too cheap, and I was very angry about the whole thing. I never wrote them back and never heard from them again. They ended up using their own poster."

Paramount commissioned designer Spiros Angelikas to design *Friday the 13th*'s theatrical poster while fantasy illustrator Alex Ebel handled the painting chores. The design featured ragged letters for

the *Friday the 13th* title, the style of which became the insignia for all of the *Friday the 13th* films released by Paramount Pictures throughout the 1980s.

The new lettering scheme was accompanied by a header, on top of the poster, that read "THEY WERE WARNED ...THEY ARE DOOMED... AND ON *FRIDAY THE 13TH*, NOTHING WILL SAVE THEM." The tagline on the bottom of the poster, underneath the title, announced *Friday the 13th* as "A 24 HOUR NIGHTMARE OF TERROR."

Befitting Paramount's sizable launch for *Friday the 13th*'s theatrical release, the studio began running television advertisements in April 1980, the appearance of which shocked many of the cast and crew. "I was in my apartment when I saw the first television commercial for *Friday the 13th* and I couldn't believe it," Mark Nelson says. "I'd almost forgotten being in the film, and here it was about to be released all across America. I flipped out. Later on, the film was playing at the Loews Astor Plaza on 44th street and I had a big party at my apartment, celebrating my first big movie role."

There were several premiere screenings for *Friday the 13th* in tandem with the film's national theatrical release on May 9, 1980, primar-

Spanish poster artwork. (Photo courtesy of Matt Hankinson)

151

ily in New York and the surrounding East Coast, the market that Paramount devoted the bulk of its promotional resources for *Friday the 13th* to in advance of the film's national launch. "At one screening, there was an ambulance outside because people were getting really scared and were freaking out," Mark Nelson recalls. "I saw Barry Moss in the elevator and he told me people had collapsed."

German poster artwork. (Photo courtesy of Matt Hankinson)

As Sean Cunningham and Tom Savini had planned, a lot of the visceral audience reaction generated by *Friday the 13th* during the film's early weeks of theatrical release was a result of the film's gory shocks, none more powerful than the Kevin Bacon throat sequence and the lake scene where Jason jumps out of the water. The latter scene evoked an especially powerful reaction from audiences, as well as the cast and crew when they saw the film with an audience.

"I knew the film would be a big success when I saw the film in a theater and saw the reaction over the last scene where Jason jumps out of the lake," Peter Brouwer says. "Before that, the villain was killed, and you could feel everyone in the theater

Australian poster artwork. (Photo courtesy of Matt Hankinson)

relax. When the monster jumped out of the water, they all screamed. It was quite something to watch. I was with my girlfriend [Brouwer's wife, assistant director Cindy Veazey] and she grabbed onto my arm."

"My brother called me up and told me that the movie was playing everywhere and that it was a big hit," Robbi Morgan recalls. "I was stunned."

"I did go to see it at Loews Astor Plaza on Broadway and 44th Street after its release (by myself)," Jeannine Taylor recalls. "The place was packed, and I remember thoroughly enjoying the audience reactions. They were absolutely riveted, and they did a lot of screaming. I thought it was a really scary movie – shockingly gory and very entertaining. I remember, just before my shower scene, a young woman sitting behind me yelled 'Don't you go in that shower, girl!' I could not stop laughing for several minutes afterward so I didn't look at the sequence very closely. I finally did watch the whole movie on TV five or six years later and I thought that, despite its lack of budget and relatively-inexperienced young cast (totally inexperienced in my case), it was really satisfying, jump-out-of-your-seat stuff. If that's your thing, you're going to love it."

"After *Friday the 13th*, I worked on the movie *Fame* in New York, and then went to Tuscaloosa, Alabama to do another movie where *Fame* played at the local theater and closed in two weeks," Robert Topol says. "*Friday the 13th* played there for six months. That's how I knew it was a big hit."

Japanese poster artwork. (Photo courtesy of Matt Hankinson)

Released on May 9, 1980, on 1127 screens across North America, *Friday the 13th* was an immediate smash hit, grossing $5.8 Million in its opening weekend.

Japanese pressbook. (Photo courtesy of Barry Abrams)

Unlike the *Friday the 13th* sequels, which made most of their money in their first ten days of theatrical release, *Friday the 13th* had "legs" at the box office. By the end of summer, *Friday the 13th* had grossed approximately $39.7 Million at the North American box office, returning $17 Million in rentals (the share that studios receive from the theatrical gross) to Paramount.

For the year of 1980, *Friday the 13th* ranked eighteenth on the yearly box office chart, falling between the Warner Bros. golfing comedy *Caddyshack* ($39.8 Million) and the Robert Redford prison drama *Brubaker* ($37.1 Million). Worldwide, *Friday the 13th* grossed in excess of $70 Million in its first year of release.

Whatever the context, whether as a low budget independent film or in competition with the various big budget studio films released in 1980, *Friday the 13th* was a certified hit.

The novelization of *Friday the 13th* was written by fantasy writer Simon Hawke and published by Signet in September of 1987. (Photo courtesy of Jason Parker www.fridaythe13thfranchise.com)

CHAPTER 11

SATURDAY THE 14TH: THE DAY AFTER

"The period after Friday the 13th was a time when I should've sat down and asked myself, 'Okay, what do you really want to do next?' I wasn't prepared for the success of Friday the 13th and I didn't have a clear idea of what I wanted to do next. I would meet with studio executives and they asked me that same question – 'What do you want to do next?' – and I really didn't have an answer. I think I was hoping they'd offer me the next Robert DeNiro or Al Pacino movie to direct."

– Sean Cunningham

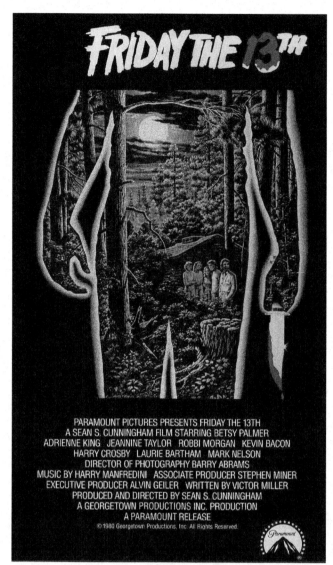

Promotional artwork that was used for *Friday the 13th*'s initial home video release. (Photo courtesy of Matt Hankinson)

Newspaper advertisement for *Friday the 13th*. (Photo courtesy of Barry Abrams)

The more public *Friday the 13th* became, the more it stood as both a lightning rod for criticism and somewhat of a scarlet letter for those involved in its making, especially the cast members. For Cunningham and Miner, the controversy and critical scorn heaped on *Friday the 13th* was offset by the fact that *Friday the 13th* made them millionaires, virtually overnight.

For the cast and crew, who only had their modest paychecks from *Friday the 13th*, and wouldn't share in any of the tens of millions of dollars of ancillary revenues, the notoriety and success of *Friday the 13th* had a lot of repercussions, both personally and professionally.

"I'm sure everyone thinks that the actors in the movie, me and Adrienne King especially, get residuals from the movie, but it's not true," Betsy Palmer says. "I get about fifteen dollars a year."

BLOOD MONEY

Friday the 13th was a ripe target for film critics and cultural commentators throughout the summer of 1980 who, almost universally, condemned *Friday the 13th* as filth and pornography, ubiquitous charges that teenagers cheerfully ignored. The most influential opponent of *Friday the 13th*, by far, was *Chicago Tribune* newspaper film critic Gene Siskel. In 1980, Siskel was co-hosting - alongside *Chicago Sun-Times* newspaper film critic Roger Ebert – *Sneak Previews*, a weekly television film review program that aired on public broadcasting. It was on this television platform, especially, that Siskel – who described Sean Cunningham as "one of the most despicable creatures ever to infest the movie business" – basically declared war on *Friday the 13th*.

Ebert, who died in 2013, and Siskel, who died in 1999, devoted an entire program to *Friday the 13th* where Siskel condemned the film for its gory violence and criticized Paramount Pictures for re-

The success of *Friday the 13th* allowed Georgetown Productions to finance and produce the slasher film *Eyes of a Stranger,* for which Georgetown partners Stephen Minasian and Philip Scuderi recruited Tom Savini to provide effects work. (Photo courtesy of Tom Savini)

leasing the film. Siskel went so far as to instigate a letter writing campaign that was directed towards Charles Bludhorn (AKA Charles Bluhdorn), chairman of the conglomerate – Gulf + Western – that owned Paramount Pictures, as well as Betsy Palmer.

Siskel even suggested that viewers disgusted by *Friday the 13th* write letters of disapproval to Palmer, care of her hometown which Siskel believed to be in Connecticut. Though maintaining a Connecticut residence, Palmer was actually born in East Chicago, Indiana. "I never got any letters, and I didn't even hear about that until years later," Palmer says. "I think he must've told people to write to Connecticut, but my actual hometown was in Indiana. I thought it was ridiculous. I don't think I ever saw one letter."

Having survived the backlash against *Last House on the Left,* Cunningham was hardened to the harsh critical reaction that greeted *Friday the 13th.* For Cunningham, the biggest impact felt from *Fri-* *day the 13th* was the money that poured into him throughout the summer of 1980, pure and simple.

As was negotiated in his deal with Paramount Pictures and Warner Bros., Cunningham received his share of profits and royalties from the two studios instead of relying on Philip Scuderi and Georgetown, and their accounting practices. In the first year of *Friday the 13th*'s release alone, Cunningham received in excess of two million dollars.

Steve Miner also became a millionaire from *Friday the 13th* and both Cunningham and Miner, Cunningham especially, continue to reap profits to this day. Meanwhile, writer Victor Miller, who was paid a "low five-figure Writers Guild scale" for his scripting chores, didn't have a profit-sharing deal on *Friday the 13th*, and doesn't receive any specific royalties from *Friday the 13th.* He has been solely entitled to the Writers Guild of America (WGA) payments that relate to *Friday the 13th*'s countless television showings and sizable video rental revenues that have accrued over the years.

While this has been a substantial stream of revenue for Miller over the past thirty plus years, it certainly pales in comparison to the millions of dollars he would have reasonably expected to have yielded as *Friday the 13th*'s co-creator.

After a long exile, Adrienne King has returned to public life and is a fixture on the celebrity autograph convention circuit. (Photo courtesy of Phil Fasso www.deathensemble.com)

In 1988, Miller filed suit against Cunningham, seeking a more complete set of payments from both Cunningham and Georgetown Productions, a company that dissolved as a business entity in 1982, but remained as a corporate entity. This is evidenced by the various lawsuits that have been filed against Georgetown in the years since

Friday the 13th's release. The case was settled and Miller received an undisclosed amount of money.

The millions of dollars that Georgetown partners Robert Barsamian, Stephen Minasian and Philip Scuderi realized from *Friday the 13th* gave them freedom to finance and produce more films. This included the immediate *Friday the 13th* sequels as well as a variety of other unrelated genre film projects the partners, jointly and separately, were involved with throughout the 1980s.

After Georgetown's formal dissolution in 1982, the same year Philip Scuderi, who had a chronic heart condition, was slowed by a heart attack, Stephen Minasian focused on a partnership he'd established with schlock film producer maestro Dick Randall. Together they produced the horror films *Pieces* (1982), *Don't Open Till Christmas* (1984) and *Slaughter High* (1986), all of which received limited theatrical releases, but have enjoyed a sizable cult following over the years.

Scuderi, who died in 1995 at the age of 66, devoted most of his energies, until the mid 1980s, to the *Friday the 13th* sequels. Scuderi was also involved with the production of the 1981 slasher film *Eyes of a Stranger* – a Georgetown production that Tom Savini worked on – and the 1983 film *Off the Wall*, a prison comedy film that was co-scripted by Ron Kurz (Kurz also wrote *Eyes of a Stranger* under the pseudonym Mark Jackson).

Robert Barsamian, the silent partner of the Boston trio, maintained his low profile throughout the 1980s with his daughter, Lisa Barsamian, assuming a prominent role in the production of the first three *Friday the 13th* sequels, serving as a credited producer on each of the films.

For the Georgetown partners, and their film production business itself, the success of *Friday the 13th* produced many tentacles, many of which led away from the *Friday the 13th* franchise. This included a real estate development empire in New England, financed by the profits from *Friday the 13th* and its sequels, in which all three of the families were – and continue to be – involved, both jointly and separately, all over the New England area and beyond.

Ironically, it's this very same real estate development that led to the slow but steady extinction of the Esquire theater chain, which is now only represented by a handful of theaters,

1980 shot of Harry Crosby in New York, in the wake of *Friday the 13th*'s release. (Photo courtesy of Harry Crosby)

under the control of Stephen Minasian who, now well into his eighties, maintains only a tangential relationship to the film and theater business.

With Philip Scuderi now deceased, a result of his chronic heart condition, Robert Barsamian, Minasian's brother-in-law who's also in his eighties, is the only other living member of the Georgetown trio. Today, Robert Barsamian, who suffers from diabetes, has retired to Florida where members of the Scuderi family also reside. In recent years, Lisa Barsamian has told friends that the family has

158

an interest in getting back into the film business.

Sean Cunningham himself filed a lawsuit against Georgetown – with whom Cunningham endured several business entanglements throughout the 1980s and 1990s, in spite of Cunningham's agreement with Paramount and Warner Bros. – several years ago seeking additional monies related to Cunningham's initial profit-sharing deal. This case was settled.

Besides ensuring the Westport home (a home that sold for $12.6 Million in 2011) that Cunningham had taken a second mortgage on prior to filming *Friday the 13th* was safe from foreclosure, Cunningham was, as anybody in his position would've been, completely startled by his newfound wealth in the wake of *Friday the 13th*'s success in 1980.

After receiving his first payment from *Friday the 13th*, Cunningham immediately splurged on a brand new Mercedes which he proudly drove around Westport. "I was talking to Sean on the phone and he told me he'd bought a Mercedes, and I was shocked because I knew that Sean hated Mercedes'," Virginia Field recalls. "I said, 'Sean, you hate Mercedes. Why would you buy a car like that?' Sean said, 'I know, but I felt like I had to buy a Mercedes, something very expensive, to make this all seem real.' For Sean, the Mercedes represented that the money and the success was real."

After *Friday the 13th*, Harry Crosby starred in the made-for-television film *The Private History of a Campaign That Failed* (1981). (Photo courtesy of David Beury)

YOU'RE ALL DOOMED

For the cast members of *Friday the 13th*, the film's notoriety had a varying impact on their careers and lives. Kevin Bacon, who had a modest body of film and television work previous to *Friday the 13th*, pivoted away fairly adeptly. But for the rest of the cast members, most of whom, save for the elder Betsy Palmer, had never made a film prior to *Friday the 13th*, the film was a professional albatross.

"Films like *Friday the 13th* are like the circus for actors," Sean Cunningham says. "The actors do a good job in these films, but you don't see them in anything else because the industry looks at them as being a dime a dozen. You know, if you're casting a part for a pretty girl in a movie who are you going to want, Cameron Diaz or the girl who was in *Friday the 13th*? You have to be really strong to jump out from the pack. No one wants to see them. They think all you can do is horror. Look at the actors who were in *The Blair Witch Project*. They gave perfect performances but you never see them anymore."

Some of the cast members from *Friday the 13th* were made to feel like they'd been part of something distasteful and repugnant, almost akin to pornography. This bias wasn't just felt from the film and television industry, but also from family and friends. "Films like *Friday the 13th* are very primitive, and nobody in the industry takes them seriously, except in terms of how much money they make," Mark Nelson says. "My mom was a first grade teacher, and a couple of years after the movie came out, there was a discussion in the school about movies that should be prohibited. Someone mentioned *Friday the 13th* and my mother wanted to hide under the table."

"When the movie was first released, the reaction was a pretty universal repugnance on the part of everyone I knew, both in and out of showbiz," Jeannine Taylor recalls. "My family. My friends. (Many just didn't mention it, trying to be tactful, which, in a way, made it worse). My agents were quite upset about the public outcry and critical scorn and concerned about the negative impact on my fledgling career. For their pure-voiced little ingénue to have this type of – and level of - exposure at the start, well, I won't speak for them but they seemed to be mortified, which I'm fairly certain they were. The fact that it was a commercial success was of absolutely no consequence to those who were monitoring or representing me. They were all, in a word, horrified."

Betsy Palmer has grudgingly embraced *Friday the 13th* over the years. (Photo courtesy of Robert Armin www.robertarmin.com)

As the star of *Friday the 13th*, and the film's heroine, Adrienne King felt the brunt of this typecasting, and would never escape the bonds of *Friday the 13th*. But the worst part for King was what happened in her personal life following *Friday the 13th*'s release.

In the summer of 1980, King found herself the victim of a madman who'd become enamored with her after seeing *Friday the 13th*. The stalking ordeal lingered into 1981, by which time King was also coping with the industry's typecasting of her as the star of *Friday the 13th*. "I had a really bad stalker and it

went on for over a year," King said. "I definitely had a hard time because of the stalker because it wasn't taken seriously in the 1980s at all. I had some really nasty stuff going on back then, and the cops and FBI told me that when something actually happened to me...physically...then they would do something."

King, in an attempt to break into non-horror roles, spent part of 1980 studying at the Royal Academy of Dramatic Arts (RADA) in London where she appeared in several Shakespearean productions, most notably a stage version of *Othello* in which she played Desdemona! Returning to New York in the fall of 1980, in anticipation of making an appearance in *Friday the 13th Part 2*, King realized that the specter of *Friday the 13th* simply wouldn't let her go. "The only thing that movie [*Friday the 13th*] did for my career was type me forever as an actress in horror films," King said. "After *Friday*, the only roles I was offered were horror films. It finally got so bad that I had to go to England [RADA] to get a non-horror offer."

Other cast members felt that the impact of *Friday the 13th* on their careers was negligible. "It was, mainly, a nice conversation piece when you'd go in

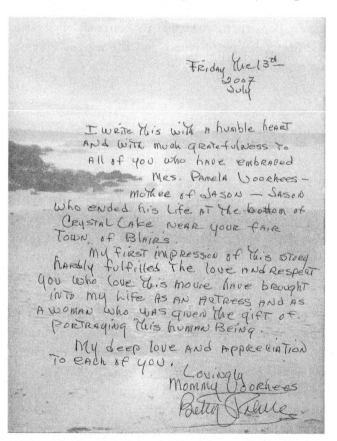

2007 letter that Betsy Palmer wrote to the Blairstown Theater Festival who held a screening of *Friday the 13th* on July 13, 2007. (Photo courtesy of Robert Armin www.robertarmin.com)

and meet with a casting director or producer," Peter Brouwer says. "Other than that, it had no effect at all on me. Before *Friday the 13th*, I was known as a soap opera actor and I did soaps after *Friday the 13th*, and no one made a big deal out of the fact that I'd been in *Friday the 13th*. I did meet Betsy Palmer several years later at a party and we laughed about the success of the movie. She was very charming. Hard to believe she could be so demonic."

"I never had a problem with having been in *Friday the 13th*, and none of my family and friends had a problem with it," says Harry Crosby. "I was thrilled, and surprised, that the movie was such a big hit, but it didn't have much of an effect on my acting career and that didn't surprise me. After *Friday the 13th*, I was cast in a Broadway play but the money fell through before we started work on it. Then I starred in a pilot for CBS called *Pony Express*, which didn't get picked up, and then I was in a television movie called *The Private History of a Campaign That Failed*, which was directed by Peter Hunt who made the film *1776*. I don't think *Friday the 13th* played a role in any of that, but it never hurts to have been in a movie that's so popular, and I'm happy that so many people love the movie."

"It didn't have that much of an effect on my career," Robbi Morgan says. "I don't think it had a negative impact. I just don't think anyone was going to cast me in a film or television show, or not cast me, because I'd been in *Friday the 13th*. I think there's two types of movies. There's *The Sixth Sense*, which is really deep and psychological and then there's the *Friday the 13th* movies which are just good fun. They're just meant to scare, and there's nothing wrong with that, so I'm not ashamed at all to have been in the movie. When the movie's on, I let my kids watch, but only the stuff when mommy's on screen. I think it might be too much for them so I wouldn't let them watch the whole thing."

Betsy Palmer, who was so skittish about doing *Friday the 13th* in the first place, was as bemused by *Friday the 13th*'s unlikely success as she was by her casting in the film. "I saw the movie once, and I haven't seen any of the sequels," Palmer says. "A few years later, I did a play in Philadelphia and one night I was in a grocery store and heard this 'ki-ki-ki, ma-ma-ma' behind me and I turned around and saw this fan who pointed at me and said, 'It's Mrs. Voorhees.'

I was doing a guest spot on an episode of *Murder, She Wrote* and one of the girls, a day-player, walked up to me and told me how much her husband loved my performance in *Friday the 13th*. Another time, a guy came over to my house in Sedona, Arizona to fix my septic tank and he just went crazy when he saw me, because of *Friday the 13th*. I was at a convention once, and there was this kid who was really nervous. I looked at him and he came over to have something signed and he asked me about Jason, and I said, 'Jason's dead. I don't know Jason. I've never seen any of the other movies.' I'm really proud that fans still think the original film is the best of them all."

Jeannine Taylor sought refuge in the world of theater in the early 1980s, in an attempt to weather the stigma of *Friday the 13th*. (Photo courtesy of Carol Rosegg)

Born again Christian Laurie Bartram had a bemused reaction to the controversy. Following the filming in Blairstown, Bartram, who'd given thought to becoming a television newscaster, returned to her apartment in Midtown New York, and kept in touch with Harry Crosby for a period afterward, as well as with Cecelia and John Verardi who lived in Staten Island. A now well-known story is that Bartram's cat died after getting into some rat poison at the Verardis' home, but there were no hard feelings about this or her participation in *Friday the 13th*.

"Laurie lived in Midtown, and we kept in touch after the filming, and Harry and Laurie had dinner at our house in Staten Island after filming," Cecelia Verardi recalls. "Laurie's mother also had dinner with us once, and she was a very nice woman. Laurie's mother brought us a cookbook from New Orleans, or somewhere in the south. Willie Adams also came to our house in Staten Island after the filming and had dinner with us. We never saw or heard from Willie again after that."

By the summer of 1980 Bartram was in the process of severing acting connections and friendships from her life in New York. It wasn't easy for her.

Following the release of *Friday the 13th*, Tom Savini was recruited to provide effects for the film *The Burning* (1981), the first – and the progenitor - of the *Friday the 13th* copycats. (Photo courtesy of Matt Hankinson)

"Laurie was an aspiring newscaster or newswoman, and I believe that she said she'd been a journalist in her hometown," Cecelia Verardi says. "One day, Laurie sent a note to us, saying that she was going away to 'fulfill her dreams' and would keep in touch. We never heard from her again. Harry also sent a note and thanked us for the good times we had, and

for our hospitality. Harry was just a really good guy."

In 1981, Bartram settled in Lynchburg, Virginia where she enrolled in Liberty Baptist College (later renamed Liberty University), a Christian school that was founded by the late Reverend Jerry Falwell. "She [Bartram] and I were on the same singing team at Liberty University, a team with an emphasis on missions, called Student Missionary Intern Training for Evangelism (SMITE)," recalls James Willis, a friend of Bartram's while they were both students at Liberty in the early 1980s. "During the school year, we toured most weekends, visiting churches in the south and southwest. She was humble. Everyone 'knew' that Laurie had once been a major star and had left that life to pursue her faith, but her previous acting career was not something she spoke about a lot."

In 1984, Bartram married fellow Liberty student Gregory McCauley. They had five children, all of whom Bartram home-schooled until Bartram – who taught dance in Lynchburg, and did voiceover work at local radio and television stations – died of pancreatic cancer on May 25, 2007 at the age of 49. "She was smart, intelligent, book-smart, and a fun person to be around," Willis recalls. "She 'had' to have her coffee. She called it her 'big eye' as in, 'I have to have my big eye in the morning, or I can't function.' She couldn't. Completely addicted to coffee when I knew her. I traveled the school year on the same singing team with Laurie, and to Brazil in the summer of 1982, where we toured the country, singing our songs in Portuguese. My favorite memory is when she sat next to me on the bus one night and I was struggling with my English homework and she offered to help. I was reading *Hills Like White Elephants* by Ernest Hemingway and didn't understand what the dialogue was talking about. She helped me to understand it and that did the trick. That was the kind person I knew, and the person I recall when Friday the thirteenth rolls around on the calendar."

With the obvious exception of Kevin Bacon, the cast members of *Friday the 13th* have accumulated a very modest list of film and television credits in the years since *Friday the 13th*'s release. Some, like Adrienne King, fell under the *Friday the 13th* typecasting curse that has also afflicted many of the cast members of the *Friday the 13th* sequels.

Mark Nelson ignored *Friday the 13th* altogether and has enjoyed a prolific stage career that has been balanced with sporadic film and television appearances. Others dropped out completely, mostly for non-*Friday the 13th* related reasons, although some of the cast members of *Friday the 13th* have endured more than their share of bad luck over the years.

Following his appearance in *Friday the 13th*, Kevin Bacon appeared on the daytime television soap opera *The Guiding Light*. Bacon's appearance on *The Guiding Light*, filmed in New York, lasted from 1980 to 1981. It was during this period that a career-conscious Bacon turned down an offer to do an *Animal House*-like television series that was going to be filmed in Los Angeles, wanting to stay close to the New York stage scene, where his career would truly be launched.

A Stranger is Watching, Sean Cunningham's follow-up to *Friday the 13th*, was a commercial and critical failure. (Photo courtesy of Barry Abrams)

After well-received turns in the plays *Flux* and *Getting Out*, both of which Bacon performed at New York's Phoenix Theater during the 1981-1982 theater season, his career had momentum. *Friday the 13th* was scarcely mentioned.

Bacon won an Obie award for his performance in the play *Forty Deuce*, after which he made his Broadway debut in the play *Slab Boys*, alongside Val Kilmer and Sean Penn. It was during this period that Bacon's film career gained life. Bacon was cast, alongside Ellen Barkin and

Mickey Rourke, in writer-director Barry Levinson's acclaimed comedy-drama film *Diner* (1982).

Following *Diner*, Bacon co-starred in the John Sayles-scripted dramatic film *Enormous Changes at the Last Minute* (1983), notable because Richard Feury, the still photographer on *Friday the 13th* and Bacon's off-screen assailant, served as an assistant director on the film. "Kevin and I worked on *Enormous Changes at the Last Minute* and we both laughed at what we'd done on *Friday the 13th*," Feury recalls. "I told Kevin he'd better be nice to me because I had pictures of me putting my hand over his face and sticking the arrow through his neck."

Footloose (1984) launched Bacon to mainstream film stardom, a status he faltered under by the end of the 1980s, after a string of commercial failures. The 1990s were a different story, however, showcasing Bacon—beginning with films like *Flatliners* (1990) and *JFK* (1991) - as an actor who could transition from leading man to interesting character actor.

Prior to *Friday the 13th*, Peter Brouwer had also been a veteran of the daytime television soap

The success of *Friday the 13th* carried no residual effect to *A Stranger is Watching*. (Photo courtesy of Barry Abrams)

opera genre. He returned to the soaps after *Friday the 13th*, appearing on *As the World Turns*, a stint that lasted from 1981 to 1982. Brouwer spent most of the rest of the 1980s and the 1990s raising a family with Cindy Veazey, while also acting in regional theater productions, as well as being an avid orchid grower.

FROM THE DIRECTOR OF FRIDAY THE 13TH...

A STRANGER IS WATCHING

R ©1982 HERON PRODUCTIONS LIMITED MGM/United Artists Distribution and Marketing

THEATRE

A Stranger is Watching's $5 Million budget was roughly ten times that of *Friday the 13th*. (Photo courtesy of Barry Abrams)

In 2009, Brouwer returned to daytime television with regular appearances on the soaps *All My Children* and *One Life to Live*. "I also work as an auctioneer," Brouwer says. "It's something that's very exciting and that I've gotten very good at it. If you're running a charity auction, I can make money for you!"

Harry Crosby gave up his earnest pursuit of a show business career in 1984 -- the year he obtained a business degree from Fordham University. From the mid 1980s, Crosby has enjoyed a successful career in the financial services/investment banking field, holding management positions at firms like Credit Suisse First Boston and Merrill Lynch. "I don't think I'd recommend that someone spend three years in England studying music and theater if they want a career in business, but I think the training I went through served me well," says Crosby who's married to a scientist and, humorously, used to incorporate a mention of *Friday the 13th* into his corporate recruitment materials. "I think acting taught me how to deal with problems and how to find creative solutions to problems. I don't regret my acting career at all. It was a great adventure."

Adrienne King also entered the crowd-

ed world of daytime television upon returning to New York from London in the fall of 1980, but what happened to King off-screen overshadowed everything else between 1980 and 1981.

After returning to New York, King was derailed by severe panic attacks that were a direct result of the disturbing stalking incident she experienced in the wake of *Friday the 13th*'s release. In the fall of 1981, King married Robert Tuckman, a New York lawyer, and then later married Richard Hassanein, an executive in the post-production film services industry, with whom King is still married to this day. By the mid 1980s, King had settled into the anonymous and peaceful life the post-production industry offers.

In the early 1990s, King reinvented herself as a voiceover performer, contributing background and looping vocals to various film titles, including *Jerry Maguire*, *Titanic*, *What's Eating Gilbert Grape?*, and many others. Today, King lives in Oregon with her husband where she runs a fledgling winery business while also being a regular on the celebrity autograph convention circuit.

Following her appearance in *Friday the 13th*, Robbi Morgan appeared in the Broadway production of *Barnum* which ran from 1980 to 1982. Following several episodic television appearances in the early 1980s, Morgan – an acrobat, actress, dancer and singer – put her performing career on hiatus to focus on her family life when she married actor and game show host Mark Walberg. "I've bumped into Betsy Palmer, who'd worked with my brother on *Peter Pan*, quite a few times over the years, in between her plays and my jobs, and she's an amazing lady," Morgan says. "Hard to believe that she could ever kill me. I'm married and have two children and haven't acted very much lately. Most of the performing I've done over the past twenty years has been as a dancer and singer, performing at revue shows, vaudeville kind of stuff, where me and other performers dance, sing, everything. I wouldn't mind doing another horror movie if the right script came along."

Mark Nelson has enjoyed an acclaimed, rich stage career since appearing in *Friday the 13th*. Most recently, Nelson has gone back to his acting roots, teaching drama at his alma mater, Princeton University. "I look at *Friday the 13th* as, quite simply, a fun two weeks of work that happened more than thirty years ago," Nelson says. "I think the actors who appear in these movies make a mistake by trying to make that kind of experience into more than it is. The best part of *Friday the 13th*, for me, was the time when the movie came out, which was a real thrill. Other than that, I think everything in my career, especially my work in the theater, has happened pretty much as it would've happened, whether I'd been in *Friday the 13th* or not."

Following the release of *Friday the 13th*, Betsy Palmer joined the cast of the daytime soap opera *As the World Turns*, where she appeared from 1981 to 1982, around the same period that Peter Brouwer was on the show, although neither Brouwer nor Palmer recall working together on the show.

Palmer, who also co-hosted several regional talk/variety shows during the early 1980s, spent the rest of the 1980s appearing on episodic television, as well as continual work in theater, her true love. Although *Friday the 13th* didn't lead to more film roles for Palmer, her most notable post-*Friday the 13th* film role being a sizable cameo in *Friday the 13th Part 2*, the success of *Friday the 13th* did raise Palmer's once dormant profile, which had been sagging from the 1960s. "There weren't any movie offers after *Friday the 13th*, but I think the success of *Friday the 13th* did allow me to do more theater, in terms of the

Barry Abrams abandoned feature filmmaking following the filming of *A Stranger is Watching* and later operated a charter plane business in the British Virgin Islands with wife Nikki Abrams. (Photo courtesy of Nalani Clark)

publicity from the film, which is my first love," says Palmer who's also a regular on the celebrity autograph convention circuit alongside King, Ari Lehman and Jeannine Taylor. "I never liked doing movies anyway. The best part of *Friday the 13th* for me has

been getting to meet all of the fans and have them tell me how much they love the film and how much they loved my character. That's very flattering."

No one benefitted more from *Friday the 13th* than makeup effects expert Tom Savini. His groundbreaking work in *Friday the 13th*, combined with his prior triumph on *Dawn of the Dead*, ushered in an era, beginning in the early 1980s, where makeup experts like Savini, Rick Baker and Rob Bottin were viewed as pseudo rock stars within filmdom circles. "When I was first hired to work on *Friday the 13th*, it was just a job, but I'm very proud of my work in the film," Savini says. "*Friday the 13th* was one of those rare experiences, rare even on independent films, where all of the effects work I did made it into the finished film. It's very flattering when fans say that the effects were the star of the film."

Savini's celebrity status was evident following *Friday the 13th*'s release when Savini was recruited by film producer Harvey Weinstein to handle the effects chores on a summer camp-themed horror film. Titled *The Burning*, it was a blatant *Friday the 13th* rip-off filmed in western New York in the summer of 1980. *The Burning* marked the first producing effort for Weinstein's then-fledgling Miramax Films banner.

The Burning had a production budget of $1.5 Million, about three times that of *Friday the 13th*. "Harvey Weinstein called me up and told me he loved the effects in *Friday the 13th* and that he wanted me to do the same thing with *The Burning*," Savini recalls. "I had a lot of fun and a lot of creative freedom on *The Burning*, but the best part was when the film was released in 1981 and the company flew me around the country to do press for the film. When was the last time you saw a makeup guy doing press for a film?"

Savini actually chose *The Burning* over *Friday the 13th Part 2*. Ever a man of creative principles, Savini eschewed *Friday the 13th Part 2* because he objected to the concept of featuring Jason in the sequel. This maverick streak has followed Savini throughout his entire career, and is one of the main reasons why Savini has never embraced – or been embraced by – mainstream Hollywood. "I turned down the sequel, because I didn't think there was any point in doing a movie about the character of Jason who was, after all, dead," Savini says. "It didn't make sense to me and it just seemed pointless."

Barry Abrams continued working on television commercials, off and on, throughout the 1980s and 1990s, and in 1985, Barry and Nikki Abrams collaborated on a Michael Jackson toy figurine commercial, for which Barry Abrams served as cameraman and director and Nikki Abrams served as producer. Nikki Abrams passed away in 1999 and her funeral was attended by several *Friday the 13th* crew members. Barry Abrams died in 2009. (Photo courtesy of Nalani Clark)

Jeannine Taylor's dearth of post-*Friday the 13th* film and television credits was a result of circumstances and fate, mostly in the form of a debilitating illness that derailed her acting career and her life for a period in the 1980s.

Following her work in *Friday the 13th*, Taylor immersed herself back in the New York theater scene, appearing in several productions between 1980 and 1982. In 1982, Taylor, like Peter Brouwer and Betsy Palmer, had a recurring role on the daytime television soap opera *As the World Turns*. That same year, Taylor made her last filmed appearance with a role in *The Royal Romance of Charles and Diana*, a movie-of the week about the courtship of Prince Charles and Princess Diana that aired on CBS. "I played the 'bad girl,' in the small role of Prince Charles' vain, spoiled love interest," Taylor recalls. "She dumps the prince because his royal duties prevent him from paying enough attention to her. The thing I remember most about that shoot was being on the same set with both Ray Milland and Olivia de Havilland, which was a major thrill!"

Taylor discovered that *Friday the 13th* cast an even wider shadow than she ever could've imagined. "My disappearance from film and TV was, I think, due mostly to the extreme critical scorn and public outcry against *Friday the 13th* at the time of its release in 1980, and for a few years immediately afterward," says Taylor who, in 1983, went to Los Angeles in pursuit of more film and television opportunities. "It was clearly something that had to be overcome professionally, and I'd begun to do that by continuing to work in stage plays and musicals, and being (mostly!) well-reviewed, so I believe I would have overcome this setback in time."

Spring Break marked the end of Sean Cunningham's professional relationships with Virginia Field and Victor Miller. (Photo courtesy of Matt Hankinson)

During her time in Los Angeles in 1983, Taylor was cast in an ABC television series pilot that fell through when Taylor's agent demanded too much money from the production. Taylor also discovered that the specter of *Friday the 13th* carried much the same powerful impact on the West Coast as it had back in New York. "One agent, a woman with a one-person office, told me to take *Friday the 13th* off my demo reel and said she couldn't work with me," recalls Taylor of her time in Los Angeles. "After two weeks, I knew I couldn't stay in LA; I was just too lonely and I felt like a fish out of water. The palm trees, the driving everywhere (For some reason, every time I got lost – a daily occurrence! – I ended up at the La Brea Tar Pits.) I was cast in a pilot for an ABC comedy. Gary Leaverton [Taylor's New York agent], my agent, who passed away some years ago, demanded $2000 more per week than they offered and negotiated me out of the job! – something he was famous for doing – and they ended up using another actress. During that trip to LA in 1983, I also met with a casting director at one of the three major networks and he was quite candid about the hit that *Friday the 13th* had delivered to my career. He told me I needed to go back to New York and 'get some momentum back into your career.' His exact words. He, in fact, verbalized what I was already feeling. I had something to live down and I had to do that in New York."

In 1985, Taylor's career and life were turned upside down when she was stricken with Graves' disease, an autoimmune disorder of the thyroid that, while rarely being fatal, has many punishing side effects. "For awhile, I had a resting pulse of 150, could not bend my wrists, knees or ankles without excruciating pain, and my eyes bulged out of their sockets so badly that I could not close them to sleep," Taylor recalls. "I wore dark glasses indoors and out for several years because it just felt more comfortable that way. There's often no fast and easy cure for Graves' disease and recovery can take several years, as it did for me. During treatment, the beta-blockers I needed to take to slow my heart rate swelled my face (and the rest of me) almost beyond recognition. My hair fell out, and for a year my face was covered in severe acne. It was a tough time. I was ill from 1985 till 1988. Meanwhile, my SAG health insurance had run out, and I needed a job with good health benefits, so I went to work at *Institutional Investor*, a financial magazine in New York. At first, it felt very strange being in a corporate setting, but it was a great company and the salary and the benefits were, quite literally, a lifesaver."

Like Barry Abrams, Virginia Field relocated to Paris, France, where Field currently teaches at a film school. (Photo courtesy of Tony Marshall)

In 1989, Taylor traveled to England and attended RADA, following in Adrienne King's footsteps. But by this time Taylor had put her acting career on the back-burner, focusing on other interests. In 1990, Taylor married James McConnell, a businessman. Taylor returned to school in the early 1990s to study art history and eventually transitioned into a career as an appraiser of antiques and art. "Having gone through a major illness, my priorities had changed, and a new man entered my life and I felt I needed a more 'family-friendly' career," says Taylor who lives and works in the New England area. "During the early 1990s, I returned to school to study art history, interned at an art museum, worked for an auction house, and eventually became an appraiser of art and antiques."

NO ONE IS WATCHING

Whatever stench *Friday the 13th* generated in society, the success made Sean Cunningham a hot commodity in money-conscious Hollywood. It was the same with writer Victor Miller. "The success of *Friday the 13th* made Sean and I very hot for a brief period of time," Miller says. "Around June of 1980, just after *Friday the 13th* had been released, I took a meeting with the head of Columbia Pictures, Frank Price, and gave him a one sentence pitch, for a project called *Asylum*, that he bought instantly. The movie never got made but I was paid very well. Looking back, I think he would've bought anything I pitched, because of the success of *Friday the 13th*."

YOU ARE CORDIALLY INVITED TO SPEND AN EVENING WITH ROGER COBB AND HIS FRIENDS.

DON'T COME ALONE!

·HOUSE·

HORROR HAS FOUND A NEW HOME.

NEW WORLD PICTURES Presents
A SEAN S. CUNNINGHAM Production a STEVE MINER film
HOUSE starring WILLIAM KATT · GEORGE WENDT
RICHARD MOLL · KAY LENZ Production Designer GREGG FONSECA
Director of Photography MAC AHLBERG Associate Producer PATRICK MARKEY
Music by HARRY MANFREDINI story by FRED DEKKER
screenplay by ETHAN WILEY produced by SEAN S. CUNNINGHAM
Directed by STEVE MINER

OPENS NATIONWIDE FEBRUARY 28TH

Sean Cunningham and Steve Miner reteamed on the film *House* on which Cunningham served as producer and Steve Miner served as director. *House* was a modest commercial success. (Photo courtesy of Matt Hankinson)

In 1980, Cunningham signed a production deal with Columbia Pictures, as well as a deal with Filmways, a film and television production company that had recently swallowed up American International Pictures (AIP). Filmways hired Cunningham to direct and produce a thriller film project called *Ridge Run*, a story about four mentally-deranged people who hijack a school bus. The project never came to pass.

Cunningham also spent the fall of 1980 talking to Metro-Goldwyn-Mayer (MGM) (before MGM merged with United Artists into MGM/UA in the summer of 1981) about an independent film project he wanted to make entitled *Stomping Ground*. The project went nowhere. "I always figured that when they let you in the club, they took you upstairs and opened a filing cabinet where they kept all these great scripts that [Jane] Fonda and [Robert] Redford were dying to do and said, 'Here, take your pick,'" Cunningham says. "It isn't that way at all. You sit at a table and they all look at you and say, 'What do you want to do?'"

In the fall of 1980, Cunningham signed a production deal with MGM and finally seemed to gain traction when he made the acquaintance of independent producer Sidney Beckerman, an adventurous, colorful film producer whose previous film credits included such eclectic titles as *Last Summer* (1969), *Marlowe* (1969), *Kelly's Heroes* (1970), *Portnoy's Complaint* (1972), and *Marathon Man* (1976).

Beckerman was in control of a project called *A Stranger is Watching*, based on a 1977 bestselling novel by Mary Higgins Clark. The story followed a young girl who's kidnapped and terrorized by the same psychopath who raped and murdered her mother. Beckerman, who died in 2008, had been looking for a director for *A Stranger is Watching* since 1978. "He [Beckerman] said he thought *A Stranger is Watching* would be just right for me," Cunningham said. "I read it and agreed with him."

With its seedy elements of child endangerment and rape, *A Stranger is Watching* seemed quite compatible with Cunningham's filmmaking sensibilities, but all of the other production elements put Cunningham well out of his comfort zone. *A Stranger is Watching* had a budget of $5 Million, which was modest by Hollywood standards but a whopping tenfold increase from *Friday the 13th*. "It was simple arithmetic," Beckerman said at the time. "I figured that if he [Cunningham] could make a $500,000 movie that grossed $70 Million, we would make a $5 Million movie and gross $350 Million."

In addition to the increased budget, *A Stranger is Watching* was an all-union production filmed on location in New York with a "professional" cast that included Kate Mulgrew, James Naughton and the notorious Rip Torn who played the film's villain. This was uncharted territory for Cunningham who was joined by *Friday the 13th* alumni Barry Abrams, Virginia Field, Braden Lutz, Robert Topol and Victor Miller, who co-wrote the script with Earl Mac Rauch.

Unlike Sean Cunningham, Steve Miner was able to escape the bonds of *Friday the 13th* and progress into mainstream filmmaking. (Photo courtesy of Laurel Moore)

"It was like night and day going from *Friday the 13th* to films like *A Stranger is Watching* and *Spring Break* because of the unions and increased budgets," Field recalls. "A guy on the crew [referring to *A Stranger is Watching*] complained about asbestos on one of my sets because he was upset about not getting overtime. That's something that never happened on the previous films. We shot in Grand Central Station and Rikers' Island prison. There were some name actors, especially Rip Torn. Everything was different."

"We did *A Stranger is Watching* and it was a bigger movie all the way around," Robert Topol

recalls. "It was more serious. There was a union crew, professional gaffers, more money, a bigger cast of actors, filming in and under Central Station. It was an entirely different experience."

Filmed in the spring of 1981, *A Stranger is Watching* was belatedly-released in January of 1982 by the newly-formed MGM/UA. The film was greeted with total indifference. It grossed a paltry $2.5 Million at the North American box office and quickly disappeared onto the ether of the cable television market thereafter. Not even the film critics, those who'd attacked *Friday the 13th* so ferociously, could seem to muster any venom to spew onto the film.

The failure of *A Stranger is Watching* was a painful rejection for Sean Cunningham, and a pow-

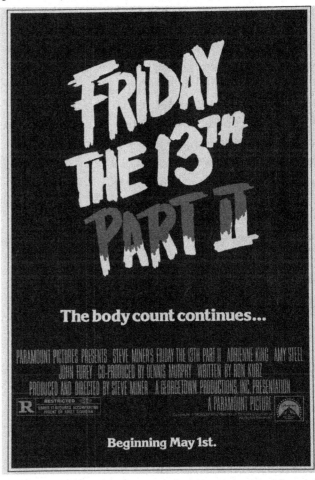

Friday the 13th Part 2 marked Steve Miner's feature directing debut. Although Sean Cunningham's role on *Friday the 13th Part 2* was uncredited, Cunningham did visit the set during filming. (Photo courtesy of Matt Hankinson)

erful dose of reality. The film marked the end of his relationship with MGM/UA, and it also marked the end of his relationship with cinematographer Barry Abrams, who left the film business all together. "*A Stranger is Watching* was a very dreary, unhappy shoot because we spent most of the time filming in an underground subway, which wasn't a fun or easy location to light," Abrams said. "At that point, I had a lucrative retainer shooting toy commercials in New York, and I had a wife and young son, so I decided to stop doing movies. I was offered *Friday the 13th Part 2* and *Spring Break*, but I turned them down to do commercials and spend time with my wife and son."

"Barry thought this [the success of *Friday the 13th*] might be his ticket to the big-time," Max Kalmanowicz recalls. "Barry left the movie business after working on the subway film, which wasn't a happy experience and wasn't going anywhere. Barry realized that the film work wasn't a dependable enough source of money. *A Stranger is Watching* went nowhere and I think that made Sean [Cunningham] realize that he had to stick with the films that made him. Sean realized that he was stuck making more *Friday the 13th* films, or films of that ilk, and Barry felt there was no future for him in doing more of those kinds of films. Barry realized that there was no dance card for him and he was just married to Nikki [Abrams' wife, Nikki Abrams, who also worked on *A Stranger is Watching*] and had a young son and needed to do toy commercials to generate a steady source of income."

Abrams continued shooting commercials, alongside Tad Page, until the late 1980s. By this time Abrams – an accomplished pilot and sailor – was in the process of moving to the British Virgin Islands where he and his wife eventually established a successful airline charter business called Fly BVI (British Virgin Islands).

Another reason Abrams left the film business – and a major reason why neither Abrams nor anyone from his crew worked on *Friday the 13th Part 2* – had to do with the union problems he faced after shooting *Friday the 13th*.

Abrams had joined the more highbrow IATSE union prior to shooting *Friday the 13th* whereas most of his crew belonged to the more rag-tag NABET union. The split caused a bit of dissention amongst Abrams and his loyal crew of followers, although this was short-lived. "When *Friday the 13th* made so much money, we thought we should sign a union contract for the second one, but Barry wouldn't have been able to work on it if it signed with NABET," Robert Shulman says. "We

thought *Part 2* would go union, and they'd spend more money, but they wouldn't go union. I think he [Abrams] was threatened with a $5000 fine for working on a non-union job [*Friday the 13th*] as it was. A different cameraman was hired [Peter Stein] who chose his own crew. So the split was about divergent interests. Barry went onto work with a very good IATSE crew on *A Stranger is Watching* and we felt unloved because he seemed to have hit the big-time without us, but the movie did pretty badly and I guess Sean went back to what he did best."

Walt Gorney and Steve Miner on the set of *Friday the 13th Part 2.* Union conflicts prevented Barry Abrams and his crew from working on *Friday the 13th Part 2.* (Photo courtesy of Virginia Field)

By 1994, Abrams – who'd been commuting from the British Virgin Islands to New York to shoot freelance commercials with Tad Page – settled into his charter airline business full-time alongside his wife. In November 1999, Abrams' life came to a screeching halt when his beloved wife, Nikki Abrams, passed away. "We had a memorial for Nikki and everyone from the crew was there because we all loved her so much," Tad Page recalls. "I don't recall seeing Sean there, but pretty much everyone else was there."

Following his wife's passing, Abrams moved to Paris, France where he learned to speak French and spent the next – and final – phase of his life teaching English as a Second Language (ESL) to aviation company executives. It was in Paris that Abrams, who also lectured at film schools in his spare-time, reconnected with Virginia Field who'd also relocated to Paris in the 1990s.

In August of 2009, Abrams, who'd battled illness for several years, died of leukemia

Friday the 13th Part 3 (AKA *Friday the 13th Part III 3-D*) was directed by Steve Miner and was the first of three *Friday the 13th* sequels to be shot in California. (Photo courtesy of Matt Hankinson)

at the age of 65. Following his death, memorials were held for Abrams, simultaneously, in the British Virgin Islands, New York and Paris.

Following the experience of *A Stranger is Watching*, Sean Cunningham hurtled right back to his bread and butter exploitation roots. Just as he had used the success of *Halloween* as a cue for *Friday the 13th*, Cunningham next turned his focus to the newly-minted teen sex comedy genre (AKA Horny Teenager genre), a genre driven by the mammoth success of the teen sex comedy film *Porky's*, which had surpassed $100 Million at the North American box office following its release in March 1982.

In the spring of 1982, Cunningham, along with Virginia Field and Victor Miller, travelled to Fort Lauderdale, Florida to study the mores of sex-crazed college students and the rituals of beer, drugs and sex that comprise the annual rite of spring break.

The result of this brainstorming was *Spring Break*, a sex comedy film project for which Miller worked on several script drafts before being summarily dismissed by Cunningham, who'd signed a production deal with Columbia Pictures. "I worked on the *Spring Break* script, but Sean didn't like the direction my script was going in and so he replaced me with another writer," recalls Miller who went on to join the massive fray of *Friday the 13th* alumni to enter the daytime television soap opera genre, serving as a writer on several soap operas between 1982 and 2006. "Sean and I haven't spoken since, which is something I feel really bad about given how close we were for so many years, working out of each other's kitchens, sharing ideas."

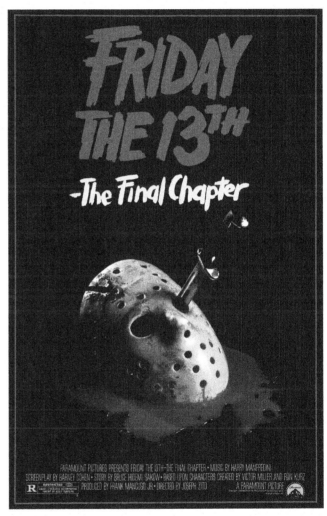

Friday the 13th: The Final Chapter's titular pronouncement proved to be false advertisement given *The Final Chapter*'s robust box office performance. (Photo courtesy of Matt Hankinson)

Released in March 1983, *Spring Break* was a modest box office success, grossing $24 Million at the North American box office which earns the film the dubious distinction of being the highest-grossing film of Sean Cunningham's directing career, outside of the *Friday the 13th* franchise.

Spring Break's modest success, however, placed Cunningham back into the waters he very much wanted to escape from. "*Spring Break* was one of Columbia Pictures' most profitable movies of that period, but it pushed me back into the exploitation genre," Cunningham says. "I just didn't know how to escape from all of this, and since no one was offering me any good projects, I felt that the only thing I could do was to try and make films that appealed to the marketplace."

Besides parting ways with Victor Miller, *Spring Break* also marked the end of Cunningham's relationship with Virginia Field. As mentioned, Field settled in Paris, France in the 1990s where she continued to serve as an art director and production designer on films, while also designing houses. Today, Field teaches at a film school in Paris. "I came to Paris and made my work reel with *Friday the 13th* on it and some of the film people over here were offended to see a horror film on a reel," Field says. "I saw the film [*Friday the 13th*] a few years ago, and it scared the shit out of me! I think it's a really effective little thriller. A student of mine, a film student, is working on a project about Jason deciding to see a shrink! I don't teach *Friday the 13th* in my film class because the budget was so low on that film and I can't show my students how to do some of the scenes in that film because it was so cheap."

Following *Spring Break*, Sean Cunningham's directing career careened through the film genre sweepstakes. Cunningham's next film was *The New Kids*, a teen vigilante thriller that he directed and produced for Columbia Pictures. Released in 1985, the film sank without a trace. "I have to apologize for that one," Cunningham said. "They [Columbia Pictures] asked me to do *The New Kids*. I didn't want to do it. They offered me a lot of money. I did it, but I hated doing it."

During the period when Cunningham was busy with *A Stranger is Watching* and *Spring Break*, Cunningham's protégé, Steve Miner, was busy directing and producing both *Friday the 13th Part 2* and *Part 3* (AKA *Friday the 13th Part III 3-D*), which were released in 1981 and 1982, respectively.

Miner took a break from the film business between 1983 and 1984, partly to develop non-*Friday the 13th* film projects and partly to decompress from the stigma of *Friday the 13th*.

In 1985, Cunningham and Miner reteamed for *House*, a horror-comedy film scripted by Ethan Wiley, which Cunningham produced and Miner directed.

Deftly combining comedy and horror within the confines of the haunted house film genre, the making of *House* was a genial experience for Cunningham and especially Miner. The film's modest financial success launched Miner's directing career, both in features and episodic television, where he would enjoy a considerable degree of success until the early 2000s.

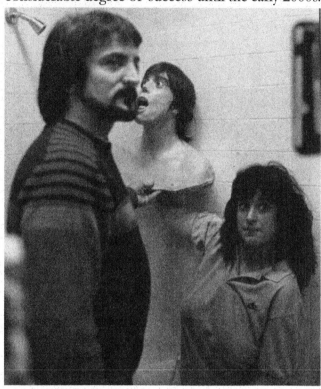

Tom Savini returned to the *Friday the 13th* film franchise to handle effects chores on *Friday the 13th: The Final Chapter* in the mistaken belief that *The Final Chapter* would be the last *Friday the 13th* film. (Photo courtesy of Tom Savini)

Released in 1986, *House* grossed $20 Million at the North American box office, a solid performance in relation to the film's $3 Million production budget. Moreover, *House* proved that while Cunningham would never escape the bonds of genre filmmaking, he didn't need to be trapped in the sleaziest corners of the exploitation and horror marketplace in order to survive.

After producing *House II: The Second Story* (1987), a dismal sequel, Cunningham returned to the directing chair with *Deepstar Six* (1989), a late entry into the crowded underwater monster film sweepstakes of the late 1980s. A commercial and critical failure, *Deepstar Six* marked the last theatrical feature of Cunningham's directing career.

Sean Cunningham's career, both before and after *Friday the 13th*, is emblematic of the businesslike, pragmatic mission statement with which he entered the film business at the dawn of the 1970s. Whereas most filmmakers measure their ultimate success by critical acclaim and the longevity of their films, Cunningham has always measured success by such basic tenets as the ability to support his family, to sustain himself financially, to stay alive.

These are the core values with which Cunningham entered the world of filmmaking, and which led to the creation of *Friday the 13th*, and this cynical, no-nonsense, workmanlike approach to filmmaking is ultimately how Cunningham will be remembered as a filmmaker, for better and for worse.

THE FRANCHISE

Of all of the *Friday the 13th* sequels, the one with the most direct connection to the 1980 film is obviously *Friday the 13th Part 2*. Originally entitled *Jason*, the sequel focused on the character of Jason, now grown. This creative decision was made primarily by Philip Scuderi, who viewed the evolution and increased prominence of the Jason character as being the key to the continued success of the *Friday the 13th* franchise, whatever the word "franchise" meant back in 1980.

Although Barry Abrams and his technical crew were absent from the sequel, Steve Miner was joined by Richard Feury, Virginia Field, Martin Kitrosser, Denise Pinckley, Robert Topol, Cecelia Verardi and a handful of other *Friday the 13th* crew members, most prominently cinematographer Peter Stein who'd shot the hospital scene in *Friday the 13th*.

Sean Cunningham's financial interest in *Friday the 13th* and its sequels meant he got paid regardless of the degree of his involvement. Cunningham had no interest in directing the sequel, choosing to focus on the development of non-*Friday the 13th* projects in his bid for mainstream commercial acceptance. But he was involved on many levels, mostly because his wife, Susan, served as editor.

In the summer of 1980, Cunningham toyed with the idea of directing a *Friday the 13th* sequel in 3-D but imagined the costs too prohibitive. In his discussions with Philip Scuderi, re-

Friday the 13th Part V: A New Beginning marked the end of Stephen Minasian and Philip Scuderi's creative involvement with the *Friday the 13th* film series. (Photo courtesy of Matt Hankinson)

garding the sequel, Cunningham expressed his objection – and bemusement – over the idea of making Jason the sequel's focus. He thought the concept was ridiculous given that Cunningham had always envisioned Jason as being a nightmare.

Cunningham was also conscious of apprentice Miner's desire to direct his own film, and he was more than happy to mentor Miner – and shepherd their investment – through this process. "I was basically just a mentor to Steve on the sequel, and my wife was the editor on the sequel," Cunningham says. "I just tried to be supportive of Steve, and give him advice, although Steve didn't need much advice because he'd clearly been waiting a long time to direct his own movie and he'd prepared very well."

Cunningham did visit the Connecticut filming location when filming commenced in the fall of 1980. The only returning cast members were Adrienne King and Betsy Palmer, although King was the only one who was actually in Con-

Although still profitable, *Friday the 13th Part VI: Jason Lives* ushered in the commercial decline of the *Friday the 13th* film series. (Photo courtesy of Matt Hankinson)

necticut during filming. This was due to the fact that the production – which was spearheaded by Robert Barsamian's daughter, Lisa Barsamian, and Miner – refused to pay for Palmer's travel.

This was just one example of the brazen frugalness that carried from the first film to the sequel, in spite of *Friday the 13th*'s success. Prior to the start of filming, Palmer recorded her dialogue for Miner in Los Angeles where a mold of her skull was also completed.

Adrienne King was originally supposed to star in the sequel, but contractual wrangling between her agent and the producers resulted in King's role being reduced. King's role in the sequel merely occupied the film's prologue sequence in which her character, Alice, is killed by Jason via an ice pick through the skull. Palmer's appearance in the sequel happens at the end of the film via a dreamlike sequence. The mold that was done of Palmer's skull was later jettisoned, after its appearance in the prologue, and a

nurse named Connie Hogan, the sister of *Friday the 13th*'s office manager, Denise Pinckley, served as Pamela Voorhees' "head" in the sequel's denouement.

Released on April 30, 1981, *Friday the 13th Part 2* grossed $21.7 Million at the North American box office, about half the total of *Friday the 13th* but still very profitable. From here, the franchise departed the East Coast milieu – the setting that so defined both *Friday the 13th* and the early careers of Cunningham and Miner – and moved to California, beginning with *Friday the 13th Part 3* which was filmed in Cali-

Sequels like *Friday the 13th Part VII: The New Blood* were so far removed from the source origin of the 1980 film so as to be unrecognizable. (Photo courtesy of Matt Hankinson)

fornia in the spring of 1982, under Miner's direction. Following the avalanche of films to be shot in 3-D throughout the early 1980s, the gimmick generated a wave of enthusiasm for *Friday the 13th Part 3* which grossed a robust $36.6 Million in August of 1982.

Friday the 13th: The Final Chapter (1984) and *Friday the 13th Part V: A New Beginning* (1985) were also filmed in California – in 1983 and 1984, respectively – and the former's titular proclamation of the series' demise made *The Final Chapter* a hit, to the tune of a $32.9 Million domestic box office gross upon the film's release in April of 1984.

Obviously, *The Final Chapter* turned out to be a false promise, and this was evidenced by the somewhat dulled reaction that *A New Beginning* received from the marketplace in March of 1985. Although *A New Beginning's* $21.9 Million domestic box office gross proved that the *Friday the 13th* franchise still had box office muscle, and a loyal fan-base, it clearly represented the slow but steady decline of the *Friday the 13th* franchise in terms of commercial popularity and fan interest.

A New Beginning also marked the end of Stephen Minasian and Philip Scuderi's hands-on involvement with the franchise. Minasian and Scuderi had been intimately-involved with the creative directions of *The Final Chapter* and *A New Beginning*, developing the stories, choosing directors, engaging in almost daily production conferences. It was the end of a colorful, turbulent era.

Throughout the early 1980s, the *Friday the 13th* film series ruled as the vanguard of the horror film genre, outlasting all of the pretenders that flooded the marketplace, especially the countless independent horror film productions – such as *The Burning* (1981), *Girls Nite Out* (1984), *Sleepaway Camp* (1983) – that appeared. None of these *Friday the 13th* copycats – most of which were financed by regional businessmen – made a ripple in the marketplace.

The horror film landscape changed in November of 1984 with the sleeper release of the horror film *A Nightmare on Elm Street*, which was written and directed by Wes Craven, Sean Cunningham's colleague and close friend. Eschewing Cunningham's *Friday the 13th* playbook, Craven's film transcended the blood-and-guts approach by interjecting a fantasy element into the well-worn slasher film genre, as embodied by the introduction of the bladed-gloved – and wisecracking – villain Freddy Krueger, a colorful contrast to the hockey-mask wearing, sullen Jason Voorhees.

Filmed on a budget of less than $2 Million, *A Nightmare on Elm Street* grossed in excess of $25 Million during its theatrical release, and is credited with launching its production company, New Line Cinema, a once tawdry film distribution company, into a major Hollywood studio power. Sean Cunningham actually assisted Craven during *A Night-*

mare on Elm Street's production, directing second unit scenes, and lending advice and support to Craven, much like Craven had done with Cunningham on *Friday the 13th* and Cunningham's previous films.

By the time *Friday the 13th Part VI: Jason Lives* arrived in theaters in August of 1986, the Boston connection had vanished from the *Friday the 13th* series with producing chores being overseen by Frank Mancuso Jr., the son of Frank Mancuso Sr. By this time, the *Nightmare on Elm Street* film series – which had since expanded to include *A Nightmare on Elm Street 2: Freddy's Revenge* – had clearly supplanted the *Friday the 13th* franchise on top of the horror film roost.

The disappointing box office performance of *Friday the 13th Part VIII: Jason Takes Manhattan* marked the end of Paramount's relationship with the *Friday the 13th* film franchise. (Photo courtesy of Matt Hankinson)

Jason Lives' $19.4 million domestic box office gross, though still profitable, revealed sharp signs of wear on the *Friday the 13th* franchise, as well as the fact that the series had moved completely away from the execution, story, style and tone of the 1980 film.

Sean Cunningham brought the *Friday the 13th* film series to New Line Cinema who released *Jason Goes to Hell: The Final Friday* to a tepid commercial response. (Photo courtesy of Matt Hankinson)

Friday the 13th Part VII: The New Blood, released in May of 1988, attempted to enliven the franchise by introducing a telekinetic heroine. But the sequel's box office performance – the film grossed $19.2 at the domestic box office – was static to that of *Jason Lives*.

It was during this period that New Line Pictures and Paramount Pictures engaged in probing discussions regarding the possibility of doing a *Freddy Vs. Jason* – or *Jason Vs. Freddy* – film and these talks would continue for several more years, with rights and territorial issues being the major stumbling points that held the project back. This turned out to be a moot point, for by the end of the 1980s, both the *Friday the 13th* franchise and the *Nightmare on Elm Street* franchise were on the verge of extinction.

Friday the 13th Part VIII: Jason Takes Manhattan was released in July of 1989 and was the least commercially-successful film in the *Friday the 13th* series, up to that point, grossing a disappointing $14.3 Million at the domestic box office. Likewise, *A Nightmare on Elm Street 5: The Dream Child* grossed

a disappointing $22.1 Million upon its release in August of 1989, which was a sharp decline from the strong box office of *A Nightmare on Elm Street 4: The Dream Master* which had grossed $49.3 Million domestically upon its release in August of 1988.

In April of 1990, Paramount cancelled *Friday the 13th: The Series*, the ancillary television series that had run in syndication since 1987. This marked the end of Paramount's relationship with the *Friday the 13th* franchise.

Released in 2002, *Jason X* failed to reignite the *Friday the 13th* film franchise but did serve to hasten the development of the long-gestated *Freddy Vs. Jason* film project. (Photo courtesy of Matt Hankinson)

Although Paramount had the exclusive right to distribute any future *Friday the 13th* sequels, they weren't interested. And Frank Mancuso Jr. – who'd shepherded the series since *Jason Lives* – was also moving on to other film projects.

By the fall of 1990, the *Friday the 13th* franchise, the property, was dormant, finished, dead. It was at this point that Sean Cunningham reentered the picture, motivated by a strong desire to produce a *Freddy Vs. Jason* film, a project in which Cunningham

Sean Cunningham served as producer on *Freddy Vs. Jason,* which proved to be more commercially-successful than any film within either the *Friday the 13th* or the *A Nightmare on Elm Street* film franchises. (Photo courtesy of Matt Hankinson)

envisioned great commercial possibilities. In 1992, Cunningham spoke to Philip Scuderi and his partners about getting the rights to *Friday the 13th* from Paramount and taking the franchise to New Line Cinema chairman Robert Shaye who was likeminded with Cunningham about doing *Freddy Vs. Jason.*

With nominal financial consideration, and still in control of the library of *Friday the 13th* films they'd released since 1980, Paramount Pictures granted Cunningham the right to take the *Friday the 13th* property to New Line Cinema who subsequently made a new deal with him and Scuderi for the rights and for the production of another *Friday the 13th* film. It was hoped this new sequel would serve as a precursor, a warm-up, for an anticipated *Freddy Vs. Jason* film.

This was *Jason Goes to Hell: The Final Friday* which was made for a $3 Million budget and was released by New Line Cinema in August of 1993 to dismal reviews and a lethargic box office take of $15.9 Million domestically. Worse, *The Final Friday* failed in its mandate to generate buzz and momentum for a possible *Freddy Vs. Jason.* Following the

release of *Jason Goes to Hell,* the *Friday the 13th* series would sink into hibernation for nearly a decade.

Cunningham spent much of the 1990s trying, unsuccessfully, to develop *Freddy Vs. Jason* with the major stumbling point being a suitable concept and story that pleased all parties involved. In this regard, Cunningham underestimated just how precious both the Freddy Krueger character and the *Nightmare on Elm Street* franchise were to New Line Cinema and especially to Shaye. Whereas the *Friday the 13th* films had been just a source of discretionary income for Paramount Pictures, Freddy Krueger was like family to Robert Shaye and the other executives at New Line Cinema.

In 2001, frustrated with the stalled progress of *Freddy Vs. Jason,* Cunningham felt like he had to make another *Friday the 13th* film to at least keep the franchise alive and relevant should New Line Cinema ever come around to the possibility of doing *Freddy Vs. Jason.* "I just felt like I had to do something, to keep the property warm until *Freddy Vs. Jason* got off the ground," Cunningham says. "It had been a long time since *Jason Goes to Hell,* and I was frustrated with the lack of progress on *Freddy Vs. Jason,* and I felt like we had to do something with the franchise or it was just going to die off."

The result was the tepid *Jason X,* released by New Line Cinema in April of 2002. The film grossed $13.1 Million at the domestic office. Budgeted at $14 Million, and filmed in Toronto, Canada, *Jason X* was set in space, a location that represented just how far the *Friday the 13th* series had drifted from its original source.

Although *Jason X* did nothing to revitalize the *Friday the 13th* franchise, the film did, in a strange way, hasten development of *Freddy Vs. Jason.* It made Cunningham and New Line Cinema realize that if *Freddy Vs. Jason* was going to happen, it needed to happen soon, or not at all.

Finally, by the summer of 2002, Cunningham and the executives at New Line Cinema had a script for *Freddy Vs. Jason* – written by Damian Shannon and Mark Swift – all sides were satisfied with, or at least satisfied enough that they were willing to go forward into production.

Budgeted at $25 Million, not including the millions of dollars spent on development over the years, *Freddy Vs. Jason* began filming in September of 2002 in Vancouver, British Columbia, under the direction of Ronny Yu. Released in 2003, *Freddy Vs. Jason* grossed a robust $36.4 Million in its opening weekend at the box office, on its way to an impressive $82.6 Million domestic box office take overall.

DON'T CALL IT A REMAKE

In the spring of 2008, New Line Cinema and Paramount Pictures joined forces to produce a belated remake of *Friday the 13th*. They were joined by Cunningham who was operating out of his production shingle, Crystal Lake Entertainment.

Cunningham's production partner on the remake was Platinum Dunes, a production company that produced the 2003 remake of the iconic 1974 horror film *The Texas Chainsaw Massacre* whose box

Although billed as a remake of *Friday the 13th*, the 2009 version of *Friday the 13th* contains more similarities with the various *Friday the 13th* sequels, as well as the teen-related horror films of the early 2000s, than it does with the 1980 film. (Photo courtesy of Matt Hankinson)

office success had been almost identical to that of *Freddy Vs. Jason*. This was fitting since the *Friday the 13th* remake would end-up being much more similar to the *Texas Chainsaw Massacre* model – in execution, style, tone - than its 1980 predecessor.

Entitled *Friday the 13th*, the $19 Million production began filming in April 2008 in Austin, Texas. It was directed by Marcus Nispel, director of the *Texas Chainsaw Massacre* remake. Damian Shannon and Mark Swift handled scripting chores, having worked with Cunningham on *Freddy Vs. Jason*.

Employing a grown, hulking, hockey-mask wearing Jason Voorhees as the film's villain, the remake relegates the entire events of the 1980 film into a brief prologue sequence, during which the character of Pamela Voorhees (played by actress Nana Visitor) makes a brief appearance. The rest of the "remake" utilizes various beats and elements from the first four *Friday the 13th* sequels.

Advertisement for the Blairstown Theater Festival's 2007 screening of *Friday the 13th*. (Photo courtesy of Robert Armin www.robertarmin.com)

Released in February of 2009, during President's Day weekend in the United States, the 2009 version of *Friday the 13th* grossed a boisterous $43.5 Million at the North American box office on its opening weekend of business. This powerful opening box office frame, however, was followed by a record-breaking fall in business that resulted in a virtual standstill.

The "remake" eventually wound up with a domestic gross of $59.8 Million. The strong opening weekend, and the precipitous decline hereafter, is clear evidence of how the *Friday the 13th* brand remains a very potent – yet divisive and polarizing – symbol in pop culture.

LEGACY

Back in 1979, before *Friday the 13th* became a brand name, *Friday the 13th* represented not a franchise but rather a state of mind for a ragtag group of cast and crew who gathered in Blairstown, New Jersey to make a low budget horror film that none of them thought would ever generate the level of interest the film continues to enjoy today.

A ticket for the Blairstown Theater Festival's July 13, 2007 screening of *Friday the 13th*. (Photo courtesy of Robert Armin www.robertarmin.com)

Too commercially successful to attain true cult status, too crude to gain mainstream acceptance, too transparent to be embraced by the horror intelligentsia, *Friday the 13th* has always been a cinematic outcast, reviled by everyone except its fans.

A shot of Roy's Hall, a historic Blairstown Theater that's visible in the film. The theater was built in 1913 as a silent movie house. Roy's Hall hosted a 2007 screening of *Friday the 13th*. (Photo courtesy of Robert Armin www.robertarmin.com)

In the more than thirty years since its release, *Friday the 13th* has risen above criticism and universal repugnance and morphed into a communal, cult-like experience for millions of people around the world, a testament to the film's visceral power and enduring relevance in pop culture.

Friday the 13th won't die.

Friday the 13th is a fact of life.

It was a much simpler time when *Friday the 13th* was filmed in 1979. There was a summer camp. There was a group of camp counselors. There was a lake. There was a killer. There was a boy named Jason. There was a cast and crew who were just happy to be alive and making a film, any film. There was no need for a hockey mask.

1979 shot of the idyllic-looking Sand Pond. (Photo courtesy of Tony Marshall)

sean s cunningham films ltd

F R I D A Y 1 3

A Screenplay

by

Victor Miller

THIRD DRAFT
August 21, 1979

155 long lots road. westport. conn. 06880 ● 203-255-0666 ● telex ¯48-411 answer back vasbt

1   FADE IN   1

        EXT.   CAMP/LAKE   NIGHT

        Establish Camp Crystal Lake at night in a cover shot
        which reveals some lighted cabins, dark patches of
        forest, a door slamming as a COUNSELLOR leaves. We
        hear NIGHT SOUNDS--creepers, an owl, a distant dog
        across the lake, some chatter from a Counsellors'
        cabin, and, in the BG, some CAMP SONGS.

            SUPERIMPOSE:

                            CAMP CRYSTAL LAKE
                            July 4, 1958

        The title holds, then we

                                            CUT TO:

2   EXT.   CABIN A   NIGHT   2

        The CAMERA, handheld in the POV of the person we shall
        call the PROWLER, moves towards the porch of one of
        the darkened cabins. Walks up the steps. Goes in.
        The THEME, a child-like melody in a strange mood,
        comes in very faintly.

                                            CUT TO:

3   INT.   CABIN A   NIGHT   3

Still hand-held, the CAMERA as PROWLER moves down
the aisle between the rows of sleeping CAMPERS.
These are the younger kids. The nearby light sources
splash a little light across their peaceful sleeping
faces.

The CAMERA looks up at the back door and sees a distant
campfire. It moves towards the light of the fire.

                                                    CUT TO:

4   EXT.   LAKE SHORE   NIGHT   4

Eight COUNSELLORS and ASSISTANT COUNSELLORS sit around
a dying fire. There are boys and girls and they are
singing "The River is Wide, I cannot cross over...."
and enjoying the last hours of the day.

The CAMERA selects two Assistant Counsellors, BARRY
and CLAUDETTE. They are both 17 hears old, very
attractive, filled with the excitement of adolescence,
and dressed in the camp uniform. Their t-shirts read:

          (Camp Crystal Lake
           Counsellor in Training)

BARRY yawns, stretches, gets up and exits. CLAUDETTE
waits three seconds, then yawns, stretches and exits.
They don't fool anybody. One COUNSELLOR jabs another
in the ribs to point out the simultaneous leave-taking.

                                                    CUT TO:

5   EXT.   FOREST   NIGHT   5

BARRY & CLAUDETTE walk along a path. He leaves the
path and goes to sit on a log in a small clearing.
CLAUDETTE hesitates, then goes to sit next to him.

                    CLAUDETTE
          You said we were special.

                    BARRY
          I meant everything. But...you know.

                    CLAUDETTE
          I can't, Barry...

                                              (Continued)

182

(Continued)

5   He puts an arm around her and draws her close. They   5
     kiss. They separate.

                         CLAUDETTE
               Does MariAnne kiss as good as I do?

BARRY decides to be polite.

                         BARRY
               I wouldn't know.

                         CLAUDETTE
               Oh, you...

She kisses him and they are locked.

The CAMERA shifts to ANOTHER ANGLE: Just beyond the
thicket of lacy vines. It is a slow tracking shot which
gives the impression that we are watching the action
from the POV of another person, an unseen visitor...
watching the two teen-aged Assistant Counsellors making
their first sexual encounters.

BARRY reaches up outside CLAUDETTE's t-shirt to hold
her breast. She reaches up to take his hand away.

                         BARRY
               Claudette...

                         CLAUDETTE
               Sombody'll see.

                         BARRY
               No, they won't....

He ends the argument by snaking his hand inside her
t-shirt so that part of her bra is exposed. He seals
her protesting lips by kissing her.

From the PROWLER's POV, the CAMERA MOVES to get a better
angle. A hand moves into FRAME and pulls back some
branches to clear the field of vision. A branch pops.

                         CLAUDETTE
                    (in a thick whisper)
               Somebody's there, BARRY.

                         BARRY
               Come on, Claudette. A man's not made of
               stone.

                              (continued)

(Continued)

5   CLAUDETTE   5
                  Let's go back, Barry...

                           BARRY
           I need you so much, Claudette.

BARRY leans in and unhooks her bra. They kiss again,
passionately.

The PROWLER pauses, then moves, never seen--except for
a bit of foot or hand--from the POV of the CAMERA, closer
and closer as the two TEENAGERS become more and more
oblivious.

In the distance a loon mourns. A faint, faint voice
cries "Help me, help me " so that we can hardly hear
it.

Closer. The THEME has snuck in. It becomes discordant.
It swells. Closer.

QUICK CUT to BARRY & CLAUDETTE's faces, their eyes
closed, the perspiration streaking their flushed skin.

Suddenly CLAUDETTE looks up into the CAMERA with terror.

A hatchet flashes into FRAME and CLAUDETTE goes down
under the blow.

The CAMERA TURNS TO BARRY. The PROWLER's powerful
hand has him by the throat. He backpeddles, trying
to get away.

ANOTHER ANGLE: as BARRY is stopped against a tree.

A hunting knife soars against the leafy sky.

BARRY grabs the knife-hand at the wrist. The knife
falls to the mossy floor of the clearing.

Two hands go for the free blade. BARRY's hand has it.

There is a confused jumble of struggle.

The PROWLER's hand has the knife. It moves quickly
forward. We can hear the blade strike.

BARRY stares up at the sky in a soundless shriek.

QUICK CUT TO: MARIANNE, a pretty Counsellor, is out
searching for the missing Counsellors. She stands at
the edge of the clearing, her hands pressing on her
temples, her throat filled with a scream of terror.
The MUSIC has stopped abruptly.

                                            (Continued)

(Continued)

5   THE SCREEN BLEEDS TO WHITE.   5

It is completely SILENT.

                                        CUT TO:

6   TITLE SEQUENCE   6

The screen is completely black. A small white shape
starts to ZOOM towards the FG. The shape becomes a
three-dimensional rendering of FRIDAY 13. Just as it
gets to its final position, the FRIDAY 13 logo shatters
a previously unseen pane of glass. There is a loud
crash. The logo shifts to the upper left corner of
the FRAME as we ROLL TITLES, white on black.

The THEME MUSIC is a reprise of the THEME we heard
during the Forest sequence, now done in a childlike
arrangement.

TITLES END and the MUSIC fades out.

                                        DISSOLVE TO:

7   EXT.   RURAL TOWN   EARLY MORNING   7

The TRACK is SILENT.

In a LONG SHOT we see the one main street. A newspaper
delivery truck drives away from the CAMERA. A GIRL
walks down the street.

Superimposed title:

                        THE PRESENT

A MEDIUM SHOT in front of the bank reveals a day/date/
time/temp sign which blinks:

                        FRIDAY, 13
                        7:01
                        61°
                        FRIDAY, 13
                        7:01
                        61°

                                        (Continued)

185

123   EXT.   CAMP AREA   NIGHT   123

ALICE, exhausted, slogs her way to the shore.

CUT TO:

124   EXT.   EDGE OF LAKE   NIGHT   124

The spot-lights toss long shadows across the shore as
ALICE makes her way down to the very edge of the lake.
She falls forward on her knees near a canoe. The paddles
are leaning against the canoe. She reaches forward and
splashes water over her face. She ducks her head under
to try to clear away the nightmare.

From her POV we look at the face in the dark water. It
is ALICE's face among the ripples of the water where
Jason had drowned. And then we suddenly see another
face!

MRS. VOORHEES with machete over her head appears in the
black mirror. The THEME shreiks again.

ALICE slips sideways as the blow comes down. She rolls
towards the canoe, picks up a canoe paddle and holds it
out like a quarter-staff.

MRS. VOORHEES smiles and winds up for another downward
blow. ALICE holds her paddle out. MRS. VOORHEES cuts
through it with a crack! It leaves ALICE with two
halves of a paddle.

ALICE tosses away the blade end, keeping the half with the
knob. She adjusts it so that it can be used like a billy-
club. MRS. VOORHEES keeps edging forward. ALICE keeps
edging backwards.

MRS. VOORHEES whistles two chops through the air that
barely miss ALICE.

MRS. VOORHEES steps towards a bowline on the end of the
painter for one of the rowboats.

ALICE looks down and sees.

MRS. VOORHEES' foot steps inside the bowline.

ALICE reaches down, snaps the other end of the painter,
and the pull trips up the older woman. MRS. VOORHEES
falls. No sooner is she down that ALICE is on top of
her, raining down blows with the paddle half.

(Continued)

124   (Continued)   124

The CUTS show bits and pieces of arms and legs and
grunts and MRS. VOORHEES struggling to throw off the
enraged ALICE.

ALICE grabs the machete and stands up. In a swift slash
of light and blade she brings it down on the woman below .
her.

MRS. VOORHEES' head rolls along the shore into the water.

ALICE breathes in and out like a steam engine, looks at
the bloody blade in her hands and tosses it into the
lake like a boomerang. It lands somewhere in the
darkness and splashes.

The lake. ALICE heads for the lake. That will be safe.
Cleansing. ALICE has a low growl in her breathing. She
is distracted. She only wants to escape now. She pushes
a canoe into the water, hops in and paddles with her
hands.

In the FG, OUT OF FOCUS, lies MRS. VOORHEES' face. In the
BG, the canoe with ALICE on it slips into the area of
shadow.

DISSOLVE TO:

125   EXT.   LAKE   DAWN   125

A red sunball spreads its fire upwards from the Eastern
horizon. The early morning birds wake up the forest.
The water laps gently at the edge of the shore.

In the middle of the lake is a single lone canoe. From
our LS it appears to be empty. It is moved by a morning
breeze.

CUT TO:

126   EXT.   CAMP/EDGE OF LAKE   DAWN   126

A car comes into view, moving slowly among the trees and
buildings.

CLOSER ON CAR: It's a police car. It stops. Two POLICE
OFFICERS get out. They look around.

ANOTHER ANGLE: POV FROM LAKE: The first POLICEMAN points out
into the water, as if seeing ALICE in the canoe.

They walk toward the lake.

CUT TO:

127   EXT.   LAKE   DAWN   127

The CAMERA looks down into the canoe and finds ALICE asleep in the bottom. She stirs a little. The birds, the lapping water.... She looks up. In CU she almost smiles. She is safe here in the middle of the lake. There is a fuzzy focus to the picture as the sun burns through the haze.

CUT TO:

128   EXT.   LAKE SHORE   DAWN   128

The two POLICE OFFICERS are standing at the edge of the water. The SECOND POLICEMAN has his hands cupped, calling out to ALICE--we see his lips moving, but don't hear the voice. The FIRST POLICEMAN is taking off his shoes as if to wade out.

CUT TO:

129   EXT.   LAKE   DAWN   129

In the canoe, ALICE sits up and reaches over the gunwhale to wet her hand and moisten her lips. As she does so, a hand reaches from beneath the water and grabs her!

STINGER! The canoe upturns.

From below the surface of the water JASON pops up, his face horribly bloated, purple, agonized! He shrieks!

                  JASON

        Mommy!!

ALICE flails her arms, screaming. The grotesque form, clutching her vice-like, drags her underwater.

SCREEN GOES BLACK, V.O. SCREAMING REMAINS.

CUT TO:

130   EXT.   HOSPITAL   DAY   130

Establishing shot that zooms to a window.

We hear OVER:

                CALL NURSE (V.O.)

        Dr. Spongberg, report to O.R.B. Dr. Spongberg, please report to O.R.B.

CUT TO:

131   INT.   HOSPITAL ROOM   DAY   131

CU ON ALICE: as she jerks up in bed, screaming.

ANOTHER ANGLE: a DOCTOR is clutching her (in much
the manner that JASON had in the water); in BG we
see a NURSE and several ATTENDANTS. ALICE is wearing
hospital clothes.

                    DOCTOR
               (trying to calm her)
          It's all right now, Alice. It's over.
          Everything's over.

                    NURSE
          You're going to be fine, Alice. Just fine.

A MAN in uniform stands with his back to the CAMERA in
the hospital room.

ALICE is quieter now. The DOCTOR leaves. The NURSE
resumes the chair where she is keeping watch over the
patient. In the BG we can hear the quiet ritual of
the hospital.

The MAN turns around. We see that it is SGT. TIERNEY.

                    TIERNEY
          Your folks are on their way up.

ALICE nods.

                    ALICE
          Are they all dead?

                    TIERNEY
          Yes, m'am. Two of my men pulled you out of
          the water. We thought you were dead, too.
          Do you remember much?

                    ALICE
          Is he dead too?

                    TIERNEY
          Who?

                    ALICE
          The boy, Jason.

                    TIERNEY
          Jason?

                                        (continued)

131   (Continued)   131

                              ALICE
           In the lake. The one who attacked me.
           The one who dragged me under the water.
           I don't remember anything after that.

                             TIERNEY
           Ma'am, we didn't find any boy.

     ALICE turns and looks towards the window.

                              ALICE
           Then he's still there.

                                          DISSOLVE THROUGH
                                          THE WINDOW TO:

132   EXT.   LAKE   DAY   132

     A canoe drifts aimlessly on the lake.

     ROLL CREDITS.

APPENDIX II: THE SHOOTING SCHEDULE

FRIDAY the 13th TENTATIVE ADVANCE SCHEDULE FOR WEEK ENDING 8/23/79

	MONDAY	TUESDAY	WEDNESDAY	THURSDAY	FRIDAY	SATURDAY
SCENE NUMBER	49 Int. 52 Int. 57aInt. 59aInt. 63 Int. 81 Int.	72 Int. 74 Int. 85 Ext. 70 Int. 86 Int. 69aInt. 71 Ext. 73 Ext. 15 Ext.	76 Ext. 77 Ext. 78 Ext. 79 Ext. 80 Ext.	53 Ext. 54 Ext. 58 Ext. 55 Int. 57 Int. 57bInt. 59 Int.	60 Ext. 61 Int. 64 Int. 89 Int.	87 Ext. 88 Int. 97 Ext. 99 Int. 69 Ext. 90 Ext.
CAST	Alice Marcie Brenda Bill Ned Jack	Brenda Alice Bill Camera as prowler	Brenda Camera as prowler	Ned Jack Marcie Camera as prowler	Marcie Brenda Alice Bill Camera as prowler	Alice Bill Camera as prowler
SPECIAL EFFECTS	52			57 57b 59	61	
RAIN	56 57a	59a 81 63	all scenes	54 55 57b 58 57 59	60 64 61 89	all scenes
VEHICLES		van				
LOCATIONS	Kitchen Main Cabin	Brenda's Cabin	Path Archery Range Electric Box	Lake Shore Path Camp Grounds Ned's Cabin	Bath House Bathroom	Jack's Cabin Main Cabin Office

	MONDAY	TUESDAY	WEDNESDAY	THURSDAY	FRIDAY	SATURDAY
SCENE NUMBER	92 93 96 106 100 101	65 91 66 94 67 83 68 82 84	1 103 2 3 5 4 95 98 95	130 131		
CAST	Alice Bill Camera as prowler	Steve Christy Sgt. Tierney Sandy Camera as prowler Extras	Camera as prowler Claudette Barry Marianne Extras	Alice Sgt. Tierney Extras Doctor		
SPECIAL EFFECTS	106	82	5			
RAIN	all scenes	all scenes	95 103 98			
VEHICLES	Camper Van	Jeep Police Car				
LOCATIONS	Parking Lot Van Generator Shed	Diner Jeep Highway Rural Rd. Police Car Camp Rd.	Lake/Camp Cabin A Path Forest Lake Shore Moon/sky	Hospital Hospital Room		

192

FRIDAY the 13th ADVANCE SCHEDULE FOR WEEK ENDING September 8, 1979/Night Shooting

	MONDAY	TUESDAY	WEDNESDAY	THURSDAY	FRIDAY	SATURDAY
SCENE NUMBER		110 Int. 121 Int. 122 Int.	112 Ext. 113 Ext. 114 Int.	115 Int. 116 Ext. 118 Ext. 117 Int. 119 Int.	109 Ext. 111 Ext. 120 Ext. 123 Ext. 124 Ext.	107 Int. 108 Int. 103 Int. 105 Ext. 104 Int. 102 Int.
CAST		Mrs. Voorhees Alice	Alice Mrs. Voorhees	Alice Mrs. Voorhees	Mrs. Voorhees Alice Brenda Steve Christy Annie	Alice Brenda
SPECIAL EFFECTS		110 122	114	119	111 124	108
RAIN		110	112 113 114	115 116	109 111	107 103 104 108 105 102
VEHICLES					109 - Jeep 120 - Van	
LOCATIONS		Main Cabin Kitchen Larder	Arts & Crafts Generator Shed Arts & Crafts	Equipment Shed Rifle Shack	Main Cabin Path/Shore Lake Shore	Kitchen Main Cabin

FRIDAY the 13th ADVANCE SCHEDULE FOR WEEK ENDING ___ September 15, 1979/Day Shooting

	MONDAY	TUESDAY	WEDNESDAY	THURSDAY	FRIDAY	SATURDAY
SCENE NUMBER	7 Ext.	24 Ext. 31 Ext.	13 Ext. 45 Ext.	41 Ext.	110A Ext.	46 Ext.
	8 Int.	25 Ext. 32 Ext.	14 Int. 20 Ext.	42 Ext.	129 Ext.	48 Int.
	9 Ext.	26 Ext. 33 Ext.	15 Ext. 35 Ext.	43 Ext.	128 Ext.	23 Ext.
	10 Ext.	27 Ext. 34 Ext.	17 Ext. 36 Ext.	44 Ext.	126 Ext.	50 Ext.
	11 Int.	28 Ext.	47 Ext. 37 Ext.	110B Ext.		51 Int.
	12 Ext.	29 Ext.	18 Ext. 38 Ext.	125 Ext.		
	19 Ext.	20 Ext.	29 Ext. 29 Ext.	132 Ext.		
			22 Ext. 40 Ext.			
			21 Ext.			
CAST	Extras	Annie	Alice	Alice	Alice Jason	Alice
	Annie	Camera as prowler	Marcie	Marcie	Marcie	Marcie
	Trudy		Brenda	Brenda	Brenda	Brenda
	Enos		Bill	Bill	Bill	Bill
	Salesman		Ned	Ned	Ned	Ned
	Cop		Jack	Jack	Jack	Jack
	Operator		Steve Christy Camera as prowler	Police #1&#2		
SPECIAL EFFECTS		29		110B		46
		34		110A		48
				129		23
VEHICLES	Delivery Truck	Jeep	Van		Police Car	
	Pick-up Truck		Jeep			
	Oil Truck					
	Car passes					
LOCATIONS	Rural Town Rd.	Highway	Lake Shore		Lake Shore	Alice's Cabin
	Gen. Store Rd./Jeep	Van/Rds.	Forest Path			Archery Range
	Town Street Rural Rd.	Camp Rd./Sign	Camp			Generator Shed
	Rural Rd. Jeep/Rd.	Camp Rd./Camp				
	Oil Truck/Rd. Rd./Camp sign	Main Area/stump				
	Rural Crossrds. Jeep/Rd	Parking lot				

APPENDIX III: SELECTED FILMOGRAPHIES

KEVIN BACON

born 8 July 1958 in Philadelphia, Pennsylvania

Kevin Bacon's acting career began in 1975 when Bacon won a full scholarship to the Pennsylvania Governor's School for the Arts at Bucknell University, where Bacon studied Theater as part of the program. At the age of seventeen, Bacon left home and went to New York to pursue a career in theater. "I wanted life, man, the real thing," Bacon said. "The message I got was 'The arts are it. Business is the devil's work. Art and creative expression are next to godliness.' Combine that with an immense ego and you wind up with an actor."

1978 NATIONAL LAMPOON'S ANIMAL HOUSE [Chip Diller]
1979 STARTING OVER [Husband]
1979 THE GIFT [Teddy]
1979 SEARCH FOR TOMORROW (daytime soap)(various episodes) [Todd Adamson]
1980 HERO AT LARGE [Teenager]
1980 FRIDAY THE 13TH [Jack]
1980-1981 THE GUIDING LIGHT (daytime soap)(six episodes)[T.J. 'Tim' Werner]
1981 ONLY WHEN I LAUGH [Don]
1982 DINER [Timothy Fenwick, Jr.]
1982 FORTY DEUCE [Ricky]
1983 ENORMOUS CHANGES AT THE LAST MINUTE [Dennis]
1983 THE DEMON MURDER CASE (TV movie) [Kenny Miller]
1984 FOOTLOOSE [Ren]
1984 MISTER ROBERTS (TV movie) [Ens. Frank Pulver]
1986 QUICKSILVER [Jack Casey]
1987 WHITE WATER SUMMER [Vic]
1987 END OF THE LINE [Everett]
1987 PLANES, TRAINS & AUTOMOBILES [Taxi Racer]
1988 SHE'S HAVING A BABY [Jefferson 'Jake' Briggs]
1988 LEMON SKY (TV movie) [Alan]
1989 CRIMINAL LAW [Martin Thiel]
1989 THE BIG PICTURE [Nick Chapman]
1990 TREMORS [Valentine McKee]
1990 FLATLINERS [David]
1991 PYRATES [Ari]
1991 QUEENS LOGIC [Dennis]
1991 JFK [Willie O'Keefe]
1991 A LITTLE VICIOUS (short film) [Narrator]
1992 A FEW GOOD MEN [Jack Ross]
1994 THE AIR UP THERE [Jimmy Dolan]
1994 THE RIVER WILD [Wade]
1994 NEW YORK SKYRIDE (short film) [Narrator]
1994 FRASIER (TV series) {Vic}
Bacon's voice was featured in the episode entitled *Adventures In Paradise: Part 2.*
1995 MURDER IN THE FIRST [Henri Young]
1995 APOLLO 13 [Jack Swigert]
1995 BALTO (voice) [Balto]
1996 SLEEPERS [Sean Nokes]
1997 PICTURE PERFECT [Sam Mayfair]
1997 DESTINATION ANYWHERE [Mike]
1997 TELLING LIES IN AMERICA [Billy Magic]
1998 DIGGING TO CHINA [Ricky]
1998 WILD THINGS [Sgt. Ray Duquette]
1999 STIR OF ECHOES [Tom Witzky]

2000 MY DOG SKIP [Jack Morris]
2000 WE MARRIED MARGO [Himself]
2000 HOLLOW MAN [Sebastian Caine]
2000 GOD, THE DEVIL AND BOB (TV series) [Himself]
Bacon's voice was featured in the episode entitled *Bob Gets Involved*.
2002 WILL & GRACE (TV series) {Himself]
Bacon appeared as himself in two episodes. The first episode, entitled *Bacon and Eggs*, aired in 2002, and the second episode, entitled *The Finale*, aired in 2006.
2001 NOVOCAINE [Lance Phelps]
2002 TRAPPED [Joe Hickey]
2003 MYSTIC RIVER [Sean Devine]
2003 IN THE CUT [John Graham]
2003 IMAGINE NEW YORK (short film) [Himself]
2004 THE WOODSMAN [Walter]
2004 CAVEDWELLER [Randall Pritchard]
2004 NATURAL DISASTERS: FORCES OF NATURE (short film) [Narrator]
2005 LOVERBOY [Marty]
2005 BEAUTY SHOP [Jorge]
2005 WHERE THE TRUTH LIES [Lanny Morris]
2007 DEATH SENTENCE [Nick Hume]
2007 RAILS & TIES [Tom Stark]
2008 THE AIR I BREATHE [Love]
2008 FROST/NIXON [Jack Brennan]
2008 SAVING ANGELO (short film) [Brent]
2009 THE MAGIC 7 [Himself]
2009 MY ONE AND ONLY [Dan]
2009 TAKING CHANCE (TV miniseries) [Lt. Col. Michael Strobl]
2010 BORED TO DEATH (TV series) [Himself]
2011 ELEPHANT WHITE [Jimmy the Brit]
2011 SUPER [Jock]
2011 X-MEN: FIRST CLASS [Sebastian Shaw]
2011 CRAZY, STUPID, LOVE. [David Lindhagen]
2013 THE FOLLOWING (TV series) [Ryan Hardy]
2013 R.I.P.D. [Bobby Hayes]

LAURIE BARTRAM

born 16 May 1958 in St. Louis, Missouri
died 25 May 2007 in Lynchburg, Virginia

Prior to her role in *Friday the 13th*, Laurie Bartram had, during her time living in New York, studied acting with the likes of Paul Gleason (of *The Breakfast Club* fame) and Gordon Hunt. As a trained dancer, Bartram had, previous to her time spent living in New York, been a soloist with the St. Louis Civic Ballet. She also appeared with the Los Angeles Ballet and at the Dance Center in London, England.

Bartram was a member of the Fall 1976 season of the Musical Theater Workshop of the Los Angeles Civic Light Opera, performing various roles, and was also a member of the St. Louis Municipal Opera, where Bartram appeared in productions of *Take Me Along, Man of La Mancha, Bittersweet, Carousel, Camelot, Funny Girl, Girl Crazy, On the Town, Kiss Me, Kate, Showboat* and *Oliver!*.

As mentioned earlier in this book, Bartram isn't to be confused with another actress named Laurie Brighton, whose identity has been erroneously attributed to Bartram through other media sources. Aside from her role in *Friday the 13th*, Bartram is believed to have appeared in an unreleased film entitled *Retrievers*, but there's no evidence of the project's existence. Bartram did appear in various commercials and industrial films/shows during her time in New York.

1978-1979 ANOTHER WORLD (daytime soap)(various episodes)[Karen Campbell]
1980 FRIDAY THE 13TH [Brenda]

HARRY CROSBY

born 8 August 1958 in Hollywood, California

Born Harry Lillis Crosby III, Harry Crosby was the fifth son of legendary actor and singer Bing Crosby, who passed away in 1977. Crosby's sister is actress Mary Crosby, best known for her role on the television series *Dallas* and especially the landmark *Who Shot J.R.?* storyline, which generated record-breaking ratings upon its conclusion in November of 1980. Although it's been suggested, by certain sources, that the cast and crew of *Friday the 13th* were aware of Mary Crosby's appearance on *Dallas*, and mentioned this to Harry Crosby, the fact is that Mary Crosby's *Dallas* episodes didn't begin airing until October of 1979, after principal filming on *Friday the 13th* had been completed.

During the considerable period of time Harry Crosby spent in London, England, where Crosby studied at the London Academy of Music and Dramatic Arts (LAMDA), Crosby played a variety of roles in productions of *View From the Bridge*, *Wedding*, *Anniversary*, *Monologue*, *The Caretaker*, *Games After Liverpool*, *The Crucible*, *Cat Among the Pigeons*, *The Fool* and *The Absolute Monarch*. As well, Crosby's mother, Kathryn Grant Crosby, is an accomplished stage actress, who has appeared in numerous stage productions over the years, both before and after the release of *Friday the 13th*. In fact, Kathryn Crosby was once slated to appear in a Los Angeles stage production of *Romantic Comedy*, alongside *Friday the 13th* co-star Ron Millkie, but the project fell through.

Following his work on *Friday the 13th*, Crosby returned to London, to LAMDA, where Crosby and a group of LAMDA players toured Great Britain and Europe, fulfilling a commitment that Crosby had made prior to his work in *Friday the 13th*.

1966-1968 THE HOLLYWOOD PALACE (TV series) {Himself}
Crosby appeared, as a singer, on three episodes of this television series, which aired in 1966, 1967 and 1968.
1977 BING CROSBY'S MERRIE OLDE CHRISTMAS (TV movie) [Himself]
1977 BING CROSBY AND FRED ASTAIRE: A COUPLE OF SONG AND DANCE MEN (documentary/TV special) [Himself]
1980 FRIDAY THE 13TH [Bill]
1980 RIDING FOR THE PONY EXPRESS (TV movie) [Albie Foreman]
This TV movie, which aired on CBS, basically served as a pilot for a would-be television series, entitled *The Pony Express*, but the project wasn't picked-up by CBS.
1981 THE PRIVATE HISTORY OF A CAMPAIGN THAT FAILED (TV movie) [Cpl. Ed Stevens]
1984 DOUBLE TROUBLE (TV series) [Steven]
Crosby appeared in a 1984 episode entitled *Heartache*.

SEAN S. CUNNINGHAM

born 31 December 1941 in New York City, New York

1970 ART OF MARRIAGE (AKA THE ART OF MARRIAGE) (director/producer)
1971 TOGETHER (director/co-producer)
1972 LAST HOUSE ON THE LEFT (AKA THE LAST HOUSE ON THE LEFT) (producer)
1973 THE CASE OF THE SMILING STIFFS (AKA CASE OF THE FULL MOON MURDERS, THE CASE OF THE FULL MOON MURDERS, SEX ON THE GROOVE TUBE, SILVER C, SILVER COCK) (co-director/co-producer)
1976 THE PEOPLE WHO OWN THE DARK (AKA ULTIMO DESEO, PLANETA CIEGO, BLIND PLANET) (co-producer)
1978 HERE COME THE TIGERS (director/co-producer)
1978 MANNY'S ORPHANS (AKA KICK!)(director/co-producer)

1980 FRIDAY THE 13TH (director/producer)
1982 A STRANGER IS WATCHING (director)
1983 SPRING BREAK (director/producer)
1984 A NIGHTMARE ON ELM STREET (un-credited second unit director)
1985 THE NEW KIDS (AKA STRIKING BACK) (director/producer)
1986 HOUSE (producer)
1987 HOUSE II: THE SECOND STORY (producer)
1989 THE HORROR SHOW (AKA HOUSE III: THE HORROR SHOW) (producer)
1989 DEEPSTAR SIX (director/producer)
1991 HOUSE IV: THE REPOSSESSION (producer)
1993 MY BOYFRIEND'S BACK (producer)
1993 JASON GOES TO HELL: THE FINAL FRIDAY (producer)
2001 XCU: EXTREME CLOSE-UP (director/producer)
2002 JASON X (executive producer)
2002 TERMINAL INVASION (director)
2003 FREDDY VS. JASON (producer)
2006 TRAPPED ASHES (anthology film)(director)
Cunningham directed the segment entitled *Jibaku*.
2009 FRIDAY THE 13TH (producer)
2009 THE LAST HOUSE ON THE LEFT (producer)

ADRIENNE KING

born 21 July 1955 (many sources list 1960) in Long Island, New York

After largely disappearing from acting in the 1980s, for reasons that are all too obvious, Adrienne King carved out a second career for herself in the 1990s as a voiceover performer on various film and television projects. A staple on the celebrity autograph convention circuit, King has recently returned to acting, appearing in several micro-budget independent genre films.

1965 HALLMARK HALL OF FAME: INHERIT THE WIND (TV movie) [Melinda]
1977 SATURDAY NIGHT FEVER (un-credited) [Dancer]
1979 HAIR (un-credited) [Dancer]
1980 FRIDAY THE 13TH [Alice]
1981 FRIDAY THE 13TH PART 2 [Alice]
1993 THE NIGHT WE NEVER MET (ADR loop group)
1993 THE MAN WITHOUT A FACE (looping voices)
1993 THE GOOD SON (looping voices)
1993 WHAT'S EATING GILBERT GRAPE? (group voices)
1993 THE PELICAN BRIEF (looping voices)
1993 PHILADELPHIA (looping voices)
1994 WOLF (looping voices)
1995 WHILE YOU WERE SLEEPING (ADR voice)
1996 JERRY MAGUIRE (looping voices)
1997 TITANIC (looping voices)
1997 MOUSEHUNT (looping voices)
2000 ALMOST FAMOUS (looping voices)

MARK NELSON

(date and location of birth withheld by request)

A 1977 graduate of Princeton University, in Drama, Mark Nelson, a New York native, has enjoyed an accomplished and distinguished stage career, as an actor, director and teacher. Prior to his appearance in *Friday the 13th*, his first feature film, Nelson's first major acting role was in the role of the Bridegroom in a production of the play *The Dybbuk* that was held at Joseph Papp's Public Theater in New York. Following his graduation from Princeton in 1977, Nelson began studying acting with the famed Uta Hagen. In early 1980, prior to *Friday the 13th*'s release, Nelson appeared in an off-Broadway production of the play *Green Fields* which was held at the Jewish Repertory Theatre.

In the years since *Friday the 13th*'s release, Nelson, who has served as a guest director at the famed Juilliard School, has acted in many acclaimed Broadway productions, appearing in Tom Stoppard's *The Invention of Love*, Arthur Miller's *After the Fall*, and Chekhov's *Three Sisters*, as well as being in the original casts of *A Few Good Men*, *Rumors*, *Biloxi Blues* and *Amadeus*. Nelson received an Obie award for his performance in Steve Martin's *Picasso at the Lapin Agile*.

1980 FRIDAY THE 13TH [Ned]
1981 THE CHOSEN [Fighting Student]
1985 REMINGTON STEELE (TV series) (in episode entitled *Gourmet Steele*) [Lino]
1989 BLOODHOUNDS OF BROADWAY [Sam the Skate]
1991 THIRTYSOMETHING (TV series) (in episode entitled *Melissa and Men*) [Leonard Katz]
1993 THE SEVENTH COIN [Librarian]
1996 THE FIRST WIVES CLUB [Eric Loest]
1996-2010 LAW & ORDER (TV series)
Nelson appeared in four different episodes, in four different
roles, that aired between 1996 and 2010
1997 LIBERTY! THE AMERICAN REVOLUTION (TV mini-series) [Loyalist]
1998 SUDDENLY SUSAN (TV series) (in episode entitled *Not in This Life*) [Paul]
1998-2000 SPIN CITY (TV series) [Therapist]
Nelson appeared in four episodes that aired between 1998 and 2000
1999 LAW & ORDER: SPECIAL VICTIMS UNIT (TV series) (in episode entitled *Payback*) [Robert Stevens]
1999 NOW AND AGAIN (TV series) (in episode entitled *A Girl's Life*)
2002 LAW & ORDER: CRIMINAL INTENT (TV series) (in episode entitled *Badge*) [Mancuso]
2002 ED (TV series) (in episode entitled *Neighbors*) {Sid Pennington]
2007 THE AMERICAN EXPERIENCE (documentary/TV series) [Nathaniel Pendleton]

BETSY PALMER

born 1 November 1926 in East Chicago, Indiana

Although Betsy Palmer, who studied Dramatic Art at DePaul University in Chicago, made countless film and television appearances throughout the 1950s, the majority of her performing career has been devoted to the genre of summer and winter stock theater, which has occupied most of Palmer's career over the past 50 years.

Palmer's "sweet old lady" image that was so visible to the cast and crew of *Friday the 13th* was an image that Palmer had cultivated through her many years as a popular television personality throughout the 1950s and 1960s, a million miles removed from the psychotic persona of Pamela Voorhees. Palmer has remained active in theater in recent years and has also been a fixture on the celebrity autograph convention circuit.

Somewhat cryptically, Palmer has also spent much of her recent career and life sharing recollections of the many show business legends she's crossed paths with in her long career, most of whom – if not all – she's outlived.

1951 MISS SUSAN (TV series)(in episode entitled *Unknown*)
1953 I'LL BUY THAT (TV series)(in episode entitled *Assistant*)
1953 DANGER (TV series)(in episode entitled *Death is My Neighbor*)
1953 CAMPBELL PLAYHOUSE (TV series)(in episode entitled *Too Little a Kiss*)
1953-1955 ARMSTRONG CIRCLE THEATRE (TV series)(two episodes)
1953-1956 THE PHILCO TELEVISION PLAYHOUSE (TV series)(four episodes)
1953-1957 STUDIO ONE (TV series)(seven episodes)
1954 INNER SANCTUM (TV series)(in episode entitled *Dark of the Night*)[Karen]
1954 LUX VIDEO THEATRE (TV series)(in episode entitled *Captive City*)

1954 THE WEB (TV series)(in episode entitled *The Bait*)
1954-1957 GOODYEAR TELEVISION PLAYHOUSE (TV series)(four episodes)
1954-1960 THE UNITED STATES STEEL HOUR (TV series)
Palmer appeared in nine episodes between 1954 and 1960, playing a variety of characters.
1955 DEATH TIDE [Gloria]
1955 MISTER ROBERTS [Lt. Ann Girard]
1955 APPOINTMENT WITH ADVENTURE (TV series)(in episode entitled *The Secret of Juan Valdez*)
1955 QUEEN BEE [Carol Lee Phillips]
1955 THE LONG GRAY LINE [Kitty Carter]
1956 FRONT ROW CENTER (TV series)(in episode entitled *Strange Suspicion*)[Emily]
1956-1957 KRAFT TELEVISION THEATRE (TV series)(three episodes)
1956-1957 CLIMAX! (TV series)(three episodes)
1957 THE ALCOA HOUR (TV series)(in episode entitled *Protégé*) [Ann Fenn]
1957 THE TIN STAR [Nona Mayfield]
1958 THE TRUE STORY OF LYNN STUART [Phyllis Carter]
1958 PLAYHOUSE 90 (TV series) (two episodes)
1959 THE BALLAD OF LOUIE THE LOUSE (TV movie)[Tina Adams]
1959 THE LAST ANGRY MAN [Anna Thrasher]
1959 SUNDAY SHOWCASE (TV series)(in episode entitled *The Practical Dreamer*)
1968 HALLMARK HALL OF FAME (TV series) (in episode entitled *A Punt, a Pass, and a Prayer*)[Nancy]
1972 LOVE, AMERICAN STYLE (TV series)(segment entitled *Love and the Ghost*)[Barbara Kreitman]
1980 FRIDAY THE 13TH [Pamela Voorhees]
1980-1981 NUMBER 96 (TV series) [Maureen Galloway]
1981 FRIDAY THE 13TH PART 2 [Pamela Voorhees]
1981 ISABEL'S CHOICE (TV movie)[Ellie Fineman]
1982 THE LOVE BOAT (TV series)(episode entitled *Isaac Gets Physical/She Brought Her Mother Along/Cold Feet*) [Millicent Holton]
1982 AS THE WORLD TURNS (daytime soap)[Suzanne Becker]
1982 MAGGIE (TV series)(in episode entitled *Maggie the Poet*)[Virginia Sullivan]
1983 T.J. HOOKER (TV series) (in episode entitled *Vengeance Is Mine*){Anne Armstrong]
1985-1989 MURDER, SHE WROTE (TV series)
Palmer appeared in two episodes, playing two different characters, which aired in 1985 and 1989, respectively.
1987 CHARLES IN CHARGE (TV series)(in episode entitled *The Egg and Us*)[Gloria]
1987 NEWHART (in episode entitled *Me and My Gayle*) [Gayle]
1987-1988 OUT OF THIS WORLD (TV series) (two episodes) [Donna's Mom]
1988 GODDESS OF LOVE (TV movie) [Hera]
1988 WINDMILLS OF THE GODS (TV movie) [Mrs. Hart Brisbane]
1989-1990 KNOTS LANDING (TV series) (several episodes) [Virginia Bullock]
1991 COLUMBO (TV series) (in episode entitled *Death Hits the Jackpot*) [Martha Lamarr]
1992 DEEP DISH TV (TV movie)
1992 STILL NOT QUITE HUMAN (TV movie) [Aunt Mildred]
1994 UNVEILED [Eva]
1998 JUST SHOOT ME! (TV series)(in episode entitled *The Walk*) [Rhonda]
1999 THE FEAR: RESURRECTION [Grandmother]
2000 HANG TIME (TV series)(in episode entitled *A Night to Remember*) [Sweet Old Lady]
2001 FREAKYLINKS (TV series) (in episode entitled *Subject: Sunrise at Sunset Streams*) [Betty]
2005 PENNY DREADFUL (short film) [Trudie Tredwell]
2006 WALTZING ANNA [Anna Rhoades]
2007 BELL WITCH: THE MOVIE [Bell Witch]

JEANNINE TAYLOR

born 2 June 1954 in Hartford, Connecticut

Between 1971 and 1976, Jeannine Taylor appeared in various stage productions around the New England area, primarily in and around New Hampshire. In 1977, Taylor appeared as Harriet Shelley in an Off-Off Broadway production of the play *Shelley*. After appearing in several more plays throughout 1978, at the Golden Apple Theatre in Sarasota, Florida, including a production of *The Sound of Music* in which Taylor was alongside acting legend Ann Blyth, Taylor headed to New York where, in 1979, she appeared as Jenny in a production of *The Umbrellas of Cherbourg* that was held at Joseph Papp's Public Theater. 1979 being a busy year for Taylor, even regardless of her work in *Friday the 13th*, Taylor also travelled to Seattle, where Taylor appeared in a production of *A History of the American Film*, and Toronto, Canada, where Taylor appeared in a pre-Broadway production of *Home Again, Home Again*.

Between 1980 and 1982, in and around *Friday the 13th*'s release, Taylor remained busy in theater, appearing in numerous stage productions that were held all over New York. In 1984, before Taylor's career was derailed by her aforementioned bout with Graves' disease, Taylor – who'd also appeared in television commercials for Arby's, Burger King, Dr. Pepper, Ultra Ban II, along with doing voiceover work and appearing in industrial film projects - appeared at the Cincinnati Playhouse, playing the role of Nina in a production of *The Seagull*. In 2007, after a long hiatus, Taylor returned to the stage, appearing in an Off-Off Broadway production of the play *A Little Experimenting*, and also appearing, in the role of Emily Dickinson, in a production of *The Belle of Amherst* that was staged at the William Esper Studio in New York.

1980 FRIDAY THE 13TH [Marcie]
1982 AS THE WORLD TURNS (daytime soap) (recurring role) [Maureen Durfee]
1982 THE ROYAL ROMANCE OF CHARLES AND DIANA (TV movie) [Samantha Edwards]

APPENDIX IV: FILMS PRODUCED BY BARSAMIAN/MINASIAN/SCUDERI

Although their names don't appear on *Friday the 13th*, the three partners behind Georgetown Productions – Robert Barsamian, Stephen (Steve) Minasian, Philip Scuderi – clearly influenced *Friday the 13th*, both in terms of the production itself and certain key creative elements that were vital to *Friday the 13th's* success.

Although the Boston trio had been involved with the production of several films prior to the making of *Friday the 13th*, most notably *Last House on the Left* (AKA *The Last House on the Left*), the success of *Friday the 13th* opened up a whole new horizon for the trio in terms of giving them the resources with which to both finance and produce more films themselves, both in and out of the *Friday the 13th* film series.

While Philip Scuderi, who was always the driving creative force amongst the three partners, spent most of his energies focusing on the immediate *Friday the 13th* sequels, alongside Stephen Minasian in this regard, the period between the early to mid 1980s saw the trio move in various directions. This was especially true of Stephen Minasian who, beginning in the early 1980s, in the wake of the formal dissolution of both Hallmark Releasing Corporation and Georgetown Productions, formed an alliance with producer Dick Randall to produce a string of genre films that were released throughout the 1980s, under the production company banner Spectacular Trading Company (AKA Spectacular Film Productions, Spectacular Trading International).

The following filmography contains a list of all the films in which the Boston partners were involved with, both jointly and separately. Not to be confused with the countless films that the partners distributed and released, under the Hallmark Releasing banner, throughout the 1970s, the following list solely details the film projects in which the partners were directly-involved with, jointly and separately, in terms of development, financing, and production.

In the context of the *Friday the 13th* film series, the following list contains only the first four *Friday the 13th* sequels, in which the partners, primarily Stephen Minasian and Philip Scuderi, were intimately-involved with from a production standpoint. The production of *Friday the 13th Part VI: Jason Lives*, as mentioned earlier in this book, marked the end of the Boston trio's creative involvement with the *Friday the 13th* film series, after which the Boston partners were relegated to being solely financial participants in the *Friday the 13th* film franchise.

This list is meant to show how *Friday the 13th*, despite its commercial success, has deep roots within various sectors of the exploitation, and horror film universe, and how the success of *Friday the 13th* influenced and launched the production of many other genre films.

1971 TOGETHER
Although Hallmark Releasing took over *Together*, after buying the distribution rights from Sean Cunningham, and Stephen Minasian received a producer credit on the film (as Steve Minasian), there's no evidence that Minasian or his partners were involved with any filming of additional footage or extra scenes.
1972 LAST HOUSE ON THE LEFT (AKA THE LAST HOUSE ON THE LEFT)
1973 EXPLOZIA (AKA THE POSEIDON EXPLOSION
Stephen Minasian was an executive producer on this action-drama film which was filmed in Romania.
1974 DEADLY WEAPONS
The Boston trio produced this film, under the Hallmark banner, whose story followed a woman, named Chesty Morgan, who possessed 73 inch breasts.
1978 HERE COME THE TIGERS
Hallmark Releasing had virtually ceased its distribution of films by the end of 1977 and had basically dissolved. *Here Come the Tigers* marked the only time that the name Philip Scuderi was credited in a film, although this related to Philip Scuderi, Jr., Philip Scuderi's son, who was cast as a deaf mute kid in the film.
1978 MANNY'S ORPHANS
As mentioned previously, the Boston investors provided financing for *Manny's Orphans*, which Sean Cunningham also had money invested in, and Philip Scuderi and his partners monitored the filming, just as they'd done on *Here Come the Tigers*.

1979 KING FRAT

This *Animal House* rip-off was financed by Philip Scuderi and his partners and was written by Ron Kurz under the pseudonym Mark Jackson, although Victor Miller recalls working on an early draft of the script.

1980 FRIDAY THE 13TH

In actuality, Philip Scuderi was an un-credited producer on *Friday the 13th*, while partners Robert Barsamian and Stephen Minasian were, at the very least, un-credited executive producers.

1981 EYES OF A STRANGER

This slasher film, which was actress Jennifer Jason Leigh's first feature film, was shot in Miami, Florida, and was directed by Ken Wiederhorn, who'd previously directed *King Frat* for the Boston partners. The film was written by Ron Kurz under his well-worn Mark Jackson pseudonym. Also, Tom Savini was recruited by Philip Scuderi to contribute effects to the film. "I got a call from the producers behind *Friday the 13th*," Savini recalls. "A movie they were handling, called *Eyes of a Stranger*, was nearing the end of shooting in Miami. It had no graphic murders in it at that time, but, after seeing how *Friday the 13th* was coming along, they wanted to hire me to go down to Florida and put some graphic murders into the film. I felt like an assassin again. I load up my car, drive someplace, and kill people."

1982 BRUCE, KING OF KUNG FU

A Stephen Minasian-Dick Randall production. Stephen Minasian is un-credited.

1982 FRIDAY THE 13TH PART 2

Philip Scuderi and his partners had much the same relationship with *Friday the 13th Part 2* as they had with *Friday the 13th*, with the notable exceptions being that Steve Miner took over from Sean Cunningham, as director and producer on the sequel, while Lisa Barsamian, Robert Barsamian's daughter, was an executive producer on the sequel and was a continual presence on the set of the sequel, monitoring the Boston investors' investment in much the same way that Alvin Geiler - a longtime associate of the Boston partners, who was a credited executive producer on *Friday the 13th* – had done during the filming of *Friday the 13th* in Blairstown. *Friday the 13th Part 2* also saw writer Ron Kurz, the un-credited co-writer of *Friday the 13th*, serve as the sole writer on the sequel. Frank Mancuso, Jr., the son of Frank Mansuso Sr., was a co-producer on the sequel. "By now, Phil [Philip Scuderi] had great connections with Frank Mancuso, Sr. at Paramount and he'd gotten a deal for *Part 2* which Georgetown would make and Paramount would distribute," Kurz recalls. "With Paramount in the game, I thought 'screw this. I'm going to go legit as a writer,' and I came clean with the Writers Guild about my errant ways [referring to Kurz having previously written under the table for Philip Scuderi and Georgetown]. It was a smart decision because I'm still getting quarterly residuals from *Part 2*."

1982 FRIDAY THE 13TH PART 3 (AKA FRIDAY THE 13TH PART III 3-D)

This was the first of three *Friday the 13th* sequels to be shot in California. Ron Kurz was originally contacted to script the film, but left the project due to a scheduling conflict and was replaced by Martin Kitrosser, the script supervisor – and Mario Bava devotee - on *Friday the 13th,* who shared scripting credit with his wife, Carol Watson. The production, which was housed in and around the Veluzat ranch in Santa Clarita Valley, California, near Los Angeles, was overseen by Robert Barsamian's daughter, Lisa Barsamian. "Phil offered me *Part III*, but I was working for CBS on a movie-of-the-week and I turned him down," Kurz recalls. "I think I did one more rewrite for him, a year later, on a teen road movie called *Off the Wall*."

1982 INVADERS OF THE LOST GOLD

A Minasian-Randall production. Stephen Minasian is un-credited.

1982 PIECES

Filmed in Spain, this slasher film stands as the most notorious, and commercially-successful, of the Minasian-Randall collaborations.

1983 OFF THE WALL

Philip Scuderi had a heart attack while mounting this prison comedy film project, after which Frank Mancuso, Jr. took over the bulk of the producing chores. Ron Kurz received a co-writing credit on the film, which starred Rosanna Arquette and Paul Sorvino. "Never seen that movie," Kurz says. "Phil had a heart attack and turned the film over to Frank Mancuso, Jr. on the West Coast. I heard it was a big mess. I had to go to arbitration with the Writers Guild to keep my credit as the beauties in Hollywood tried to screw me out of it."

1983 LA BELVA DALLE CALDA PELLE (AKA EMANUELLE, QUEEN OF THE DESERT)

A Minasian-Randall production. Stephen Minasian is un-credited.

1983 LOS NUEVOS EXTRATERRESTRES (AKA EXTRATERRESTRIAL VISITORS)

Filmed in Spain, this Minasian-Randall production was a blatant rip-off of the blockbuster 1982 film *E.T. - The Extra-*

Terrestrial. Stephen Minasian is un-credited.

1984 BRUCE THE SUPER HERO

A Minasian-Randall production. Stephen Minasian is un-credited.

1984 DON'T OPEN TILL CHRISTMAS

A Christmas-themed slasher film produced by Stephen Minasian and Dick Randall.

1984 FRIDAY THE 13TH: THE FINAL CHAPTER

Stephen Minasian and Philip Scuderi handpicked *The Final Chapter*'s director, Joseph Zito, and engaged in numerous phone conferences with Zito throughout the filming schedule while the production itself was overseen by Lisa Barsamian.

1984 MEATBALLS PART II (AKA SPACE KID)

Produced by Lisa Barsamian, representing the Boston partners, *Meatballs Part II* was originally called *Space Kid* and was intended to be a jokey rip-off of *E.T.- The Extra-Terrestrial*, with no relation to the hit summer camp comedy film *Meatballs* that had been distributed by Paramount Pictures in 1979 and which, in fact, made more money at the domestic box office than *Friday the 13th*. After acquiring the rights to the *Meatballs* title, the producers of *Space Kid* changed the name of their film project to *Meatballs Part Ii*, and shot the film at the Veluzat Ranch in California, the same location where *Friday the 13th Part 3* had been filmed. The film was directed by Ken Wiederhorn, who'd previously directed *Eyes of a Stranger* and *King Frat*, and co-scripted by Martin Kitrosser.

1984 THE MAKING OF A HORROR FILM

This promotional documentary, about the making of the film *Don't Open Till Christmas*, featured Stephen Minasian's only on-screen appearance as he talks about the making of *Don't Open Till Christmas*.

1985 FRIDAY THE 13TH PART V: A NEW BEGINNING

Stephen Minasian and Philip Scuderi were involved with every element of *A New Beginning*'s production, beginning with their choice of filmmaker Danny Steinmann to direct and write the sequel. According to film historian, and *Last House on the Left* scholar, David A. Szulkin, Minasian and Scuderi infused *A New Beginning* with various elements of the 1973 S.F. Brownrigg-directed splatter film *Don't Look in the Basement* (AKA *The Forgotten*) which Hallmark Releasing had distributed in 1973. "The ax murder at the beginning is most definitely modeled on the scene at the beginning of Hallmark's *Don't Look in the Basement* (the S.F. Brownrigg film)," Szulkin says. "Actually, the whole setting of *Friday 5* seems to be inspired by *Don't Look in the Basement*. Gene Ross, the actor who swings the axe in *Don't Look in the Basement*, had a bit role in *Friday the 13th: The Final Chapter*."

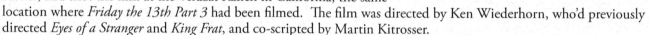

Minasian and Scuderi also contracted Steinmann to direct and write a sequel to *Last House on the Left* – to have been called either *Beyond the Last House on the Left* or *Last House on the Left II* – which was to have been filmed in Wisconsin in April of 1985. Although the would-be sequel was promoted on *Last House on Left*'s 1985 video release, from Vestron Video, the sequel obviously never materialized, primarily due to an inability to come-up with a workable script.

1985 SPACE WARRIORS 2000 (TV movie)

A Minasian-Randall production.

1986 SLAUGHTER HIGH (AKA APRIL FOOL'S DAY)

Filmed in England, this slasher film was originally called *April Fool's Day*, but the title was changed to *Slaughter High* when it was revealed that Paramount Pictures had a horror film project that was also entitled *April Fool's Day*. Paramount ended up paying Stephen Minasian and Dick Randall to switch the title of their project.

1989 DON'T SCREAM IT'S ONLY A MOVIE (documentary)

Stephen Minasian and Dick Randall co-produced this compilation documentary, which was hosted by Vincent Price and chronicles the history of horror films, from the silent film era to the splatter films of the 1980s. The documentary features clips from the Minasian-Randall films *Pieces* and *Don't Open Till Christmas*.

1989 THE URGE TO KILL

A Minasian-Randall production. Stephen Minasian is un-credited.

1990 LIVING DOLL

A Minasian-Randall production. Stephen Minasian is un-credited.

APPENDIX V: BIBLIOGRAPHY

BOOKS

Bouzereau, Laurent. *Ultraviolent Movies*. New York: Citadel Press, 1996.

Bracke, Peter M. *Crystal Lake Memories*. London: Titan Books, 2006.

Clover, Carol J. *Men, Women and Chainsaws: Gender in the Modern Horror Film*. Princeton, New Jersey: Princeton University, 1992.

Dika, Vera. *Games of Terror: Halloween, Friday the 13th, and the films of the Slasher Cycle*. Rutherford, New Jersey: Fairleigh Dickinson University, 1990.

Grove, David. *Jamie Lee Curtis: Scream Queen*. Albany: BearManor Media, 2010.

Grove, David. *Making Friday the 13th: The Legend of Camp Blood*. Godalming: FAB Press, 2005.

Hawke, Simon. *Friday the 13th*. New American Library, 1987.

Howarth, Troy. *The Haunted World of Mario Bava*. Godalming: FAB Press, 2002.

Lucas, Tim. *Mario Bava: All the Colors of the Dark*. Cincinnati: Video Watchdog, 2007.

McCarty, John. *The Official Splatter Movie Guide*. New York: St. Martin's, 1989.

Rebello, Stephen. *Alfred Hitchcock and the Making of Psycho*. New York: Dembner, 1990.

Rockoff, Adam. *Going to Pieces: The Rise and Fall of the Slasher Film, 1978-1986*. Jefferson: McFarland & Company, 2002.

Savini, Tom. *Grande Illusions*. Charlotte: Morris Costumes, 1994.

Skal, David. *The Monster Show: A Cultural History of Horror*. Penguin USA, 1994.

Szulkin, David A. *Wes Craven's Last House on the Left: The Making of a Cult Classic*. Godalming: FAB Press, 1997.

Thrower, Stephen. *Nightmare USA: The Untold Story of the Exploitation Independents*. Godalming: FAB Press, 2007.

Waller, Gregory A. *American Horrors: Essays on the Modern American Horror Films*. University of Illinois Press, 1988.

Wells, Paul. *The Horror Genre*. Wallflower Press, 2001.

MAGAZINES AND NEWSPAPERS

Buckley, Tom. "A potboiler of gold at the end of his rainbow." *The New York Times*, January 23, 1981.

Chute, David. "Tom Savini: *Maniac* (special effects in horror films)." *Film Comment*, July-August 1981.

Gire, Dann and Paul Mandell. "*Friday the 13th*: Horror's First Franchise." *Cinefantastique*, November 1989.

Grove, David. "Crystal Lake Memories." *Fangoria*, May 2002.

Grove, David. "New Line wraps on *Freddy Vs. Jason*." *Rue Morgue*, January-February 2003.

Mandell, Paul. "Jason Lives! The Birth of a Slasher." *Cinefantastique*, November 1989.

Martin, Bob. "*Friday the 13th*: A Day for Terror." *Fangoria*, June 1980.

Martin, Bob. "Tom Savini: A Man of Many Parts." *Fangoria*, June 1980.

Miller, Victor. "*Friday the 13th* is Miller's first horror effort." *Anchorage Daily News*, June 24, 1980.

Rogal, James C. "Just Taking Off as An Actor, Bing Crosby's Son Harry Finds '*Friday the 13th*' a Bloody Good Omen." *People*, June 30, 1980.

Schreger, Charles. "Formula For Success." *Sarasota Herald-Tribune*, September 30, 1980.

Scott, Vernon. "Bing's boy, Harry, makes it on his own." *St. Petersburg Times*, April 16, 1980.

Shapiro, Marc. "The Six Faces of Jason – Part One." *Fangoria*, October 1987.

Shapiro, Marc. "The Women of Crystal Lake – Part One." *Fangoria*, June 1989.

Siskel, Gene. "Gross profits – looking at a man who distributes gore by the score." *Chicago Tribune*, April 17, 1977.

"Betsy Palmer's number comes up." *The Telegraph*, January 3, 1981.

Waddell, Calum Robert. "Crystal Lake Chronicles: An Interview With Director-Producer Sean S. Cunningham." *Shock Cinema*, Winter 2005.

MISCELLANEOUS

Friday the 13th Pressbook (Paramount Pictures, 1980).

Here Come the Tigers Pressbook (American International Pictures, 1978).

A Stranger is Watching Pressbook (MGM/United Artists(UA), 1982).

ONLINE

Black Saint, The. "Interview: Adrienne King (*Friday the 13th*)." *www.horrornews.net*, October 26, 2010.

Caretaker, The. "Tom Savini interview." *www.HouseofHorrors.com*, July 1997.

"Where Are They Now? Ari Lehman." *www.fridaythe13thfilms.com*, February 4, 2004.

Gencarelli, Mike. "Interview with Ari Lehman." *www.mediamikes.com*, January 26, 2011.

Kat. "Ari Lehman." *www.campblood.net*, May 20, 2004.

Keehnen, Owen. "The First Jason Voorhees: Talking with Ari Lehman." *www.racksandrazors.com*.

King, Adrienne. "Bio/credits." *www.adrienneking.com*.

Kirst, Brian. "Adrienne King: *Walking the Distance* with the Original Final Girl." *www.horrorsociety.com*, September 23, 2008.

O, Jimmy. "Interview: Adrienne King." *www.joblo.com*, February 5, 2009.

Perry, Scott W. "Adrienne King." *www.slickdevilmoviehouse.com*.

SOURCES

The vast majority of quotes in this book are taken from interviews that were conducted by the author during the period ranging from 2000 to the present. These interviews were variously conducted in person, by E-Mail, by phone conversation, by fax, and sometimes through handwritten correspondence. In addition, the author has respected the wishes of those interview subjects who spoke on the condition of anonymity or on the condition that their correspondence was off the record.

The following source notes identify all of the quotes in the book that were taken from secondary sources, namely books, magazine and newspaper articles, online articles and miscellaneous sources, primarily press notes.

1

1 *I like pictures*: Gene Siskel, "Gross profits – looking at a man who distributes gore by the score," *Chicago Tribune*, April 17, 1977.

1 *To think*: Dann Gire and Paul Mandell, "*Friday the 13th*: Horror's First Franchise," *Cinefantastique*, November 1989.

2 *All I was trying to do*: Tom Buckley, "A potboiler of gold at the end of his rainbow," *The New York Times*, January 23, 1981.

2 *After producing Last House on the Left*: Paul Mandell, "Jason Lives! The Birth of a Slasher," *Cinefantastique*, November 1989.

7 *We hardly looked like a film crew*: David A. Szulkin, *Wes Craven's Last House on the Left: The Making of a Cult Classic*.

8 *to psychologically prepare his audience*: *Friday the 13th* Pressbook.

8 *If you examine it*: Szulkin, *Wes Craven's Last House on the Left: The Making of a Cult Classic*.

9 *The violence in Friday the 13th*: Szulkin, *Wes Craven's Last House on the Left: The Making of a Cult Classic*.

9 *The scary things*: Mandell, "Jason Lives! The Birth of a Slasher."

2

11 *You don't have to pass a bar exam*: Szulkin, *Wes Craven's Last House on the Left: The Making of a Cult Classic*.

12 *I became interested in the theater*: Szulkin, *Wes Craven's Last House on the Left: The Making of a Cult Classic*.

12 *I went to grad school*: Szulkin, *Wes Craven's Last House on the Left: The Making of a Cult Classic*.

12 *Theater is an anachronism*: Szulkin, *Wes Craven's Last House on the Left: The Making of a Cult Classic*.

13 *At the time*: Peter M. Bracke, *Crystal Lake Memories*.

13 *I was in completely uncharted waters*: Bracke, *Crystal Lake Memories*.

13 *We were trying to do anything*: Szulkin, *Wes Craven's Last House on the Left: The Making of a Cult Classic*.

16 *bullets over Broadway*: David A. Szulkin to DG.

16 *Phil saw what I saw*: Bracke, *Crystal Lake Memories*.

16 *There was a scene*: Szulkin, *Wes Craven's Last House on the Left: The Making of a Cult Classic*.

17 *After that*: Bracke, *Crystal Lake Memories*.

17 *It was almost instant*: Szulkin, *Wes Craven's Last House on the Left: The Making of a Cult Classic*.

17 *We resisted*: Gire and Mandell, "*Friday the 13th*: Horror's First Franchise."

19 *Last House became*: Szulkin, *Wes Craven's Last House on the Left: The Making of a Cult Classic*.

19 *Wes and I*: Bracke, *Crystal Lake Memories*.

19 *Wes and I made*: Szulkin, *Wes Craven's Last House on the Left: The Making of a Cult Classic*.

20 *That wasn't a movie*: Calum Robert Waddell, "Crystal Lake Chronicles: An Interview With Director-Producer Sean S. Cunningham," *Shock Cinema*, Winter 2005.

20 *It was a bizarre experience*: Szulkin, *Wes Craven's Last House on the Left: The Making of a Cult Classic.*

21 *In Spain*: Bracke, *Crystal Lake Memories.*

21 *When I came home*: Bracke, *Crystal Lake Memories.*

21 *I thought it would be fun*: Waddell, "Crystal Lake Chronicles: An Interview With Director-Producer Sean S. Cunningham."

22 *My conversation with the producers*: Waddell, "Crystal Lake Chronicles: An Interview With Director-Producer Sean S. Cunningham."

3

28 *I'm sitting around thinking*: Adam Rockoff, *Going to Pieces: The Rise and Fall of the Slasher Film, 1978-1986.*

29 *You have to understand*: Gire and Mandell, "*Friday the 13th*: Horror's First Franchise."

31 *I was more like a naughty kid*: Laurent Bouzereau, *Ultraviolent Movies.*

33 *I was trying to get support*: Gire and Mandell, "*Friday the 13th*: Horror's First Franchise."

33 *I got an idea*: Mandell, "Jason Lives! The Birth of a Slasher."

34 *I ran the ad in the summer*: Rockoff, *Going to Pieces: The Rise and Fall of the Slasher Film, 1978-1986.*

36 *There was a movie*: Bracke, *Crystal Lake Memories.*

37 *They were theater owners*: Mandell, "Jason Lives! The Birth of a Slasher."

37 *I had gone away*: Bracke, *Crystal Lake Memories.*

37 *They came back to me*: Bracke, *Crystal Lake Memories.*

38 *We tried to negotiate*: Bracke, *Crystal Lake Memories.*

38 *That was a very troubled night*: Bracke, *Crystal Lake Memories.*

4

51 *In the summer*: Adrienne King, "Bio/credits," www.adrienneking.com.

52 *What I liked*: Marc Shapiro, "The Women of Crystal Lake – Part One," *Fangoria*, June 1989.

52 *They brought in every young actress*: Bracke, *Crystal Lake Memories.*

52 *Originally*: Shapiro, "The Women of Crystal Lake – Part One."

54 *He thought it would be fun*: Bracke, *Crystal Lake Memories.*

5

64 *I was trying to make something*: Rockoff, *Going to Pieces: The Rise and Fall of the Slasher Film, 1978-1986.*

67 *My fondest memory*: The Black Saint, "Interview: Adrienne King (*Friday the 13th*)," www.horrornews.net, October 26, 2010.

70 *We were shooting*: Rockoff, *Going to Pieces: The Rise and Fall of the Slasher Film, 1978-1986.*

71 *Motel 96*: Shapiro, "The Women of Crystal Lake – Part One."

75 *There was no way*: The Black Saint, "Interview: Adrienne King (*Friday the 13th*)."

6

87 *I was strongly aware*: Bracke, *Crystal Lake Memories.*

93 *They built a fake neck*: Bracke, *Crystal Lake Memories.*

94 *I was extremely nervous*: Bracke, *Crystal Lake Memories.*

94 *I don't want to sound*: Mandell, "Jason Lives! The Birth of a Slasher."

95 *I have to give*: Mandell, "Jason Lives! The Birth of a Slasher."

7

97 *When my agent urged me*: "Betsy Palmer's number comes up," *The Telegraph*, January 3, 1981.

99 *Originally, we had planned*: Bob Martin, "*Friday the 13th*: A Day for Terror," *Fangoria*, June 1980.

8

115 *It sounds so low-rent*: Bracke, *Crystal Lake Memories*.

117 *Talented, tenacious, endearing*: Scott W. Perry, "Adrienne King." *www.slickdevilmoviehouse.com*.

122 *I was like*: Brian Kirst, "Adrienne King: *Walking the Distance* with the Original Final Girl," *www.horrorsociety.com*, September 23, 2008.

122 *We really got away*: Shapiro, "The Women of Crystal Lake – Part One."

123 *The strip Monopoly pages*: Perry, "Adrienne King," *www.slickdevilmoviehouse.com*.

9

128 *Kevin Bacon and Harry Crosby*: Kirst, "Adrienne King: *Walking the Distance* with the Original Final Girl."

129 *I worked with Tom Savini*: Mike Gencarelli, "Interview with Ari Lehman," *www.mediamikes.com*, January 26, 2011.

129 *Working with Tom Savini*: Kat, "Ari Lehman," *www.campblood.net*, May 20, 2004.

130 *We worked for weeks*: Owen Keehnen, "The First Jason Voorhees: Talking with Ari Lehman," *www.racksandrazors.com*.

131 *The only disturbing moment*: Bouzereau, *Ultraviolent Movies*.

131 *The movie had no emotional impact*: Bouzereau, *Ultraviolent Movies*.

137 *The first time we tried it*: Perry, "Adrienne King."

138 *Sean hadn't gotten the exact shot*: Perry, "Adrienne King."

138 *It took us three months*: Shapiro, "The Women of Crystal Lake – Part One."

138 *Sean Cunningham was very apologetic*: Shapiro, "The Women of Crystal Lake – Part One."

10

142 *My children are proud*: Victor Miller, "*Friday the 13th* is Miller's first horror effort," *Anchorage Daily News*, June 24, 1980.

145 *I was shocked*: Mandell, "Jason Lives! The Birth of a Slasher."

145 *We have in the MPAA*: Gire and Mandell, "*Friday the 13th*: Horror's First Franchise."

148 *I'm shocked*: Mandell, "Jason Lives! The Birth of a Slasher."

149 *I took it to Warner Bros.*: Buckley, "A potboiler of gold at the end of his rainbow."

11

160 *I had a really bad stalker*: The Black Saint, "Interview: Adrienne King (*Friday the 13th*)."

160 *The only thing that movie did*: Shapiro, "The Women of Crystal Lake – Part One."

168 *He said he thought*: Buckley, "A potboiler of gold at the end of his rainbow."

168 *It was simple arithmetic*: Buckley, "A potboiler of gold at the end of his rainbow."

172 *I have to apologize*: Gire and Mandell, "*Friday the 13th*: Horror's First Franchise."

INDEX

ACKNOWLEDGEMENTS

There are many people who helped me to bring this book to life. Foremost, I want to thank Barry Abrams (1944-2009), whose friendship and support provided the happiest moments for me on this journey, which has now spanned over a decade.

Thanks to Barry, I was able to interview most of the technical unit that joined him on *Friday the 13th*, as well as many other adjoining adventures and projects. Special thanks to Tad Page and Robert Shulman in this regard. I also want to thank James Bekiaris, Richard Berger, Max Kalmanowicz, Richard Murphy and David Platt.

I have a special thanks for Virginia Field who introduced me to Barry Abrams back in 2004. I also want to thank Daniel Mahon and Robert Topol for their invaluable recollections. Special thanks also to Tony Marshall for sharing with me his personal photographs from his time spent in Blairstown during the filming of *Friday the 13th*.

I want to thank Cecelia and John Verardi for their special help and wonderful stories that sent me in directions I otherwise never would've discovered.

I want to thank Sean Cunningham, who I interviewed in 2001, and again in 2003. Thanks also to Steve Miner.

A special thanks to Tom Savini for continually answering my many questions and putting up with my special annoyance. Thanks also to Taso Stavrakis.

Thanks to Victor Miller for also putting up with my continuous pestering and answering my stream of questions. Special thanks also to Ron Kurz for his invaluable help.

Thanks to Barry Moss and Julie Hughes for sharing their casting recollections with me and also to Richard Illy who was kind enough to share his *Friday the 13th* photographs with me, with the invaluable assistance of Steve Minnick.

Special thanks to Harry Manfredini for helping me understand his musical contribution to *Friday the 13th*.

Amongst the cast members, I want to thank Peter Brouwer, Ronn Carroll, Harry Crosby, Ari Lehman, Ron Millkie, Robbi Morgan, Mark Nelson, Betsy Palmer and Jeannine Taylor.

Thank you to Leona Bartram for sharing some memories with me about her daughter, the late Laurie Bartram (1958-2007).

Special thanks to Peter Nussbaum at Sure Copy in Burnaby, British Columbia, Canada without whom this book would never have been completed.

Thank you to Michael Aloisi for publishing this book. Thank you to Loretta Kapinos for editing the book.

Thank you to the following people who either answered my questions, or helped me with information, or helped with the writing of this book in various other ways: Jesse (Jessie) Abrams, Carlton J. Albright, Glenn Allen, Robert Armin, John Ballard, David Beury, Martin Blythe, Jimmy Bradley, Lammert Brouwer, Alison Buehler, Nalani Clark, Caron Coplan, Alex Ebel, Phil Fasso, Harvey Fenton, Richard Feury, David Fuentes, Sondra Gilman, Celso Gonzalez-Falla, Kim Gottlieb-Walker, Henri Guibaud, Matt Hankinson, Jason Hawkins, Troy Howarth, Kat, Sean Kearnes, John Klyza, Abigail Lewis, Tim Lucas, George Mansour, Brett McBean, James McConnell, John Mikesch, Jane Minasian, Laurel Moore, Dean Orewiler, Jason Parker, Jason Pepin, Denise Pinckley, Carol Rosegg, Elisa Rothstein, Chris Stavrakis, Peter Stein, David A. Szulkin, Stephen Thrower, Christine Torres, Robert Tramontin, Reuben Trane, Tony Urban, James Willis and Mommy.

CPSIA information can be obtained
at www.ICGtesting.com
Printed in the USA
BVOW09*2319190117

474019BV00003B/3/P